D0046603

LANGUAGE AND THE

DISCOVERY OF REALITY

LANGUAGE AND THE DISCOVERY OF REALITY

A Developmental Psychology of Cognition

by

JOSEPH CHURCH

with a foreword by
ROBERT B. MacLEOD

VINTAGE BOOKS
A Division of Random House
New York

FOREWORD

It is a pleasure to write a brief foreword to what promises to be a significant book. Professor Church is writing about human language, how it develops in the human individual, how it serves as a means of communication between humans, how it participates in the processes of human thinking. He has a somewhat unconventional point of view, which deserves serious consideration. He has facts to present, plus some interesting speculations, which even adherents to other camps will find worth pondering. I regard this as a notable contribution, not only to the psychology of language but also to the general psychology of human behavior.

I recommend that the whole book be read and that it be read continuously from beginning to end. One cannot jump back and forth among the chapters without missing some of the essence of the author's theory. I recommend, too, that it be read carefully. Professor Church's style is clear, effortless, and pleasing, so much so as to be almost deceptive. Let the reader not be deceived, however, by the graceful cadence and the apt metaphor. The case that is being presented is closely reasoned and is buttressed by solid scholarship. The book will undoubtedly provoke some vigorous reactions. This is all to the good, but one hopes that these will be reactions to what the author has actually said rather than to superficial impressions based on a hasty skimming.

"Why don't animals speak?" it has been asked, and the oft-quoted answer is "Because they have nothing to say." This is quite wrong, of course, for animals have much to say; and they say it, in squawks and barks and purrs, in ways that are intelligible to their friends and enemies. In the animal world we find a multitude of expressive sounds and movements to which there are appropriate reactions, and many of these we are only beginning to understand. In some animal forms there is impressive evidence of intentionality in communication, which goes beyond mere expression; and this, too, deserves further study. It may well be that we have underestimated the range of communication in the sub-human world. No one can challenge the statement, however, that the gap between animal and man is tremendous. Even if this great difference be merely one of degree rather than of kind, man is unique among the species in his ability to transform grunts and groans into complex symbolic systems that relay more than states of need or anticipations of something dangerous. Not even the most brilliant chimpanzee (or porpoise?) has ever been able to reply to a request for directions with, "Down the hill to the first traffic light; two blocks to the right; then left about seven blocks. You can't miss it." Humans can abstract and generalize; and humans can salt away their abstractions in words and expressions that will form a basis for further abstractions and generalizations. Humans have developed languages, from one of which it is possible to translate to another; no sub-human animal has ever developed a true language. What is the psychological basis of human language? This is the question which Professor Church is trying to answer.

The growing interest in the psychology of communication is a sign of the times. If we are to have peace among the nations and peoples of the earth we must learn to communicate with one another, and languages are the most obvious media of communication. There is thus a practical motive for the study of language, and teachers are being pushed to accelerate their pupils' mastery of their own and other tongues. But there is also a theoretic motive. Psychologists are becoming increasingly aware of the fact that an understanding of man's higher thought processes requires an understanding of his language. And even the philosophers, in their current preoccupation with linguistic analysis, concede that it might be helpful to know something about the ways in which language becomes an instrument, or a mediator, or an organizer of thought. It is clear that we have a great need for an account of the ways in which language develops and becomes functional in human communication.

The psychology of language goes back, of course, at least as far as Plato's discussion of the problem in the *Cratylus,* and no philosopher since then has failed to have his say. In modern times there have been two main streams of thought. The *Geisteswissen-schaftler,* represented in the early nineteenth century by Wilhelm von Humboldt and more recently by Benjamin Lee Whorf, have argued that man's thinking is in its essentials structured by his culture, of which his language is the most significant component. Reacting against the cultural approach were the *Junggrammatiker,* represented ably by Hermann Paul in his *Prinzipien der Sprachgeschichte* (1898), whose goal was the establishment of linguistic study as a *Naturwissenschaft,* with its explanatory constructs drawn from physics, physiology, and associationist psychology. We find the same emphasis in contemporary "information theory" and "behavior theory." For the *Geisteswissenschaftler* the central problem for the psychological student of language is that of the communication of meaning, and the focus is consequently on semantics and syntax. The *Naturwissenschaftler* is more interested in analysis, and is likely to begin with phonetics and phonemics and to regard "meaning" as either no problem at all or else as a problem of secondary importance. On the one hand, we have an emphasis on content, on the other an emphasis on form.

In my opinion the formalists are at present in the ascendant, especially since we have coined the word "psycholinguistics" to signal the recent rapprochement between psychology and linguistics. This is one of my reasons for welcoming Professor Church's book so heartily. It serves to restore balance and, I think, to chart a course which a productive psychology of language must follow.

I should be inclined to classify Professor Church as a neo-Humboldtian but not a Whorfian. Humboldt was interested in the content of communication and in the linguistic forms dictated by what is communicated. Whorf was interested in content, too, but he developed a theory which many of us think has been pushed too far in the direction of a complete relativism. Nevertheless, Whorf presents us with a challenge. He invites us to pry into the meanings that are represented in language—not just the meanings of words, which are rather arbitrary, but also the meanings conveyed by accent, word order, metaphor, and style. What we need in the psychology of language is an insight into what is actually being conveyed by a speaker through a medium to a hearer. And this is why Church is so stimulating. He is not concerned about the imposition of a formal theoretical structure on the phenomena of linguistic behavior; he is interested in the actual process of communication. Like Werner and Piaget, from whom he draws liberally, he is curious about that which lies behind the machinery of communication, namely the phenomenal world of the individual.

A final word about psychological phenomenology. Many psychologists are interested only in the prediction and control of behavior. There are some of us, however, who believe that the word "understanding" represents something more. To understand another person is to reconstruct the world of the other person in such a way that it can be related to one's own. We can have complete communication only where there is full understanding; and this is never really achieved. Language presents so many obstacles that one sometimes wonders how it is that we understand one another at all. The astounding fact is, however, that we do succeed in understanding one another reasonably well and that we can transmit and receive meaningful messages through linguistic barriers that seem to be almost impermeable. Compare English and Chinese, Kwakiutl and Swahili. The linguistic structures are totally different, yet we can translate quite efficiently from one to another. How can the psychologist explain this?

Professor Church asks us to take another look at the child,

who faces the world and the language he is about to learn without any preconceptions. Whorf would say that the child's world becomes structured in accordance with the language he is taught. Church would say, I think, that the world batters its way through and demands representation, in one form or another, in any language.

This may be unfair to Professor Church. Let his book speak for itself. I heartily endorse his implied thesis that if we are to understand the psychological basis of human communication we must begin at the beginning, not with phonemes but with children.

Robert B. MacLeod

PREFACE

This book is about the way human beings, in the course of growing up, come to discover reality: people, things, attributes of people and things, space, time, values, opinions, ideas; their own bodies, feelings, wants, needs, and intentions; and the multifarious functional and formal relations among all these. It is, in short, about the acquisition of knowledge and the way behavior changes in keeping with new knowledge. It is most particularly concerned with the acquisition of language and the kinds of behavior that language makes possible. But this book cannot be simply a factual, descriptive account of the developmental psychology of language and cognition. The facts take on meaning only as they are ordered according to systematic principles. And the principles that seem best to suit the facts of cognitive development are not the accustomed principles of general psychology. For this reason, the book occasionally roams afield from its home terrain to show that the principles of cognitive development are consonant with the facts, if not the principles, of psychology as a whole. Although the book's aim is factual, there are facts we do not know, and it has a secondary purpose of defining areas of ignorance and uncertainty as a prelude to further empirical investigation.

This book avoids, as well as it is able, metaphysical and metatheoretical debate. Its assumptions are few. It assumes that there is a physical reality and that people are capable of coming to know it. It assumes that human knowledge has an inevitable component of ambiguity, since we repeatedly discover that properties found in reality are in fact reflections of ourselves—projections, if you will. It assumes that we are able to reconstruct from what a person says and does something of his inner workings, of the "logic" by which he operates. It assumes the principle of intentionality: that all behavior has an object, whether a substantial thing, an event, a situation, a hallucination, an arrangement of symbols, or the behaving organism itself. Thus, the principles that we shall invoke do not represent absolute properties of the organism but forms of organism-object relationships. Finally, this book repudiates—although it may have to talk about them—the archaic metaphysical antinomies that still may hobble psychological thinking long years after its supposed liberation from philosophy: materialism-spiritualism, determinism-voluntarism, biologism-environmentalism, central-ism-peripheralism, optimism-pessimism. People are what they are, and it is the task of the behavioral sciences to define and conceptualize the facts of human behavior without regard to a priori commitments.

There are eight chapters in this book, divided into two parts of four chapters each. Part I sets forth some basic principles of cognitive development along with the kinds of facts that point to the principles. Chapters 1 and 2 deal with facts and principles of cognitive organization prior to the acquisition of language. Chapter 3 describes the way in which children come to understand and to use language, and Chapter 4 deals with the transformation of human functioning that comes with language and the cognitive operations it makes possible. Part II is devoted to an elaboration and extension of the views contained in Part I. Chapter 5 is concerned with a psychological approach to problems of meaning and reference, and with the associated problems of linguistic determinism and cultural learning. Chapter

6 discusses the relationships of language and thinking. Chapter 7 deals with intelligence and its assessment, and with techniques for the study of symbolic functioning. Chapter 8, an epilogue, gives a brief account of a cognitive approach to problems of emotion and motivation, and seeks to locate the viewpoint of this book relative to the theoretical orientations prevailing in present-day psychology.

This book owes a great deal to many people besides its author. The two who have contributed the most are among the least mentioned, since to give them credit in every instance would have made these pages a litany to the names of Heinz Werner and Maurice Merleau-Ponty. To the former I am indebted for a vision of psychology, to the latter for one of philosophy. As usual, though, I give credit without assigning responsibility. This book departs in several important ways from the thinking of its mentors, and they are not to blame for any of its inadequacies. I have used the ideas of Jean Piaget freely, but in ways that he would perhaps not countenance. I am grateful to Robert B. MacLeod both for introducing me to the phenomenological point of view and for a critical reading of the manuscript. Again, he is not to blame if I have failed to profit from his insightful comments. I give thanks to my friend and colleague L. Joseph Stone for his sound criticisms and suggestions. Eric G. Heinemann has in many hours of discussion staunchly upheld a quite different view of language and cognition and has kept me alert to the kinds of criticism I must anticipate. The published works of B. F. Skinner have served a like function, and I must acknowledge my gratitude. My students have contributed immeasurably through their questions, objections, and suggestions in class discussion, through their comments on earlier versions of the manuscript, and through the numerous experiments—for the most part assimilated without specific acknowledgment—that they have carried out. I am grateful to Vassar College for a Faculty Fellowship, which gave me a period of uninterrupted work on this book, and I take this occasion to salute the College on its hundredth anniversary.

CONTENTS

CONTENTS

CONTENTS

PART I

Principles of Cognitive

Development

1

PREVERBAL EXPERIENCE:

1. PERCEPTION

It is quite clear that human adults behave in ways very different from those of children. It is less obvious that we need two sets of principles to account for these two ways of behaving. What is more, we need still a third set to describe the pattern of transition from immature to mature behavior. Although our concern is with development, our presentation is not consistently chronological. We shall shuttle back and forth between childhood and adulthood with a view both to sharpening the contrasts and to demonstrating the persistence of primitive qualities in adult behavior. For, as we shall see, the emergent principles of mature behavior only partially supersede those of immature behavior. Our thesis is that developmental change can best be accounted for in cognitive terms, that is, in the way the individual perceives, conceptualizes, and thinks about reality. And central to the individual's grasp of reality is the use of language and symbols. Much of what the individual knows—or thinks he knows—about reality is known only implicitly and is simply taken for granted. This means that we shall have to spend much of our time making explicit the implicit features of experience, a reversal of figure and ground that the reader may find hard to adjust to.

We must begin by attacking an assumption widely held by persons who are not specialists in human development, and even by some who are. This is the notion that the material world, together with all its physical attributes and objective relationships, is given to us perceptually from the beginning, so that in order to see it, all we have to do is look. In this view, language is in effect a set of labels to be attached to this pre-existing perceptual reality. Gestalt psychology, with its theory of innate organizing factors in perception, assumes a primary experience of pure, objective objects not yet shrouded in or animated by labels, values, and meanings. The baby's-eye view of the nursery shown in many psychology books assumes that the world lies open to our gaze from birth, with only the necessary adjustment of perspective for the baby's small size. It seems to be the opinion of many semanticists that language is even an impediment to perception, obscuring an otherwise direct contact with things as they really are. It is our thesis, to be documented at greater length in the pages that follow, that the individual discovers the characteristics of reality as he goes along, that there are predictable regularities in the sequence of discoveries, and that language, including both what other people tell him and what he tells himself, plays an intimate part in this discovery and in enabling him to perceive the world as a coherent, stable place in which to live and act.

Let us now make explicit the major principles underlying the preverbal child's perception of reality and the way perception changes with experience. It is obvious that the child from the beginning perceives things in terms of figure and ground, since perception of objects or groups of objects would otherwise be out of the question. But figure-ground organization is dictated neither by stimulus intensities (except at disruptively high levels of contrast) nor by the formal organizational laws of Gestalt theory. Those objects, and those properties of objects, stand out which offer some relevance to the child himself, in terms of promise or threat or concrete action. Those things which are meaningless seem also to be beyond perception. The young infant is oblivious to the screaming sirens of the fire trucks that go racketing past, to the hubbub of the thunderstorm, to the clamor of the telephone or doorbell; but he may wail in distress when his mother sneezes in the next room. Here we are saying two things: that the child perceives only personally meaningful objects, and that what he perceives is not so much the objects as their meanings. Developmentally and microgenetically, meanings precede objects in perception. As Flavell and Draguns [1] have noted, it is this principle that enables us to understand "subliminal perception," the fact that we can react affectively to something without being able to identify the something to which we are reacting.

Physiognomic Perception

We must not conclude that the infant's perception is subliminal. There can be no doubt that he perceives things, but he sees their physiognomic meaning-qualities rather than their objective attributes. Such objective properties of an object as size, shape, and color are at first submerged in the object's global identity—what we shall call its *physiognomy*—and do not emerge as isolable perceptual dimensions until almost age two. Here we must note two things. First, an object is rich in qualities which resist definition in terms of the usual physical dimensions. We shall have more to say about these qualities later. Second, not only is an object figural with respect to its background, but there is a kind of figure-ground organization within the object such that some qualities are figure and others ground.

It should not be supposed that physiognomic perception inefficient or ineffective. It has limitations which we will take later on, but it serves the child very well. Lorenz,[2] for example tells how his daughter was able to recognize species kinships among birds differing markedly in their objective characteristics. Long before he can read, the child distinguishes phonograph records that the adult can tell apart only by reading the labels.

What is more, the child can peel the labels off cheaply made records and still recognize them unerringly, apparently on the basis of total physiognomies; that he is not relying on particular small distinctive marks is shown by the rapidity with which he selects a record, without detailed inspection. One twenty-month-old learned to recognize letters and numbers as classes of objects distinct from other abstract forms. Here, obviously, we are approaching problems of generalization and concept-formation which we shall talk about later.

We must realize, too, that adults rely heavily on the physiognomic properties of objects. Most obviously, our impressions of people—whether we find them attractive or repulsive, beautiful or ugly, interesting or drab—are based on physiognomic qualities; a girl of quite ordinary or even unfortunate configuration can create a stir among the males at a cocktail party by the skillful use of personal adornment. We might note the importance of physiognomic qualities in art. The painting that reproduces its subject with exact geometric and chromatic fidelity is likely to seem stiff and lifeless; it is for this reason that a caricature may be a better portrait than a photograph. Illegible handwriting may become legible as soon as we stop trying to puzzle out the individual letters and just glance briefly at the words. The ease with which we miss typographical errors reminds us that we read physiognomically, without taking note of how the words are constituted. It is evident that there can be physiognomic perception in which the physiognomy includes properties not accessible to the very young child, such as the meaning of a printed word. The difference between physiognomic and objective perception stands out clearly when we look at an inverted word: We know instantaneously what the word is, but, at the same time, the letters look wholly unfamiliar. It is only when we scrutinize an object analytically or judgmentally or contemplatively that we cease to perceive physiognomically. Unless we have some reason to analyze an object, we can live with it for years without ever noting many of its readily perceptible objective properties.

Movement and Space

The traditional study of object-perception has dealt for the most part with the perception of static, two-dimensional, abstract forms. Recent studies by Johansson [3] of the perceptual fusion of discrete movements, by Michotte [4] of the perception of causality, and by Heider and Simmel [5] of the "apparent behavior" of geometric forms, all indicate that movement may endow objects with qualities they lack entirely when at rest. This fact becomes important when we realize that in everyday situations the organism is in movement among objects many of which also move.

Movement is important as a carrier of physiognomic properties. It is important in signaling the existence of an object: immobility is an excellent form of camouflage, as many animals "know" and as soldiers must be taught. Indeed, as the work of Riggs and his associates [6] has shown, a truly static object cannot be seen at all for more than a fraction of a second. Movement at a moderate rate of speed is important in making an object perceptually clear: When we want to examine an object, we scan it, we turn it back and forth, we circle it, and so forth. Gibson and Gibson [7] have shown that subjects asked to estimate the degree of slant of a plane figure whose shadow is visible on a screen can do so with considerable accuracy when they have watched the shadow during rotation of the figure, but not when they are shown simply the shadow in its final position.

We have suggested that movement can be in either the object or the individual. The role of the individual's own behavior in the definition of space is beautifully shown by Kohler's experiments [8] with inverting lenses. When the lenses are first put on, the world is seen as firmly upside down, and the subject must grope his way through space as best he can on the basis of nonvisual cues. Later, even though the surrounding world remains inverted, the particular objects the subject is dealing with resume their normal visual orientation; as soon as he stops dealing with them actively, they go back over on their heads. Still later, space in general rights itself as long as the subject is moving around, as when he rides a bicycle, but inverts itself as soon as he stops. Eventually, the world is once more seen in its normal orientation, even though its retinal image remains inverted from normal. These and other findings by Kohler on the effects of distorting lenses contradict the customary neural theories of perception and call for an account in terms of the total organism in communication with the environment.[9]

It would appear that for the human baby, space is at first no larger than the capsule that contains him and whatever he may be in communication with. One can see his space beginning to expand when, within a few weeks, he begins orienting to sounds and following people's comings and goings with his eyes. The polarization of space into the accustomed dimensions of up-down, left-right, forward-back seems to begin with the vertical dimension, often manifested shortly before age one in an almost compulsive concern with righting overturned objects.[10] Horizontal space, however, continues for some time as a space-of-action, polarized according to concrete goals and pathways rather than formal coordinates. Creeping or walking, the child can detour around obstacles and stops short at the brink of beds and staircases.[11] Space in back of him, though, is less well articulated, and he may, thinking to flop backwards onto the bed, instead tumble over the edge. Similarly, creeping feet-first down a flight of stairs, the toddler must keep twisting himself around to orient himself visually. In familiar territory, such as his own house, the child, once mobile, can go unhesitatingly and unerringly from any point to any other point and knows where his playthings are kept or where he has left them. But it is not until the school years, as demonstrated by Maier's famous swastika-maze experiment,[12] and illustrated by the accompanying map by a five-year-old of the apartment in which she had lived since birth, that the child has any over-all notion of how his home is laid out. In Tolman's term, he has not yet formed a cognitive map; in the terminology which we shall develop, he has schematized space pragmatically but not conceptually.

We must insist on the difference between space given as a field of locomotion and space given visually or as a container for objects other than oneself. Although the baby confines his

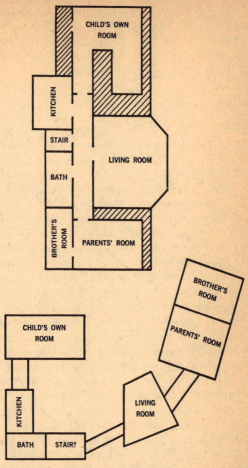

FIGURE 1. *Actual house layout (above) and its representation by a five-year-old (below). Shaded portions of drawing above represent storage space not a regular part of child's play space. Both drawings greatly simplified.*

own first locomotions to horizontal or gently sloping surfaces, he has to learn by trial and error that he cannot set his playthings down on vertical or steeply pitched surfaces. Not much before age three can the child *see* a stick as a tool for retrieving an otherwise inaccessible object. We shall have more to say in a moment about visually perceived relationships.

Three-Dimensional Space

It must be stressed that the baby's first perceptions of objects are of solid forms in voluminous space, and that two-dimensional perception comes later. As soon as he is able, the child in exploring a new object systematically inspects its hidden sides, indicating that his early perceptions contain the "implicit" datum that objects continue around out of sight. More striking is the child's first reaction to two-dimensional patterns such as the design on a playpen pad, spots of sunlight on the floor, or a stain on the woodwork: he tries, stubbornly and persistently, to pick them up. The child cannot at first recognize pictured objects. When he does, he distinguishes poorly between pictures and the objects they represent. Not only does he try to lift them off the printed page, he pets the pictured animal and tries to hear the ticking of the pictured watch. We shall return to such behavior in our discussion of "realism."

Such observations conform closely to Gibson's notion [13] that it is three-dimensional perception which is basic, and that, in spite of the numerous cues to three-dimensionality that have been defined, it is for the perception of two-dimensionality that we need cues. In the absence of such cues, we see things in the round. Experiments on the perception of a Ganzfeld, a wholly homogeneous surface, indicate that it yields the impression of a space-filling fog.[14] Without the frame or edge that bounds off a picture from the world of solid objects, and without such surface cues as reflections and the contrast between the illumination "in" the picture and that in the room in which it is viewed, the picture appears three-dimensional. This principle has been applied in the motion-picture technique known as Cinerama, which, by "surrounding" the spectator with the picture, abolishes the frame and so permits—not creates—an impression of depth.

Color, Shape, Size, and Number

The chromatic colors that, for the adult, are so important a feature of objects and that differ so sharply both from the achromatic colors and among themselves seem to play a negligible role in the baby's experience. This is not because the baby is color-blind. If color is given some relevance, as in experiments where the child is fed a normal formula from a bottle of one color and a salty formula from a differently colored bottle, he very rapidly learns to discriminate colors.[15] Also, according to Valentine and others,[16] babies as young as age three months show color preferences, and casual observation suggests that children prefer brightly colored toys to drab ones. But the child is late in recognizing color as a relatively independent dimension of objects and in being able to distinguish colors reliably. Since color is not manipulable, we should expect the perception of color to stabilize later than that of form, and Brian and Goodenough's findings [17] that form is genetically prior to color as a basis for concept-formation makes good sense.

Below age two, however, visual form perception seems poorly developed. The child adapts his grasp nicely to the shape of things, but he cannot match the forms on a form-board. He can be taught form discriminations, at least from age fifteen months or so, but spontaneous awareness of form seems to lag.[18]

We see yet another example of the discrepancy between perception attached to direct action and judgmental perception in the matter of size. The young child's size perception is obviously adequate when it comes to adapting his grasp or his embrace to take hold of something. But children up to about age two may be observed trying earnestly to fit ludicrously large things into ridiculously small ones.

By late infancy, we can observe a rudimentary, preverbal sense of number, manifested in the baby's behavior with respect to things that come in 2's, such as diaper pins: when the child finds one member of the set, he looks about for the second one. Observational data are lacking on sets of more than two things; it seems likely that Preyer's reports [19] of number perception in infants record reactions to disturbances in a familiar pattern rather than any awareness of number.

Synesthetic Perception

For most adults, the experiences given by vision, hearing, touch, taste, and so on, are clearly distinguishable. The young child's perceptions, by contrast, are *synesthetic*. That is, there are no clear dividing lines among the various sense modalities. Closely allied to synesthesia in this strict sense are a number of other phenomena, to be discussed in a moment, which can perhaps best be grouped together under the heading of *organismic effects*.

Most writers assume that synesthetic experience arises by association. This view overlooks both the evolutionary history of the senses, which indicates that specialized modalities have differentiated out of a *sensorium commune*, or generalized (probably electrochemical) receptor surface, and the evidence indicating that synesthetic effects are far more common in children than in adults. It is hard for adults, in whose experience vision is dominant, to grasp the nature of synesthetic experience. It may help to realize that dogs, for instance, have very poor vision but still manage to get about very well, or that rats blinded at birth learn to navigate complex mazes about as well as seeing rats,[20] or that bats and porpoises and probably many other species can find their way very effectively by echo-ranging.[21] In any event, the adult's experience is by no means free of synesthetic effects. Apart from special cases, such as people who have a life-long gift for synesthesias like color-hearing, whereby auditory stimulation gives rise to the experience of colors, our senses often work in concert without our being explicitly aware of it. We all know, for instance, that much of what is experienced as taste is actually smell, so that a stopped-up nose during a cold radically alters many familiar flavors. It can be shown, too, that color affects taste [22]—as food-processors know to their profit—that posture affects spatial localization,[23] and so forth. Furthermore, the special senses are not nearly so specialized as we usually think. A study by Stone [24] indicates that thermal receptors in the skin are also sensitive, if only crudely and with a low degree of accuracy, to differences in shape. Recent investigations into the perception of pain cast doubt on the notion of specialized skin receptors for pain, of specialized conduction pathways, or of specialized brain centers, and show that pain, too, contains a pictorial element.[25]

It is not clear whether these spatial, object-depicting aspects of thermal, algetic, and olfactory (one does, after all, smell a thing or a substance, and often with a locus) perception should be called synesthetic, but they certainly go beyond the data provided by the modality as it is usually conceived. In the same way, when we hear someone walking down the corridor we do not hear merely the noise of shoe striking on flooring, nor yet the meaningful pattern named "footfalls," but *somebody* walking down the corridor—as often as not, some particular person. Babies can often be observed pulling a parent's hands apart to see the handclap they have just made, or looking around the room in search of the chord that has just been struck on the piano. The physiognomy of an object is largely made up out of synesthetic qualities. When we look at something, we *see* whether it is sleek and glossy or rough and gritty to the touch, we see its leadenness or airiness, its brittleness or resiliency, the kind of sound it makes when struck. The cross-sensory metaphors of poetry, of artistic criticism, and of everyday parlance play upon our synesthetic capacity, as do the sensory metaphors we use to describe people: warm, cold, bitter, blue, and so forth. That synesthetic metaphors such as "a velvety tone" actually have communicative value has been shown experimentally by Brown, Leiter, and Hildum,[26] and in the semantic differential studies by Osgood and his associates (see p. 185).[27]

Perceived Relationships

The world as perceived by adults includes not only objects and the space that encloses them but also numerous relationships that bind objects to space, to each other, to past and future, and to the observer. Perhaps the chief difference between primitive and mature experience is in the relational structure of reality. We shall have more to say about the relation of subject and object when we come to the topic of egocentrism; for the moment we are concerned mostly with relationships in the external environment. Leaving out of account such formal relationships as those having to do with kinship, social and economic status, clock and calendar time, means and ends, political organization, and so forth, all of which are learned linguistically, there are numerous spatial features which are objectively obvious to adults and seemingly nonexistent for the young child. The six-month-old cannot see that he can obtain a distant, desired object by pulling on the string that lies within easy reach. If he does discover, in playing with the string, that he can pull the object nearer, he can utilize this discovery only to the extent of a single sweeping yank—he is wholly incapable of reeling in the string hand over hand. The toddler may doggedly, like Simple Simon, try to fetch water in a sieve. Even a three-year-old may confidently expect that he can cut out, one by one, two pictures printed on opposite sides of the same piece of paper. Even a five-year-old may not be able to see the "good continuation" of an interrupted line or a pattern with a piece left out, or trace a line representing a tangle of string, or solve a simple T-maze.

Causation

We shall have more to say shortly about temporal relationships and sequences, and here we need only point out that these are not initially clearly perceived. One kind of temporal sequence of special importance is that of cause and effect. Certain sorts of cause-effect relationships are obviously not accessible to the

child, as when there is a long delay between cause and effect—
for example, between the watering of a plant and its blooming,
or between an injury and the victim's eventual revenge (in
general, psychological causation and its devious ways are closed
to the child), or when either the causal agent or the resultant
event is hidden, as with the striking of a clock or the immunity
that follows an inoculation.

At a more direct level, the child learns a number of pragmatic
sequences: If he strikes a block tower, it topples; if he bumps his
milk glass, it spills; if he steps on the cat's tail, the cat screeches;
if he pulls the light chain, the light goes on or off, and so forth.
But it never seems to occur to the child to wonder about the
mechanics by which effects are produced. Like the generations
that preceded Galileo and Newton, he does not discover gravity,
but lives with it. The television set may do interesting things, but
there is nothing intrinsically remarkable in the fact that meaningful images and sounds should emanate from a glass-and-metal
case. Children of four or so, questioned about the workings of
a television set, seem to assume quite matter-of-factly that the
characters they see are actually contained within the set. At this
age, however, one sees the beginnings of a growing ambiguity:
on the one hand, the child accepts as real the marvels he sees on
television or hears about in stories; on the other, he knows from
his own experience that such things cannot be—yet, to complete
the circle, how can he disbelieve the things he has seen happen
with his own eyes or heard described from books?

Realism, Phenomenalism, and Dynamism

There appear to be three components in the child's causal—
or acausal—experience. The first of these is what Piaget calls
realism. Realism as a characteristic of primitive experience does
not mean sensitivity to the harsher or seamier realities of
existence, as in what is called realistic fiction, nor does it mean
hardheaded practicality. Rather, it refers to the fact that initially
all things are equally real and real in the same sense and on the
same plane: pictures, words, people, things, energies, dreams,
feelings—all are equally solid or insubstantial and all mingle in

a common sphere of experience. It is this realistic intermingling of realities that permits a three-year-old child, "cooking" in the sandbox or at the beach, actually to sample, for one brief mouthful, his sand-cake, even though he knows perfectly well the difference between sand and cake. Realism does not imply fatalism or passive resignation, but simply a failure to doubt the reality of whatever comes into awareness. The adult does not lose his realism, but retains it ambiguously. Thus, we can at the same time weep at the melodramatic movie and tell ourselves that "it's only a picture." In general, we keep our critical faculties turned low, and are willing to accept, say, a phonograph recording as the equivalent of a live performance. As the frantic quest for ever higher fidelity shows, electronic reproduction falls just short of total convincingness for those of highly discriminating taste. In general, however, we are far more likely to mistake the effigy for the real thing than to dismiss a reality as unreal. Realism comes in several special varieties. The child's early reaction to pictures as real objects has already been mentioned. Later, we shall take up the phenomenon of word realism.

Realism is closely allied to *phenomenalism*, or accepting things as given, without inquiring beneath the surface or looking for influences outside the focal event. Phenomenalism is another of Piaget's terms. It should not be confused with the philosophical doctrine of phenomenalism, even though a certain kinship will be apparent. Many of the child's first attempts at causal (rather than motivational) explanation are phenomenalistic—that is, in terms of juxtaposition of things which occur together and may in fact have some causal linkage, as in "The thunder makes it rain" or "Trees make the wind blow." When two events do coincide, there is an all but irresistible tendency to experience them as causally connected. A striking example comes from a survivor of a ship collision who switched off her stateroom light at the moment of impact; she was convinced that she had applied the emergency brakes.[28] The same principle may underlie the "superstitious" behavior reported by Skinner: If, for instance, a pigeon pirouettes just before receiving food, the pirouette is incorporated into the operant chain of food-seeking behavior.[29]

Similar behavior can be seen in young children. For instance, a toddler learning to operate his phonograph begins by unlatching the cover; but he always works the latch before turning on the phonograph even when the cover is already open.

We are all prone to phenomenalism, as when, watching the trained chimpanzee on television, we credit him with almost human intelligence, forgetting that his trainer stands just off camera, cueing every move. In general, we are easily taken in by what we see on the movie or television screen simply because it seems to be the whole picture. Phenomenalism seems almost to be a sacred creed in certain branches of behaviorist psychology, which dispense with mediational constructs, speaking, instead, of "empty organisms" and "little black boxes," and which treat stimulus, response, and reinforcement as so many monads, synchronized but without any explicit connections. We must emphasize, because there has been some confusion on the point, that phenomenalism is not the same as phenomenology. An amusing example of phenomenalism is to be found in the way many people (100 percent of elementary-school children tested, 40 percent of college-educated females, 14 percent of college-educated males) conceive of an island: it floats unattached to solid ground. Nor should it be assumed that the only alternative to a detached island is the correct idea of a mountain thrusting up from the ocean floor. Certain islands are depicted as floating but moored in place by roots or seaweed; some are supported on pilings; some run inconclusively off the page; and some rest on a point, like a spinning-top or upholsterer's tack.

The third component, along with realism and phenomenalism, in the child's—and adult's—causal experience is what we might call *dynamism*. This term has been used in so many ways that it is freighted with connotations irrelevant to the present context. Nevertheless, the author has not been able to think of a better word and he begs the reader's indulgence. Dynamism seems to be an implicit term in the child's thinking and is revealed in the *absence* of curiosity about causal connections, as though these were self-evident. The child's world seems to be pregnant with and activated by some generalized "energy" that links together all objects and events. This is not unlike the notion found in

Hopi and other cosmologies, that all of nature forms a kind of organismic unity so that any event may reverberate to the far reaches of the universe and everyone is constrained to play his role with the utmost circumspection lest he upset the cosmic equilibrium. Not all our dynamistic thinking is on such a grand scale, of course. The average woman driver's conception of how her car works, for instance, is dynamistic: one does thus-and-so and such-and-such ensues; but what intervenes between action and reaction could equally well be attributed to gnomes, an arrangement of pulleys, or the force of animal magnetism, for all the driver knows or cares. A man reports how he and his wife had an agreement not to turn on the water elsewhere in the house while the other was taking a shower, lest the bather be frozen or scalded; he found that he hesitated to switch lights on and off while his wife was in the shower, as though to do so would affect the water pressure.

Dynamism sometimes becomes explicit, as in the Hopi cosmology, or in animism (attributing animal, particularly psychological, characteristics to inanimate objects), anthropomorphism (attributing human qualities to infrahuman creatures—the "pathetic fallacy"), magicalism (attributing to human or other agencies the power to act upon reality via energies transcending those accepted by science), and spiritualism (belief in supernatural entities).

As the child learns more about how things work, dynamism gives way to more sophisticated causal notions—although not, as we have seen, entirely. Until reality has been stratified into levels of causation, however, contiguity ineluctably implies causality, and the child cannot grasp the notion of accidental coincidence. Similarly, he cannot understand that events can be meaningless and purposeless. Here, of course, he is joined by some Freudian theorists who may be inclined to attach great significance to miscellaneous bits of behavior, forgetting that just because everything must have a cause of some kind, it does not also have to have a reason. It is easy to see how realism, phenomenalism, and dynamism go together. In a "realistic" world, where images and feelings have the same status as objects, their interactions can only be dynamistic. Phenomenalistic explanations make sense because implicit dynamic forces fill in the logical gaps and obviate inquiry beneath the surface.

It is worth noting the historical progression from dynamic cosmologies to mechanical models of man and the physical world (exemplified by Descartes' pneumatic theory of neuromuscular functioning and the billiard-ball concept of the atom), back to the kind of dynamism found in the field theories of modern physics and biology. This is not to say, however, that field theories are a regression to primitive conceptualization. Field theories are articulated and dimensionalized, and relationships, if not explained, are at least explicated and systematized.

What we have said so far has, of course, raised serious epistemological problems of the kind faced by every student of perception. How can we correlate dimensions of experience with stimulus variables and with neurological variables such as patterns of excitation upon the receptor surface, transmission pathways, central projection or integration areas, message codes, and isomorphic projections? Do we really perceive objects, or, as suggested by the sense-datum theorists,[30] are what we take to be objects really inferences from or reconstructions of physical processes, projected back into the outside world? If we can assume the presence of a reality populated by objects, how can we tell which features are really there and which are the perceiver's contribution to a physically rather bleak environment? Do we really see an object move, or do we, as in viewing a motion picture, "piece together" a series of snapshots? How, indeed, can we speak of perceiving an event, when, at any given moment, part of the event lies in the past, dissolved and gone forever, whereas the rest has yet to happen, and all we have to work with is memory, anticipation, and a tissue-thin instant of present time?

Such questions are tantalizingly unanswerable. But in point of fact, we do not need to answer them. Our aim is not an explanation of how human experience is possible, but a systematic description in terms of developmental principles of what it is like and of how it changes with learning. Even a descriptive system, however, needs a standard of reality. We take as our index the reality of the adult, experienced, educated, sane, sober,

alert Western European viewing the world under the freest and
most favorable conditions. This does not imply that our ideal
perceiver has an absolute grasp on reality. All our experience has
a necessary component of ambiguity. Nevertheless, our every
act—as human beings, as citizens, as scientists—is founded on
the assumption that there is a reality and that we can perceive
it. At a fairly advanced stage, as "realism" diminishes, we
become aware that some of our presumed factual knowledge is
in error and that some of our perceptual experience is illusory,
but only the schizophrenic seriously calls into question his basic
contact with the real. The normal individual, recognizing his own
fallibility, does everything possible to guard against particular
errors but otherwise assumes, and with good reason, that he
knows what is what. The existence of illusions and hallucinations
is not a reason to question the validity of our perceptions; quite
to the contrary, our ability to recognize such phenomena as
"nonveridical" means that we have a standard of reality with
which to compare them. In short, we begin with the common-
sense assumption that people perceive objects and not pallid
simulacra of objects, otherwise called "percepts." This line of
reasoning will not satisfy the metaphysically inclined, but science,
if it is not to founder in impotence or absurdity, must take the
pragmatics and let the metaphysics go.

NOTES

(1) J. H. Flavell & Juris Draguns, A microgenetic approach to perception and thought, *Psychological Bulletin*, 1957, 54: 197–217. For
a general survey of perceptual development see: J. F. Wohlwill,
Developmental studies of perception, *Psychological Bulletin*, 1960, 57:
249–288.

(2) K. Z. Lorenz, Morphology and behavior patterns in closely allied
species. In B. Schaffner, ed., *Group Processes* (New York: Josiah
Macy, Jr., Foundation, 1955), pp. 168–220.

(3) Gunnar Johansson, *Configurations in Event Perception* (Uppsala:
Almqvist & Wiksells Boktryckeri AB, 1950).

(4) Albert Michotte, *La Perception de la Causalité* (Louvain: L'Institut Supérieur de Philosophie, 1946).

(5) Fritz Heider & Marianne Simmel, An experimental study of apparent behavior, *American Journal of Psychology*, 1944, 57: 243–259.

(6) L. A. Riggs, Floyd Ratliff, Janet C. Cornsweet, & T. N. Cornsweet, The disappearance of steadily fixated visual test objects, *Journal of the Optical Society of America*, 1953, 43: 495–501.

(7) J. J. Gibson & E. J. Gibson, Continuous perspective transformations and the perception of rigid motion, *Journal of Experimental Psychology*, 1957, 54: 129–138.

(8) Ivo Kohler, On the development and transformations of the perceptual world, *Psychological Issues*, 1961, 2, no. 4. See review of German-language edition by E. G. Heinemann, *American Journal of Psychology*, 1953, 66: 503–505. See also the symposium on the role of movement in development in *Enfance*, 1956, 2, no. 1, especially articles by Wallon, Piaget, de Ajuriaguerra, and Koupernick.

(9) H. Werner & S. Wapner, The Innsbruck studies on distorted visual fields in relation to an organismic theory of perception, *Psychological Review*, 1955, 62: 130–138.

(10) We might note the finding by Lila Ghent & Lilly Bernstein (The influence of orientation of geometric forms on recognition in children; paper given before the Eastern Psychological Association, 1960) that older children show marked preferences for particular orientations of abstract forms. See also: Irvin Rock & Walter Heimer, The effect of retinal and phenomenal orientation on the perception of form, *American Journal of Psychology*, 1957, 70: 493–511.

(11) E. J. Gibson & R. D. Walk, The "visual cliff," *Scientific American*, 1960, 202: 64–71. The "brinksmanship" practiced by Gibson & Walk's subjects is quite apparent in the everyday behavior of human infants.

(12) N. R. F. Maier, Reasoning in children, *Journal of Comparative Psychology*, 1936, 21: 357–366.

(13) J. J. Gibson, Pictures, perspective, and perception, *Daedalus*, Winter, 1960, 216–227.

(14) Walter Cohen, Spatial and textural characteristics of the *Ganzfeld*, *American Journal of Psychology*, 1957, 70: 403–410.

(15) Experiments by Raehlmann & Krasnogorski, cited in H. Werner, *Comparative Psychology of Mental Development* (Chicago: Follett, 1948), p. 100.

(16) C. W. Valentine, The colour perception and colour preferences of an infant during its fourth and eighth months, *British Journal of Psychology*, 1913–14, 6: 363–386; R. Staples, The responses of infants to color, *Journal of Experimental Psychology*, 1932, 15: 119–141.

(17) C. R. Brian & F. L. Goodenough, The relative potency of color and form perception at various ages, *Journal of Experimental Psychology*, 1929, 12; 197–213. Somewhat different findings are reported by E. F. Elting, An experimental study of color and form perception at various ages, *Vassar Undergraduate Studies in the Behavioral Sciences*, 1958, 1: 33–39. The difference probably reflects differences in sampling.

(18) N. L. Munn, *The Evolution and Growth of Human Behavior* (Boston: Houghton Mifflin, 1955), pp. 243–244.

(19) Wilhelm Preyer, *The Mind of the Child*, Part II, *The Development of the Intellect* (New York: Appleton, 1914), p. 8.

(20) J. F. Dashiell, The role of vision in spatial orientation by the white rat, *Journal of Comparative and Physiological Psychology*, 1959, 52: 522–526. Note that Gibson & Walk, *op. cit.*, find the rat very sensitive to visual depth cues. Similarly, one would assume that the squirrel's climbing and jumping are heavily dependent on visual information, yet these animals, like the rat, seem to have very poor eyesight. It would seem that spatial vision is in some way independent of object vision.

(21) D. R. Griffin, *Listening in the Dark: The Acoustic Orientation of Bats and Men* (New Haven: Yale, 1958). Griffin points out, following Dallenbach and his students (M. Supa, M. Cotzin, & K. M. Dallenbach, "Facial vision": The perception of obstacles by the blind, *American Journal of Psychology*, 1944, 57: 133–183; P. Worchel & K. M. Dallenbach, "Facial vision": Perception of obstacles by the deaf-blind, *Ibid.*, 1947, 60: 502–553), that human beings are capable of echo-location, too. See also W. N. Kellogg, Echo ranging in the porpoise, *Science*, 1958, 128: 982–988. For a survey of some recent findings on synesthetic effects see: I. D. London, Research on sensory

interaction in the Soviet Union, *Psychological Bulletin*, 1954, 51: 531–568.

(22) The relevant literature is cited by R. M. Pangborn, Influence of color on the discrimination of sweetness, *American Journal of Psychology*, 1960, 73: 229–238.

(23) See, for instance, J. H. McFarland, The effect of body tilt on tactual sensitivity. Paper given before the Eastern Psychological Association, 1959.

(24) L. J. Stone, An experimental study of form perception in the thermal senses, *Psychological Record*, 1937, 6: 235–337.

(25) T. X. Barber, Toward a theory of pain: Relief of chronic pain by prefrontal leucotomy, opiates, placebos, and hypnosis, *Psychological Bulletin*, 1959, 56: 430–460. See also H. K. Beecher, Increased stress and effectiveness of placebos and "active" drugs, *Science*, 1960, 132: 91–92.

(26) R. Brown, R. A. Leiter, & D. C. Hildum, Metaphors from music criticism, *Journal of Abnormal and Social Psychology*, 1957, 54: 347–352.

(27) C. E. Osgood, G. J. Suci, & P. H. Tannenbaum, *The Measurement of Meaning* (Urbana: University of Illinois, 1957).

(28) Alvin Moscow, *Collision Course* (New York: Putnam's, 1959). Cited in a review by Walter Lord, *New York Times Book Review*, March 15, 1959, pp. 1, 30.

(29) B. F. Skinner, "Superstition" in the pigeon, *Journal of Experimental Psychology*, 1948, 38: 168–172; W. H. Morse & B. F. Skinner, A second type of "superstition" in the pigeon, *American Journal of Psychology*, 1957, 70; 308–311.

(30) See, for example, Sir Russell Brain, *The Nature of Experience* (London: Oxford University, 1959). Note that Gestalt theory is at least in part a sense-datum theory: since space, objects, and events have their own material organization, we do not need laws of perceptual organization to account for our seeing such physical organization; therefore, the autochthonous laws must be laws for the organization of sense-data.

2

PREVERBAL EXPERIENCE:

2. ORGANISM AND ENVIRONMENT

So far, we have been talking about the perceived characteristics of the preverbal child's environment. Now it is time to look at the patterning of relationships between child and environment and how these change during development.

Egocentrism

The things we have said about early perception could be summarized as indicating that in the course of development one's experience becomes increasingly objective and decreasingly "projective." "Projective perception" refers to the fact that some things which we take to be attributes of reality seem actually to be attributes of ourselves. If, for instance, we see the objects in Heider and Simmel's film on the apparent behavior of geometric forms as possessed of purpose and feeling, it is certainly not because they have purposes or feelings; therefore, we must be supplying this component.

The occurrence of projective perception is usually taken to imply that we somehow project our inner states onto external objects and then proceed to perceive them there. A different, simpler account of projective perception (for which we need a new name) is provided by Piaget's notion of *egocentrism*. Since this term has generated considerable controversy, based largely on misunderstanding, we must begin by saying what it does not mean. Here again, a new name may be called for; what is important is that we understand the mode of functioning to which it refers. Egocentrism does not mean preoccupation with self, for which reason experiments which seek to measure ego-centrism by number of explicit self-references rather miss the point. Egocentric behavior stems from limited awareness of self, as when the toddler cannot correct the movement by which he keeps kicking away the ball he is trying to pick up, or when he plants himself in front of the television set, blocking every-one else's view, or when the preschool child fails to realize that he is obstructing a doorway, or when the adult shouting in anger is unaware that he is shouting, or when a mother is unable to grasp that some undesirable form of behavior in her child is a direct reaction to the way she treats him. This does not mean that a person who behaves egocentrically is never aware of him-self, but only that when self-awareness is submerged in action, egocentric behavior is likely to appear. The notion of egocentrism has been attacked on the grounds that egocentric behavior occurs in adults as well as in children. But as we have said and will say again, adults show all the immaturities of children; but, in addition, they behave in ways never found in children. Adults sometimes take metaphors literally, but young children never take metaphors metaphorically. In the same way, although adults often behave egocentrically, they have also a capacity for detached relativism not found in young children.

Egocentrism does not imply selfishness—although its practical consequences may look like selfishness. An example of egocentric generosity is supplied by a college student who, wanting to give her mother an especially nice birthday present, ignored her mother's repeated assertions that what she needed and wanted most was a new set of gardening tools and bought her an elegant cashmere sweater instead; the student was quite chagrined at her mother's less than wholehearted enthusiasm. (In school-age children, of course, such gifts often reflect a half-formulated anticipation that the adult will find the gift unusable and return it to the giver.) Seeming selfishness results from egocentrism when there is a difference of opinion or a conflict of interest, and the child—or adult—is egocentrically incapable of understanding the other person's point of view or feelings, as when a child interrupts a conversation or is outraged that an adult cannot comply instantly with some wish.

Egocentrism means embeddedness in one's own point of view, without any awareness that one has a point of view rather than an instantaneous, unlimited, exhaustive, and infallible grasp of reality as it actually is. The child does not know his experience as the impact of the world on a sentient organism anchored to a particular point in space, time, and understanding, but simply as *the* world, obvious and unquestionable. Here we can see the kinship between egocentrism and realism. We are not saying that the child has no experience of himself, but only that he does not experience himself experiencing. As we shall see in more detail later, even the infant has some measure of self-knowledge. But when the child is active, his self-awareness is overwhelmed by his awareness of the objects he is dealing with. The toddler, tugging heroically to pick up a stick or a length of rope, cannot see that his task would be considerably easier if he would move his feet off whatever it is that he is trying to pick up. His awareness is of the object defined by those properties that are personally relevant to him, but he does not suspect that he has an orientation or that it colors how things look to him. Stated more simply, the child's total experience is not clearly differentiated into inner (self) and outer (object), largely because inner experience is amorphous and unlocalized by comparison with outer experience. Outer experience is the prototype, and the demarcation of clearly defined inner experiences, such as feelings, attitudes, the representations of body states, and so forth, must await the process of schematization, to be discussed later. Projection, then, refers to the fact that under conditions of realistic and egocentric awareness, some of the individual's inner states may be localized perceptually in the outer world. In general, the child tends to "objectify" strong but insubstantial experiences, as when he hallucinates an imaginary companion.

Egocentrism, like all the other developmental categories to which this book refers, is not an absolute. As an example of behavior midway between egocentrism and relativism, a four-year-old girl asked her father what "that" was, pointing to a place on the side of his jaw. The father guessed he had cut himself shaving and asked if that was what it was. The little girl replied, "I don't know. Here, you look," and turned her father's head in the appropriate direction. What the infant lacks at birth and, hopefully, acquires in the course of development is a dual perspective whereby he not only perceives reality but is aware of himself perceiving and is thus able, within limits, to discount and compensate for his own biases, blind spots, and restricted vision. At the same time, he learns that other people have feelings, sensibilities, passions, and vulnerabilities similar to his own, but may, nevertheless, have geographical, moral, and cognitive perspectives very much unlike his. Egocentrism is obviously closely allied to the geocentrism of early astronomies and the ethnocentrism of most people everywhere.

The shift from egocentrism to relativism requires the establishment of a certain distance between organism and environment; that is, an autonomy of the organism that allows it to resist stimulation, or to defer response pending an act of assessment, or to replace action by contemplation or thought—in sum, to react mediately rather than immediately and to act toward a remote situation rather than a present one. Distance comes with the development of concrete schemata of self and world which we shall discuss later in this chapter. But while distance is essential to autonomy, and autonomy to relativism, these are not enough. True relativism requires the ability to place oneself, by an act of thought, in somebody else's place, to see the world as it looks to him. Relativism can only be attained, then, with the acquisition of language, and further discussion will have to wait until the next chapter.

Behavioral Mobilizations

It follows from all that we have said that perception is not simply the registration upon the organism of energies or messages from without, and that action is not merely the release of an isolated muscle response. Both perception and action entail, initially, a total organismic *mobilization*. Later in development, perception does indeed become a relatively autonomous function, and we can act without having to give ourselves wholly to each single behavior. But in early experience perceptual mobilization is identical with response mobilization—that is, to perceive is to unify oneself with the object. This leads us to the notion, which we shall develop shortly, that there are several different levels of perception. For the moment, though, we must dwell on the notion of mobilization and the kinds of evidence that support it.

Mobilization is akin to *set*, except that set ordinarily implies a narrowing of the range of action, as in the water-jar problem or in a reaction-time experiment, whereas mobilization can be not only toward a particular stimulus or in preparation for a particular kind of response but to a whole sphere of activity. For instance, when we shift from speaking English to speaking another language, even one that we know well, we can almost feel the change of mobilization—professional interpreters, of course, such as those who work at the United Nations, become highly practiced at such transitions, and may even be able to maintain two simultaneous mobilizations. It is interesting to note that truly bilingual people, when switching languages, may undergo a transformation in personality, taking on the national characteristics that go with the new language. It is a common complaint among men that when they come home from work they are not given time to "catch their breath" or to "unwind" before being plunged into the turmoil of domesticity; in effect, they have the problem of putting off their office mobilization and putting on their family one. Similarly, when people "relax" at the end of the day, they are shedding the roles—the mobilizations—they have assumed. The process of mobilizing for action is often revealed in the "intention movements" and rituals of animals, such as the dog's need to circle three times before lying down. Human analogues of intention movements are the pitcher's windup, the orchestra's warmup, the toddler's rocking from foot to foot as a prelude to walking, the orator's clearing of the throat, and the threats and insults with which two drunks work themselves up to physical combat.

Mobilization is akin to *attention*, except that, just as set neglects the input side of the behavioral circuit, attention neglects the output side. However, recent research which shows that auditory nerve responses in the cat are inhibited in the presence of a compelling visual stimulus such as a mouse, or an olfactory one such as the odor of fish, nicely illustrates the organic nature of attention and the kind of mobilization we are talking about.[1] Similarly, studies by Gardner, Licklider, and Weisz [2] indicate that loud noise can effectively suppress pain. Common-sense observation, too, tells us that when we are absorbed in one kind of activity, we may be almost wholly impervious to extraneous stimulation. Conversely, experimental evidence tells us that recognition thresholds are lowered when we have been alerted to expect stimulus-objects belonging to a certain class; such findings also point to the nonspecificity of mobilizations.[3] We should point to the kinship between mobilization and the somatic counterparts of thinking discussed by Humphrey.[4]

The most satisfactory evidence for a concept of mobilization is, of course, the demonstration of a corresponding biological phenomenon. If we are to take a biological view of behavior we must stop thinking of the organism as a collection of autonomous physiological subsystems to be studied individually in their basal, or resting, states and collectively only as they work together homeostatically. Instead, we must see how the body's subsystems are subordinated to and organized in the service of the organism's communication with reality, so that the characteristics of their functioning change in different behavioral contexts. A fine start in this direction is to be found in studies of autonomic functioning by Wenger,[5] Lacey,[6] and others. Above all, we must stop localizing psychology in the central nervous system, vital as it is to human functioning. The work of Lacey, and of Davis and associates,[7] shows that any kind of stimulation, no matter how simple, can reverberate throughout the organism, and the studies in sensory-tonic perception by Werner, Wapner, and collaborators [8] emphasize the importance of extraneural conditions.

Obviously, if one does not look for such organismic effects, as most students of perception have not, one stands a good chance of not detecting them. The study of psychosomatic effects—from the autonomic turbulence of the infant's crying, the acute discomfort produced by the squeal of chalk on blackboard, the emergency reactions described by Cannon, the ulcers of the business executive, to psychogenic abortion in mice [9]—is relevant to an understanding of mobilization. We should also mention the special kind of psychosomatic relationship expressed in the oft-demonstrated potency of the placebo effect.[10] There is evidence, too, that biological mobilization to present stimuli may be important not only for immediate behavior but for physical growth, as in Matthews' finding [11] that the female ring dove does not ovulate until shown another pigeon. If this kind of effect is general, it would imply that theories which assume that ontogenetic changes in behavior are produced by maturational changes must take account of the possibility that many maturational changes are in turn induced by perceptual stimulation.

It is a commonplace to say that the baby's activity involves a total somatic mobilization. As we have just mentioned, when he cries, he cries with his whole body. When he eats, his entire being is centered in the act. In the course of development, our mobilizations become more circumscribed and efficient, so that we can do two or more things at the same time or in rapid alternation, as when a woman knits while watching a movie, or someone carries on a conversation while driving a car. Vestiges of mass action persist, of course, as seen in the writhings and contortions of the school-age boy trying to thread a needle or of the adult trying to solve a difficult problem.

It will be seen that the notion of mobilization is somewhat similar to that of habit-family hierarchy. It should not be necessary to point out, however, that there is an important conceptual difference between the mobilization of an organism and the mobilization of hypothetical constructs called response habits.

Empathy and Participation

One of the most neglected observations of philosophers and early psychologists is the fact that we participate directly and overtly in the behavior of others.[12] The common examples are the spectators at a track meet "helping" a pole-vaulter over the bar, and the motion-picture audience which, seeing the hero sway over the edge of a precipice, leans in the opposite direction to help him recover. Psychology textbooks call such participation "empathy," and although the dictionaries are obscure or inconsistent in their definitions,[13] especially in the distinction between empathy and sympathy, we shall retain the term. It is easy to find other examples: the body English by which we try to steer a pool ball telekinetically, the jolt of pain we feel when we see someone fall down, the way we strain forward as our car labors up a steep incline. Yawns are notoriously contagious, and the frog in someone else's throat makes us want to clear our own. The contagiousness of moods and emotions and atmospheres likewise probably belongs to the same class of phenomena. We all know the experience of saying something and having it go unheeded, only to hear our words coming back to us a few minutes later as our interlocutor's own. When people listen closely, their mouths often move in unison with the speaker's. It is likely that the discomfort we feel when we see a picture hanging crooked, or when we see a precariously balanced stack of chinaware or even a badly balanced design, is an empathic reaction.[14] Swarming behavior, whether of bees, rooks, or human mobs, may have an empathic basis.[15] Needless to say, our empathy may be misplaced. American adults, watching a baby being tightly swaddled, cannot resist a sense of suffocating confinement; if they take the trouble to look more closely, however, they see that the baby himself actually is soothed rather than frustrated by swaddling.

Empathy, in spite of logical arguments such as Koffka's,[16] cannot be considered a second-order, mediated response, if only because of timing: the empathic reaction often anticipates the stimulus behavior; it is we who pull the pole-vaulter up and over. There may, of course, be a lag during which we become mobilized to respond, but, once mobilized, we keep pace with the stimulus, as in photic driving or in our response to music, whether it be in such externals as the tapping of a foot or in such internal reactions (presumably somatic as well as esthetic) as the crescendo of ecstasy that accompanies a crescendo of music.

Empathic phenomena are in keeping with the kind of behavior assumed in the James-Lange theory of emotion, which says, in effect, that we are frightened because we run, we are angry because we strike out, rather than the other way around. However, James and Lange saw the felt emotion as a secondary response based on the perception of our own somatic, especially visceral, reactions to the original stimulus. In the present view, somatic response and feeling are both part of the same global reaction to the stimulus object and so strictly simultaneous. The important point, however, is that the stimulus acts directly on our effector systems, without benefit of perceptual representation or other mediation.[17] This is not to say that we do not perceive the object; but our conscious perception is again contemporaneous with our behavioral and affective mobilization. That is, full conscious awareness is sluggish by comparison with somatic reactivity. It is only when we have already begun to orient ourselves somatically to the object that the object is explicitly perceived. Here we must mention again the principle of microgenesis. As we become explicitly aware of the object, then we may modify our behavior towards it—we may realize, for instance, that we have been frightened by a shadow, or that it would not be politically expedient to display the rage we feel toward a superior. But this kind of modification is highly sophisticated, and we hardly expect it of the animal or the preverbal child.

Strictly speaking, empathy refers only to the behavior of a bystander who becomes vicariously involved in the action of another person or thing. In this strict sense, empathy would be of little help to us in defining prototypical communication with the environment, since there seems to be an increase in empathy with age. There are two points to be made here. First, part of the increase in empathic behavior is a function of the child's expanding cognitive and behavioral scope; that is, there are simply numerically more things and activities with which he is capable of being empathically involved, more things that have meaning for him. Second, with increasing age, the child is increasingly likely to assume the role of observer, without plunging into action every time he is stimulated. More important, however, the same empathic-like process seems to underlie all communication. Realism, dynamism, egocentrism, organismic mobilization, all converge in a state of being where organism and environment interpenetrate each other and act on each other, not from outside but from within. Werner has given the name of "vital experience" to such conditions.[18] To avoid further confusion of terms, we shall refer to this more general kind of field relationship, including both empathic behavior, where one is a participant observer, and reciprocal adjustment, as when one dodges a blow, as *participation*. Here we are following the usage of Lévy-Bruhl and Piaget, but again not necessarily that of the dictionaries.

Later in life, of course, participation is thickly overgrown with mediated forms of behavior, but it still forms the basis of our affective responses. There is every reason to suppose that participation plays an essential part in what we call identification, whether the primitive kind that comes about through imprinting or the more advanced cultural identification found in human beings and, we are beginning to suspect, in other mammals.

Imitation

While imitation—and, we believe, sympathy—has its origins in empathy, it is not the same thing. Empathic behavior is approximately simultaneous with the stimulus behavior, while imitation follows it. Imitation seems rather less blind and automatic than empathy and often serves as a device for mastering, comprehending, or assimilating a piece of behavior or a personal style. In addition, imitation early becomes a vehicle of playful communication between child and adult. Like empathy, imitation is hard to explain, since it requires that the organism find the behavioral counterpart of an external, perceptually given action. This, of course, is a logical difficulty which arises from the dichotomization of subject and object, so that perception and action become two different modes; we prefer to rest on our axiom of participation and so shun the problem.

The developmentally earliest imitation that has been reported is of tongue-protrusion, at ten to twenty days of age.[19] This behavior has something of the character of both imitation and empathy. Like imitation, it follows the stimulus, although it may continue perseveratively for some time. Like empathy, it has a blind, reflexive quality. With increasing age, successive kinds of imitation have less of the quality of forced movements and more closely resemble "voluntary" acts. Within a few months of birth, the baby appears to be enjoying imitation as a form of social interchange. Later, imitation is increasingly divorced from the immediate stimulus situation and may not crop out until hours after the model behavior has come and gone.

The kinds of imitation that appear in the first year or so are represented by the following, drawn from Stern's excellent compilation [20] and our own observations and those of cooperating parent-observers: 0:1½—voice sound, a brrr, with much contortion and straining (observed by Scupin; many infants at this age seem to be trying to imitate such sounds but are unable to utter them); 0:2—lip-smacking and other mouth movements; 0:3—lip-pursing (Preyer); 0:3—crooning to music (may not be imitation, but simply vocalization expressive of pleasure; quite unlike baby's other vocalizations, however); 0:6—large gestures, such as movement of breaking eggs into a bowl; 0:8—functional acts involving large arm movements, e.g., dusting furniture, wiping up floor; 0:8—holding piece of paper above head (Major); 0:8—voice sounds, a, a-a (Stern); 0:10—baba in response to "dada"; 0:9-1:0—inanimate sounds, e.g., ding! of kitchen timer, machine-gun fire on radio, airplane; waving bye-bye, playing pat-a-cake; affective cries, e.g., "Whee!"; 0:11-1:2—words.

It is odd that modern learning theorists who make imitation an important part of their theories seem never to have encountered the extensive literature on imitation, or else to have dismissed it as of no scientific consequence without any attempt at empirical verification. It is especially important to point out, as we shall have occasion to repeat in the next chapters, that although the child imitates various kinds of sounds during infancy, and although certain of these sounds may later be incorporated into speech, the child is incapable of imitating true speech sounds until late infancy or early toddlerhood.

The importance of early imitation is less the particular acts acquired than the familiarization, through action, with different styles of activity and with one's own range of behavioral capacities. Even in later learning, the role of imitation is not the emission of particular responses, which can then be reinforced and stabilized or "shaped," but as an aid to perception and feeling. The child can grasp more clearly what the adult is doing or saying if he repeats it himself. This is analogous to stages in learning to read. The child at first can read only by pronouncing the words aloud; even after he has begun reading silently, one can see from the movements of his mouth and throat that he is still sounding the words to himself; it is only after much practice that people learn to read purely visually. The perception—and comprehension and retention—of difficult material is often a two-stage affair: one first echoes blindly and then attends to the inner reverberations of one's echoes. The preschool child's play, which is clearly imitative, seems to serve the same function: by concretely re-enacting scenes from adult life, the child can grasp and identify with, if only partially, a style of life which he finds simultaneously alien, baffling, and attractive. Needless to say, there is a magical component in the dramatic play of young children, just as there is in the role-playing of older children and adolescents; but in both cases it is a magic that works.

In addition to imitation that produces learning, there is imitation that reflects prior learning. Here we have a distinction between active learning, learning by doing, and learning by absorption, latent learning that enables the child to act appropriately, if imitatively, on some later occasion. This distinction is important to what comes later, particularly as regards learning language.

Learning and Schematization

It is apparent that preverbal behavior is not all of a piece. The one-year-old is a very different creature from the neonate, the one-year-old child is very different from the adult monkey, and so on down the phylogenetic scale. While some part of the change that occurs in infancy can be accounted for in terms of physical maturation, we know that maturation stands in a circular, feedback relationship to experience—the things the organism does, feels, and has done to it. This is not to disparage the role of maturation; it is only to insist that we cannot view it as a simple blossoming of predestined biological characteristics. We must also oppose the notion that it is specific functions that mature. The baby does not walk because his "walking mechanisms" have come into flower, but because he has achieved a kind of orientation to space whereby walking becomes a possible mode of action.

The baby's experience—what he learns—is consolidated as knowledge, and the most fundamental form of knowledge is the *schema*. The notion of schema was first introduced by Head as a neurological construct, and figures prominently in the theories of Bartlett and Piaget. The schema is akin both to Cantril's very broad "frame of reference" and Tolman's narrower "cognitive map," but is, we hope, more susceptible of precise definition.

Stated logically rather than psychologically, a schema is an implicit principle by which we organize experience. Psychologically, the schema has two faces. On the environmental side, we become sensitive to regularities in the way things are constituted and act, so that we perceive the environment as coherent and orderly, in ways that the adult can make explicit as principles but that, for the baby, exist only in the sense that here is the world and things are under pretty good control. On the organismic side, schemata exist in our mobilizations to act and react, which in turn reflect the environmental properties to which we are sensitive.

It is obvious that schemata can be very general or very specific. Most generally, all our activity assumes orientation to a very broad spatial and temporal and situational framework. This orientation, which might be termed our sense of identity, is embodied in a mobilization that can be thought of as our basic consciousness. This basic consciousness is not wholly lost even in sleep, when, as we know, we still remain vigilant to certain signals. Indeed, it is so stubbornly ingrained and pervasive that we may have to resort to drugs in order to loosen its grip enough for us to get to sleep. A genuine loss of basic consciousness occurs only in pathological conditions. Our more specific schemata are of particular objects, of classes of objects—what are sometimes called concepts or categories—and of kinds of relationships, all of which exist in the environment but become accessible to us as they speak to our concrete capacities for feeling and behavior, our competences. But all such specific schemata are subsidiary to more general patterns of orientation which we might call attitudes; these show up both in the valuative coloring of the environment and in the way we carry ourselves, in our personal style.

We have said that the end effect of all learning—whether by insight or accretion or classical or operant conditioning—is schematization. The issue of place learning versus response learning is resolved by saying that all learning involves both. Obviously, some response patterns become so thoroughly habituated that they run themselves off as though directed by a computer program. Habituation is a blessing, since we can turn over many routines to the automatisms of habit, but it can also be a nuisance, as when we neglect to detour on our way home to pick up some ice cream. Unlike Carr and Watson's rats, which obstinately tried to enter a maze alley that was no longer there,[21] human beings can, fortunately, substitute deliberate for habitual action.

Even where the end-product of learning is habituation—habituation to a region of space, to a kind of situation, to the use of habitual, stereotyped acts—we do not have to assume that the learning took place via habit-formation. We may solve a problem once insightfully, but thereafter we cope with it and related problems routinely; routinization, of course, may blind us to the fact that the problem has changed and that we are now responding inappropriately, as in Luchins' water-jar test. As we have implied, however, learning is rarely restricted to a particular act or a particular situation; the animal "learns to learn," and the human being becomes "test-wise" or develops a "problem-solving orientation." It would appear that the more general kind of learning reflected in transfer of training and in the kind of non-specific transfer called "learning sets" is based on schematization.

Schemata exist perceptually in the stability of the environment and, occasionally, in our self-perceptions. They occasionally take on a quasi-imaginal existence of their own, particularly when they let us down, when our expectations are violated. It is only when the comedian delivers his punch-line that we realize that he has carefully constructed a schema, or used an established schema, to lead us to expect one conclusion for which another, perhaps equally logical, has been substituted. We laugh when we see a midget car stop and disgorge an endless throng of occupants. When, climbing a staircase in the dark, we put our foot on the final step and come jolting down through empty air, we realize that we have been steering ourselves by a schema. The low doorway signals itself to us by a tingling of the scalp, perhaps at the point of the impact that taught us this particular schema. We feel shaken and disoriented when we discover that it is Thursday, whereas we have been acting all day as though it were Friday. Clothing fashions of a few years back seem ludicrous because they clash with current schemata. In conditions of strong emotional arousal, schemata may take forthright perceptual shape as hallucinations.

There are schemata that tell us that the environment continues beyond our immediate perceptual ken, that the model whose nude shoulders appear above a screen continues behind the screen and continues *nude* behind the screen. As we have said, the young child is not always certain about the region of space immediately to his rear, but we recognize it as pathological if an adult must constantly look around as though to reassure himself that nothing untoward is going on behind his back. Babies younger than eight or nine months of age show no signs of frustration if an activity is abruptly broken off or a plaything taken away. Children as old as three show limited drive to closure and can stop a song in the middle of a phrase, or a drawing in the middle of a stroke, while an adult feels very uncomfortable until the schematic design has been fulfilled; here, of course, we see a developmental difference in susceptibility to the Zeigarnik effect.[22] It follows, too, that logical implication is a product of the schematic structure of a proposition.

Our awareness of the strange, the odd, the incongruous, the incredible, the impossible, stems from a lack of fit between phenomenon and schema. The infant's fear of strangers develops only after he has had a chance to come to know the members of his own family. It should not be supposed, of course, that strangeness is merely the absence of familiarity. Phenomenologically, strangeness is a positive attribute. The development of fearfulness in the young chimpanzee likewise seems related to the establishment of schemata. The infant chimpanzee plays carelessly with assorted anatomical fragments of a mannequin, but at a somewhat later age, when he has some "idea" of their normal organization, they become terrifying.[23] We seldom tell ourselves explicitly that our next-door neighbor is not a criminal, but it is because this assumption is implicit in our schematization of him that we react with shocked disbelief to the news that he has been arrested for embezzlement or dope-peddling. It is apparent that schematization is central to what Festinger calls "cognitive dissonance."[24] Children are largely immune to cognitive dissonance, as seen in their insensitivity to contradictions, paradoxes, and logical (as opposed to factual or moral) inconsistencies. Our so-called "stereotypes" of thought can be described as schemata.

The phenomenon of "imprinting" seems to involve a schematization both of a talismanic object and of a style of behavior. So conceived, imprinting (as it occurs in birds) becomes a special case of a more general process of species, social, and personal identification. There is, of course, some question as to whether one should apply the term *imprinting* to the attachments formed by human babies; there are analogies, however, although the human baby's attachment develops over a period of five or six months. Thus, the behavioral deterioration seen in infants following separation from the mother (and without opportunity for substitute attachments) would reflect destruction of a primary schema, while the more diffuse pathology and retardation of institution-reared and other deprived children would reflect defective schematization because of the lack of a primary "imprinting" object through whom early experience is mediated.

It is now time to look at some of the specific schemata acquired by the human infant. Schematization occurs in the course of having his needs attended to, being played with and talked to, and, increasingly, of actively exploring the environment. We should note, too, that the taboos the baby encounters, for his own safety or for parental comfort, enter into his schematizations. It is customary to say that babies, once they have gained the use of their hands and, later, their feet, have a strong "exploratory drive." It is probably more accurate to say that the environment exerts a strong pull on the baby. Certain objects, substances, and qualities seem to be especially attractive. Human beings take first priority, and animals may be a close second. Water seems to be a truly elemental substance, and it is a rare—or mishandled—baby who does not delight first in immersion and then in water play. There are forms that ask to be grasped, textures that invite palpation, and holes and crevices that invite probing with a forefinger. It is the way the environment feeds back to his actions that forms the baby's schemata: the paper that crackles or tears, the plastic toy that skitters away from his awkward fingers, the chair that refuses to budge, the toy car that rolls backward and forward but not sideways, the food that sticks to hands, the flavors and odors and sounds that come from everywhere, the pliancy and resiliency and heft and intractability of things.

Schemata of Objects, Space, and Time

The schematization of objects should be expressed in their constancy—of identity, size, shape, color, and brightness—under widely varied viewing conditions. We know that constancy of identity appears quite early, and is seemingly independent of constancy of the component dimensions. The toddler who has never seen a horse except in a horizontal view has no trouble recognizing a picture of a horse seen from above; that is, "horseness" is a property of horses viewed from any angle. Note, however, that identity can be destroyed by changes that to the adult seem trifling. The baby, for instance, may not recognize his mother the first time he sees her dressed up—and made up—to go to a party.

This is not to say that the child's perception of other visual dimensions is inconstant. First, as we have said, the child initially takes no explicit note of these dimensions, so that the question of constancy does not arise. Second, when he does begin to take explicit note of size, shape, and color, his discriminations are quite crude, and the determination of constancy is very difficult. Preliminary findings from a study of constancy of pictured objects in two-year-olds suggest that development is not from inconstancy to constancy (noting that perception is seldom perfectly constant or inconstant) but from ambiguity to constancy. There are some oddities, however. The two-year-old may refuse to guess at the shape of a square foreshortened in one-point perspective to a trapezoid, but instantly recognize it as a square when it is shown in two-point perspective. Somewhat older children tend to call the square in one-point perspective a rectangle, suggesting that foreshortening alters the proportion of base to altitude but not the rectangularity of the corners. A severely foreshortened square seems to lose its identity for the two-year-old, whereas a similarly foreshortened circle does not.

We must note, of course, that studies of constancy in children ask that the subject make a purely visual judgment divorced from any practical action, which is quite difficult for a child. In everyday situations, children, like animals, show excellent constancy. Again, however, there are ambiguities. The two-year-old seems uncertain whether to call his toy dump truck big, because it represents something big, or tiny, which it in fact is. Once he has learned colors, the child has no difficulty with color constancy and names without hesitation colors built up out of juxtaposed elements, as in a tachiste painting.

We would guess from children's drawings that apparent size and other properties are partly determined by emotional factors. People loom larger than houses, and faces are bigger than torsos (which, in the beginning, are omitted altogether). In general, though, children's drawings, and those of naïve adults, suffer from an excess of constancy rather than a lack: surface colors are not modulated in keeping with the play of light and shadow and reflections, distant objects are as large as near ones, tabletops are resolutely rectangular, and the child does his best to depict all four vertical faces of a house.

Size constancy, of course, is related to distance. A recent study by Jenkin and Feallock, which seems to show a developmental trend from inconstancy to constancy, suffers from the fact that stimuli were presented at eye level, thus abolishing many of the situational cues to actual distance.[25] Equally important, the age differences found by Jenkin and Feallock reflect both a small degree of under-constancy on the part of the younger subjects and a small degree of over-constancy on the part of the older ones. Possibly the best summary statement that can be made about the development of constancy is that—assuming the attribute to be a perceptible one—the child's constancy is more vulnerable to loss of information than the adult's. We must also add that even adult size constancy breaks down beyond a certain distance, and it may well be that there is a developmental extension of the range within which size constancy works.

We have already said a good deal about early spatial schematization, so let us turn now to the schematization of time, which begins at birth. Our knowledge of time has its foundations in the biological rhythms of activity and repose, of feeding and digestion, and the external events with which these rhythms are coordinated. All animal organisms, and at least some plants, have daily and seasonal cycles, which are to some degree under the control of external stimulation (such as the alternation of daylight and darkness, the rise and fall of the tides, the phases of the moon, and so forth), but which also become stabilized, under fairly constant conditions, as "biological clocks" which regulate the organism's activities from within.[26] Our habitual human rhythms can be a nuisance. High-speed air travel can land us halfway around the world without an opportunity to adjust our schedules, so that our sleeping and eating patterns are 180° out of phase with our surroundings. Night-shift workers on vacation try to live on normal schedules but spend most of their holidays feeling sleepy; by the time they get back to normal, they have to return to work and make another adjustment. The human child's "biological clock" stabilizes more slowly than that of other species, but by two or three months of age he can be induced to sleep the night through, by six months his digestive cycle is attuned to our three-meals-a-day pattern, and by eight or nine months his somewhat erratic pattern of daytime sleeping and waking becomes one of wakefulness punctuated by two clear-cut naps. (Obviously, we are talking here about the kind of schedules that prevail in our own society.)

But from an early age the child's time is psychological as well as physiological. This can best be seen in his behavior at the age of a month or so, when he begins to *wait* to be fed. It is a very active kind of waiting, the baby holding himself tense, allowing an occasional whimper or bleat to escape, and, if he is being carried about the house (as is usual), straining toward the kitchen where his bottle is warming or toward the room where he is customarily fed. This is, obviously, but a tiny first step toward an orientation to time that comes to include the abstraction of time from space and activity patterns, a massive vocabulary of words with a temporal index, an understanding of the scales which we use to measure time's passage and accumulation, a knowledge first of growing up and then of growing old, a sense of how time slips by at an ever faster rate as one ages, a sense of history and destiny, and the ability to coordinate activities and events in rational sequences and fit them into the larger time scheme.

The Body Schema

We have spoken of the schematic framework which helps tie the environment together in a coherent, familiar, dependable whole. But the schematization of the environment is only half the story. Along with it goes a reciprocal schematization of the self, of one's own capacities for feeling and action, of one's powers and vulnerabilities, and, in a still-diffuse way, one's identity. Before we examine the process of early body schematization, we would do well to recall some of the observations that have been made of the adult's experience of his own body. As adults, our bodies are always with us, mutely and in the background but nonetheless reliably there. At any given moment, we are probably not explicitly aware of where all our members are—is my left leg crossed over the right, or the right over the left, or do I have my feet hooked in the rungs at the side of my chair? am I sitting up straight or slouching? am I scratching myself? is my free hand supporting my cheek as I write or is it lying idle on the tabletop?—but they work together smoothly in every change of posture, they are instantly and without question at our service (unless, of course, our foot has gone to sleep). We count on our bodies in exactly the same way that we count on finding the familiar world at our doorstep when we leave the house. It is usually only in case of malfunction due to sickness or fatigue that our bodies come spontaneously into explicit awareness, but we can at any moment conjure up sensations from any major area of our bodies; we can, if we wish, feel (without touching) our left thigh, or our back, or our fingertips. We might mention the phrase with which Karl Dallenbach used to begin his course in introductory psychology: "Until I told you, you were not aware that your shoes were full of feet." [27]

It is interesting, though, that except under conditions of extreme fatigue we experience ourselves as very nearly weightless. The young child, we would judge, has absolutely no con-

ception of his own weight, since he entrusts himself to the
flimsiest supports and seems oblivious to the fact that the adult
must exert himself and make postural adjustments in order to
carry him. We do not have to measure ourselves against a
doorway in order to know whether we can get through. We do,
however, leave ourselves a considerable margin of error, and individuals asked to estimate the width of their shoulders or their
heads usually overestimate generously. Birdwhistell's observations [28] indicate that we maintain a zone of sensitivity within
which we tolerate intrusion only by those people with whom we
want to be intimate; when two people stand talking, they stay a
fairly constant distance apart, and if one moves forward, the
other immediately moves back. (There are, however, wide
cultural variations in this respect; the Balinese, for instance, love
to huddle together, while we find it intensely disagreeable to be
in a crowded subway train or elevator.) Wapner, Werner, and
Krus [29] have shown that success leads us to experience ourselves
as taller, and failure as shorter, than ordinary. As Schilder [30] has
pointed out, the boundaries of our experienced body are not
defined by our skin. The clothes we wear, the tools we use, are
assimilated to and become extensions of our body schemata—
when we write, we feel the friction of pencil against paper at
the tip of the pencil, not in the finger surfaces that touch the
pencil.

In general, awarenesss of our body boundaries represents an
interruption of smooth communication with the environment and
so is distracting and unpleasant. It is probably for this reason
that young children dislike having sticky fingers, and not because
of any guilt over fecal play. This is not to say that body awareness as such is disagreeable; both generalized body experience, as
in swimming, and more concentrated experience, as in coitus, can
be highly pleasurable.

The body schema is made conscious in the case of the phantom
limb, the member that persists in experience after amputation.
The existence of the phantom limb clearly illustrates how a body
schema is built out of our capacities for pragmatic action. The
phantom limb disappears gradually by telescoping in upon itself,
as though the failure of feedback leads to successively more

restricted definitions of the member's reach.[31] It would be interesting to test the hypothesis that the phantom limb persists
longer in amputees who are bedridden or otherwise restricted
in mobility than in those who are active and so have more
opportunity to redefine the body schema. It is worth noting that
dogs which have lost one or two legs rapidly develop a new and
effective system of balance and locomotion, but if a stump
remains, the partial feedback seems to disturb the process of
readjustment. The reverse of the phantom limb is the paralyzed
member which is denied as part of the body (anosognosia).
Here the limb enters into the body's sensory schema but not
its operational schema and so is ambiguously both present and
absent for its owner.

The newborn baby seems to have a very limited knowledge
of his own body. The only parts of his body that he uses in any
sense volitionally are his mouth and his hands. (He can, of
course, turn his head as an incidental part of the movement
of pursuing something with his mouth.) His hands come into
play when he tries, like his simian cousins, to cling to parental
fur when he is held against an adult body, when he clutches at
breast or bottle while nursing, and when he grasps and holds
on to an adult finger. The author's observations are incomplete
at this point. As far as we have been able to discover, the baby
makes no attempt to grasp anything except a finger up to about
age three months; if one wants to put a rattle into his hand, one
must first pry open his fist. Some babies can suck their thumbs
expertly from birth on, but a great many babies can at first only
jam their fingers into their mouths, and this only laboriously. One
can induce various reflex movements of the legs, but the baby
moves them himself, somewhat ambiguously, only as part of his
rooting behavior. Even when the baby begins to gain control of
his hands as instruments for reaching out and grasping, they are
still only partially his. When, shortly before six months, he discovers his hands explicitly and visually, it is as external objects:
the two hands reach out and grasp each other and carry each
other up to his eyes for examination. More striking still is the
baby's discovery of his feet, which he treats as alien entities
which sometimes drift into view and which his now-active hands

capture and bring to his eyes for inspection and to his mouth for tasting. When he bites on his toes, he seems surprised that it hurts. After a while there is a certain complicity in the performance, the baby bringing his feet to where his hands can reach them easily but still seeming unaware that hands and feet have any internal connection. As an example of how the baby's self-schema may be tied to external spatial arrangements, one nine-month-old, who could perfectly well pick up pieces of food from his table top and put them in his mouth, when confronted with the same food in a bowl was at a loss how to grasp it, and finally lowered his mouth to the bowl like an animal.

Up to about age six months the baby pays no attention to his own image in the mirror, although by this time he recognizes the reflection of the person who is holding him. At about six months he studies his own reflection earnestly; within another month he plays with it and greets it with smiles and kisses; and before age ten months shows clearcut recognition of his image, reaching up to touch his reflected hat or looking back and forth from reflection to clothing.[32] (It is not until about age eighteen months that the baby recognizes photographs of himself.)

Although the baby's pleasure in babbling is undoubtedly contingent on auditory feedback, it is doubtful that he hears his own voice. One child discovered his own voice at age ten months when, screeching to be fed, he suddenly forgot about supper and began a pattern of screech-listen-laugh, which he repeated several times. Discovery of the genitals may be long delayed or may occur only by accident. One boy, just under a year old, in his bath, noticed something in the water, seized it curiously, and then grinned with delight at the resulting sensation.

Shortly after the age of a year, the baby may explore the adult's facial features and then touch his own face in search of corresponding ones. It is worth noting that the baby knows that some features come in pairs. If he is inspecting an adult ear, he then turns the adult's head to bring the other ear into view; when feeling his own features, he touches both eyes and both ears. Although he knows at one level that he has two eyes, he experiences them functionally as one: when he tries to peer through a cardboard tube, he plants it squarely between his eyes and is helpless to do anything about his inability to see through. This "Cyclops effect" continues well into the preschool years, long after the child can say in words that he has two eyes and draws faces with two eyes. When the one-year-old discovers his facial features, he may be able to point them out on demand. It is interesting, however, that they are not precisely localized: he has to grope a bit before he finds them.

Even in toddlerhood, when the child has developed considerable skill in the use of his body, touch localization on the body is still very poor. Young children's two-point touch thresholds are very broad, and when asked to point to a spot touched by the experimenter, the child may miss by a wide margin. Similarly, although there is no doubt that the child feels pain, he may be unable to say where it is. When the child begins using his hands for rotary movements, as in turning a radio on or off, or screwing or unscrewing a bottle cap, he characteristically uses his right hand for clockwise rotations and his left for counterclockwise, even though he can use either hand either way. We have already mentioned that the toddler may not realize that he is standing on something that he wants to pick up; similarly, if he catches his foot under the edge of a rug, he may have no notion of what is holding him back. The development of sphincter control is yet another step in bringing the body and its functions into consciousness and schematizing them in a total pattern of experienced competence—which, in the toddler, sometimes verges on omnipotence.

All these observations point to the essential ambiguity of our knowledge of our own bodies: we know them both as subject and as object. Our bodies are at once instrumentalities for knowing and things known. It is evident that while the body has to play the dual role of subject and object, its knowledge of itself can never be anything like complete.

The process of body schematization is, obviously, closely implicated in ego-world differentiation. Given the primary ambiguity of experience, it is not hard to understand how the boundaries between self and world can be defined in pathological ways, so that what is objectively outside is taken to be inside, and one's own body parts and functions are felt as external to oneself. Many individuals feel that their own wishes, feelings, thoughts, and actions are produced by alien and even repugnant agencies, sometimes conceived of as mysterious forces and sometimes as material beings or mechanical devices which act from without or are implanted inside the body. There is some evidence that auditory hallucinations may be actual perceptions of the schizophrenic's own subvocal speech. Here again we are reminded of the egocentrism that prevails until the stratification of consciousness whereby we not only experience reality but experience ourselves experiencing it, even if only implicitly and in the background.

Levels of Perception

It is time to summarize and make more explicit the contrast we have drawn between immature and mature forms of perception. We can recognize two major kinds of perception, each of which has a mature and an immature version, and each of which represents a way of being mobilized toward reality. The first kind is what we have called *participation*, where we respond organismically in an unmediated, reflex-like way to the dynamic, affective, physiognomic properties of the environment. The second is *contemplative perception*, where action is suspended in favor of inspection, judgment, and analysis. It is this kind of perception which the psychologist studies, although it is the first kind which predominates in real life, even among adults.

The distinction of maturity-immaturity that cuts across these two kinds of perception (which themselves are developmental in nature) is in terms of relativism and egocentrism, of the varieties of attributes accessible to the perceiver, of the degree of schematization and consequent stability of perception and flexibility of action, of the extent of ego-differentiation whereby feelings are internalized and object properties objectified, and of abstractness and concreteness. Thus, even the infant may contemplate something visually, instead of concretely doing something with it, but we expect that the experienced object is still a compound of subjective and objective, that properties obvious to the adult are either invisible or but dimly felt, and so forth. The adult, on the other hand, reacts immediately to objects, without really looking at them, almost absent-mindedly, but his action takes place within a stable framework of time and space and expectation and is correspondingly orderly and efficient. The primitive dynamic properties are still there, but they have been overlaid by the systematic relational dynamics given through wider understanding, and by the objective properties that the adult has discovered.

We cannot contrast the contemplative and participative modes in terms of active-passive or of active-inactive. Participation implies activity, but it may be the relatively passive activity of empathy or stimulus-bondage, or a truly reciprocal activity between subject and object (or subject and subject), or an activity in which the individual dominates the object—the pleasures of sadism are said to derive in part from participation in the victim's masochism. Nor does contemplation imply inaction. Apart from the "mental" action of analysis or judgment that may be involved, contemplative perception is often coordinated with concrete action, as in solving a problem. Since contemplative perception is sluggish by comparison with participation, and since the action that goes with it may be mediated by conscious thought, the contemplative orientation usually leads to a delay in response.

There is, of course, still a third mode of perception, the sensorial, exemplified by the artist's retinal vision of reality or the phonetician's attention to speech sounds. Such perception is not found in everyday life and, indeed, requires considerable practice. Even after much training, the artist still has to resort to squinting, to reduction screens, and to measuring devices as counterbalances to his human tendencies to constancy. Even the trained phonetician may have difficulty detecting familiar phonetic elements in an unfamiliar context. Sensorial perception is interesting, but it is not of basic theoretical concern for us as it is for those who consider—without evidence—that all perception begins with pure sensation.

In closing this chapter, we want to stress once more that sophisticated behavior is rooted in the same kind of organism-environment relationships as primitive behavior. Differentiation is not the same as alienation. Various kinds of early experience can disrupt the normal affective bonds between individual and environment, or produce abnormal attachments as in fetishism, or deprive the individual of opportunity to form normal attachments, but such patterns should not be taken as prototypical. Differentiation refers to an ability to stand apart from the environment, to contemplate it perceptually or to ignore it in favor of excursions into past or future or hypothetical time. But such behavior is always effortful; the present situation exerts a constant tug on the individual, which is why abstract thinking is so hard and why, probably, the adolescent finds it hard to maintain his lofty idealism in a not particularly idealistic society. The most sophisticated adults, in their everyday lives and especially in personal matters, show evidence of egocentrism, of realism, of anthropomorphism and animism, of behaving on the basis of affective intuitions rather than logical judgments or careful empirical study, of instability and inconsistency, and of failures of symbolization. There are always segments of reality about which we are ignorant, whether because we are not interested—some people feel no urge to study history, or geology, or chemistry—or because we have had no opportunity to learn —what could the Eskimo know of life in the tropics?—or because nobody has yet remarked, investigated, and called attention to a particular fact—Semmelweis was assailed as a crackpot and a subversive when he suggested that midwives could halt the spread of puerperal fever by washing their hands between cases. Our different bits of knowledge are never perfectly correlated; most people, for instance, study American and European history separately, and it may not occur to them, say, that the founding of Jamestown coincides with the time of Shakespeare. We may have a double standard for the concrete and familiar and for the remote and unfamiliar: we know from experience that people are only human, and so imperfect, yet we have no trouble idealizing public heroes and celebrities and crediting them with superhuman powers. We may have a hard time coordinating our concrete practices with our abstract knowledge; we know that it is bad policy to slam on the brakes when the car starts to skid, but there is a powerful impulse to do so nonetheless. As we can see, the adult's orientation to reality contains endless possibilities for primitive thought and action. In the next chapters, however, we shall stress the less primitive aspects of behavior and the way the individual develops toward them.

NOTES

(1) Raúl Hernández-Peón, Harald Scherrer, & Michel Jouvet, Modification of electric activity in cochlear nucleus during "attention" in unanesthetized cats, *Science*, 1956, 123: 331–332.

(2) W. J. Gardner, J. C. R. Licklider, & A. Z. Weisz, Suppression of pain by sound, *Science*, 1960, 132: 32–33.

(3) D. W. Chapman, Relative effects of determinate and indeterminate *Aufgaben, American Journal of Psychology*, 1932, 44: 163–174; D. H. Lawrence & G. R. Coles, Accuracy of recognition with alternatives before and after the stimulus, *Journal of Experimental Psychology*, 1954, 47: 208–214.

(4) George Humphrey, *Thinking* (London: Methuen, 1951), ch. 7.

(5) M. A. Wenger, The measurement of individual differences in autonomic balance, *Psychosomatic Medicine*, 1941, 3: 427–434.

(6) J. I. Lacey, The evaluation of autonomic responses: Toward a general solution, *Annals of the New York Academy of Sciences*, 1956, 67: 123–164.

(7) R. C. Davis, A. M. Buchwald, & R. W. Frankman, Autonomic and muscular responses, and their relation to simple stimuli, *Psychological Monographs*, 1955, 69, no. 405; R. C. Davis, L. Garafolo, & Kolbjørn Kveim, Conditions associated with gastrointestinal activity, *Journal of Comparative and Physiological Psychology*, 1959: 52, 466–475.

(8) A bibliography, complete to 1957, of sensory-tonic studies conducted at Clark University may be found in S. Wapner and H. Werner, *Peceptual Development* (Worcester: Clark University, 1957).

(9) H. M. Bruce & D. M. V. Parrott, Role of olfactory sense in pregnancy block by strange males, *Science*, 1960, 131: 1526.

#102 2006-03-23 3:02PM
Item(s) checked out to Han, Zi D'arcy.

TITLE: Pragmatics of human communication
BARCODE: 39015006908281
DUE DATE: 06-04-18

TITLE: Language and systems / [by] Neil
BARCODE: CBM50020504086
DUE DATE: 06-05-06

TITLE: Language and the discovery of rea
BARCODE: 39345002735341
DUE DATE: 06-05-06

TITLE: The origins of unhappiness : a ne
BARCODE: 39450102721277
DUE DATE: 06-04-13

TITLE: Telepathy : the surrender of cul
BARCODE: 39345010173739
DUE DATE: 06-04-13

(10) See, for instance: David Rosenthal & J. D. Frank, Psychotherapy and the placebo effect, *Psychological Bulletin,* 1956, 53: 294–301; A. K. Shapiro, A contribution to a history of the placebo effect, *Behavioral Science,* 1960, 5: 109–135.

(11) L. H. Matthews, Visual stimulation and ovulation in pigeons, *Proceedings of the Royal Society of London,* 1939, 126 (B): 557–560. See also: C. J. Smith, Mass action and early environment in the rat, *Journal of Comparative and Physiological Psychology,* 1959, 52: 154–156 (see p. 143); F. A. Beach, "Psychosomatic" phenomena in animals, *Psychosomatic Medicine,* 1952, 14: 261–276.

(12) An exception to this neglect is a paper by C. F. Haner & E. R. Whitney, Empathic conditioning and its relation to anxiety levels (given before the American Psychological Association, 1960), which indicates that conditioned responses can be acquired empathically. See also: J. V. Murphy, R. E. Miller, & I. A. Mirsky, Interanimal conditioning in the monkey, *Journal of Comparative and Physiological Psychology,* 1955, 48: 211–214.

(13) For instance, H. B. English & A. C. English, A Comprehensive Dictionary of Psychological and Psychoanalytical Terms (New York: Longmans, Green, 1958), p. 178: "While the empathic process is primarily intellectual . . ." As will be seen, this view is widely at variance with the present author's.

(14) Theodor Lipps, *Ästhetik. Psychologie des Schönen und der Kunst* (Hamburg: Leopold Voss, 1903, 1906).

(15) J. B. S. Haldane, Animal ritual and human language, *Diogenes,* Autumn 1953, 61–73. See also the discussion on behavioral contagion in Bertram Schaffner, ed., *Group Processes* (New York: Josiah Macy, Jr., Foundation, 1959), pp. 83–131.

(16) Kurt Koffka, Problems in the psychology of art, *Art: A Bryn Mawr Symposium* (Bryn Mawr: Bryn Mawr College, 1940), pp. 180–273.

(17) The contemporaneity of movement and sensation is stressed by F. A. Hayek, *The Sensory Order* (Chicago: The University of Chicago, 1952), following Boring and, especially, V. von Weizsaecker, *Der Gestaltkreis. Theorie der Einheit von Wahrnehmen und Bewegen* (Stuttgart: Georg Thieme, 1940).

(18) *Comparative Psychology of Mental Development,* pp. 96–103.

(19) René Zazzo, Le problème de l'imitation chez le nouveau-né, *Enfance*, 1957, 2: 135–142.

(20) William Stern, *Psychology of Early Childhood*, 2d ed. (New York: Holt, 1930), pp. 90–95.

(21) H. A. Carr & J. B. Watson, Orientation in the white rat, *Journal of Comparative Neurology*, 1908, 18: 27–44. Similar behavior can be seen in real life, as when a flying squirrel, returning to its nest in a tree that had been knocked down, soared to its accustomed landing place, braked, and fell clawing at the air. Instead of climbing up the stump to where the nest was still waiting, the squirrel ran off and repeated the same futile approach pattern half a dozen times until the human observers propped the felled tree back up and so provided a landing place.

(22) Such a trend has been shown in older children. See R. N. Sanford, Age as a factor in the recall of interrupted tasks, *Psychological Review*, 1946, 53: 234–240.

(23) D. O. Hebb & A. H. Riesen, The genesis of irrational fears, *Bulletin of the Canadian Psychological Association*, 1943, 3: 49–50.

(24) Leon Festinger, *A Theory of Cognitive Dissonance* (Evanston: Row, Peterson, 1957).

(25) Noël Jenkin & S. M. Feallock, Developmental and intellectual processes in size-distance judgment, *American Journal of Psychology*, 1960, 73: 268–273. See also: V. R. Carlson, Overestimation in size-constancy judgments, *American Journal of Psychology*, 1960, 73: 199–213.

(26) F. A. Brown, Jr., Living clocks, *Science*, 1959, 130: 1535–1544. See also: Paul Fraisse, *Psychologie du Temps* (Paris: Presses Universitaires de France, 1957), chs. 1 & 2.

(27) E. G. Boring, Karl M. Dallenbach, *American Journal of Psychology*, 1958, 71: 1–40.

(28) R. L. Birdwhistell, Kinesic analysis of filmed behavior of children, in B. Schaffner, ed., *Group Processes* (New York: Josiah Macy, Jr., Foundation, 1956), pp. 141–144.

(29) S. Wapner, H. Werner, & D. M. Krus, The effect of success and failure on space localization, *Journal of Personality*, 1957, 25: 752–756.

(30) Paul Schilder, *The Image and Appearance of the Human Body* (London: Kegan Paul, 1935).

(31) W. B. Haber, Reactions to loss of limb: Physiological and psychological aspects, *Annals of the New York Academy of Sciences*, 1958, 74: 14–24.

(32) These observations vary slightly in timing, but not in principle, from those reported by Ruth Griffiths (*The Abilities of Babies*, New York: McGraw-Hill, 1954) and by J. C. Dixon (Development of self recognition, *Journal of Genetic Psychology*, 1957, 91: 251–256).

CHAPTER

3

THE ACQUISITION OF LANGUAGE

Now that we have stressed the pervasiveness of primitive modes of experience, it is time to look at some characteristics of mature experience. This will serve as our introduction to the acquisition of language, since our chief concern is with the role of language in effecting the transition from primitive to mature functioning.

We can begin our summary of adult experience by saying that, in spite of flaws and lacunae and inconsistencies, the world of the adult is broader, more variegated, more coherent, and more predictable than that of the child. His tendencies to primitive realism apart, the adult recognizes that the world contains several sorts of reality. A muscular ache is just as real as a muscle, but they belong to different orders, the subjective and the objective; a muscle belongs to the order of "thing," muscle tissue to that of "substance," and the contraction of a muscle to that of "process" or "event." Since, of course, most people are not professional logicians, they may make such distinctions only schematically and implicitly, rather than verbally and explicitly. The adult knows that the name of an object is an arbitrary label, and that object and name belong to two different realms. Similarly, he knows that the same object can be described at different levels of analysis. We can describe a human being in terms of his chemical composition, as an anatomical assembly, as a homeostatic system, as a behavior system, as a person, or as an anonymous component in a higher-order system such as a discussion group, a mob, or a society. The adult knows also that one can distinguish between objects and attributes of objects, and between central, essential attributes, which cannot be altered without changing the object's identity, and peripheral, incidental or accidental ones.

The adult, if only because he has lived longer and seen more than the child, has a broader perspective and a stronger sense of continuity. He can see further into the past and future than the child, and knows, in a way that the child cannot, that the world preceded him and will survive him. Because of his perspective, he is likely to have a sense of direction, of purpose and meaning, in his life; that is, his present actions are often addressed to remote future outcomes as well as to immediate effects.

Just as the adult has acquired a perspective on time and space, so has he acquired perspective on himself. Ego-differentiation, we must remember, has two aspects, differentiation of self from environment and of self from self. The progress of self-perspective shows up clearly in our feelings about our own past. To most adults, it seems incredible that they might once have taken seriously their ability to skin the cat, or worried about how many times they could chin themselves, or felt a deep, days-long depression because they were not allowed to buy a particular article of clothing; the novels that shook us to the roots of our being in adolescence now seem, upon rereading, wholly banal and contrived and superficial; the classic movies, nostalgically revisited, prove to be technically crude, archaic in sentiment, and wholly without power of illusion; our youthful ambitions and projects now seem pathetically romantic and idealistic.

The various spheres in which the adult operates are described by Merleau-Ponty [1] as spatialities. Thus, there is not only the familiar geographical space in which we live and move, but also a body space, a sexual space, a historical space, a human space, a social space, a (for believers) religious space, and so forth. That these have a spatial character for us may be implicit in our choice of generic metaphors: "sphere," "realm," "area," "domain," "field." As Merleau-Ponty points out, certain "spaces" may be developmentally prior, as with human space, to everyday geographical space; but they are all coordinated—if imperfectly —in terms of the space in which we move and act. Indeed, according to Merleau-Ponty, each space is defined by a particular style of bodily movement, by a mobilization that sensitizes us to certain kinds of stimulation and enables us to act in certain ways. It will be seen why this formulation is congenial to the present approach, since it permits us to found the most abstract and abstruse schematizations of the adult on our concrete schematizations of space.

Stages in the Acquisition of Language

Now that we have had a glimpse of where the baby's cognitive development is headed, let us return to the problems of learning to talk. The individual's learning of language has its origins in early infancy, long before he has said a word. Within a few weeks after birth the baby's cries of distress, and then of anger and aversion, change from the symptomatic to the expressive and communicative. Further rudiments of communication can be found in the baby's early social play, particularly the conversation-like exchange of babbles that goes on between parent and child. The first quasi-symbolic communication appears in the second half of the first year, when the infant devises ways to tell people that he wants something and what it is he wants. He does this by a process of concrete enactment: to be picked up, he holds out his arms to an adult; to reinstate a round of merriment at the dinner table, he simulates laughter; to get an adult to operate a plaything, he hands it to the adult or moves the adult hand to the toy; to initiate the game in which the adult chases and catches him, he starts paddling away on all fours, looking back over his shoulder for the adult to follow. At about age nine months, he begins to shriek as a way of getting things.

If he wants something within view, he reaches toward it; otherwise, the adult is obliged to guess, offering him likely satisfiers. Wrong guesses are met by further shrieks, the right one by a satisfied grunt. At a more advanced level of communication, in early toddlerhood, we find the child using objects as tokens of what he wants to say: if he wants an adult to play the phonograph for him, he gets a record and brings it to the adult; if he wants to go out, he brings his coat. Behavior of all these kinds is within the range of the higher mammals: the dog who wants to be let out scratches at the door; if he wants to be taken for a walk, he fetches his leash; if he is hungry, he brings his dish; the home-raised chimpanzee, faced with too difficult a problem, directs his master's hand to the task.

Active and Passive Language

So far, we have been describing the child's first attempts at active communication, but, as far as genuine symbolic language goes, passive understanding long precedes active speech. The baby's first reactions are largely to commands and requests (what Skinner [2] would call "mands") of the form "Give me the . . . ," but he also responds appropriately to a variety of cue words connected with familiar games (peek-a-boo, this little piggy, etc.), with routine activities (lunch time, bath time), and with people and things ("Give it to Daddy," "Where's the block?"). By the end of the first year, the child may also respond appropriately to "Show me your eye," "Show me your mouth," etc. The author has not been able to discover a fixed sequence of passive understandings, and for the moment we can say only that all these reactions appear more or less simultaneously, late in the first year and early in the second.

Again, responses of the sort described are not unknown among animals, but there is a difference. Most essentially, the child learns to respond to requests and cue words without specific training and without reward; at a given point of experience, he simply knows what they mean. Both animal and child learn to respond to commands ("Stay!" "Sit!" "Wait!" "Beg!"), to signals, as in classical conditioning experiments where a word becomes

the conditioned stimulus for food or electric shock, and to
referential words ("stick," "ball"). Like animals, too, the child
at this stage distinguishes various tones of voice: the soothing
and loving, the joshing and jocular, the matter-of-fact, the angry
and reproachful, the hurt and pathetic, and so forth. The baby
much earlier, perhaps from age three months, could distinguish
between mock anger and real anger; now he distinguishes
between things said in a spirit of travesty and things said in
earnest. Indeed, some children learn to feign emotions play-
fully before they learn to talk. One child, age fourteen months,
having bumped his head on a cupboard door and been solaced
by his mother, returned to the cupboard three successive times,
circumspectly bumped his head, screwed up his face in a
grimace of pain mixed with a self-pleased grin, and, whimpering,
went to his mother to be comforted. It is interesting to note,
however, that children do not understand irony or sarcasm until
the school years.

The phenomena of passive language lead us to agree in part
with Skinner's assertion [3] that a verbal stimulus does not differ
in any essential way from any other kind of stimulus. The
human voice seems to be intrinsically meaningful, at least from
a few weeks of age, and language comes to the baby via a
medium charged with affect and in a context of facial expressions, gestures, actions, and behavioral objects. Like a traveler in
a foreign land, or like someone listening to a radio through static,
the baby begins to get the gist, the global sense first of what is
said directly to him and then of what is said in his presence.
There is no logical reason why an infant should find a word any
less meaningful than, say, a chair, a flower, or a dog. We must
remember, though, that material objects in the material world
belong to visual and tactual space, which means that they have
an objectivity, a solidity, a permanence, a locus, a manipula-
bility denied to sounds, however freighted with vital experience
and synesthetic qualities these may be. The baby is oriented to
action, not to contemplation and ratiocination, and what, after
all, can he *do* with a word? Ephemeral though language may be,
words do come to stand out as meaningful parts of the familiar

objective environment, although still closely implicated with the people who speak them and the objects they denote. That is, the child does not at first understand what words mean, but what the person using them means; he does not learn that such-and-such an object is *called* such-and-such, but that this thing *is* chair or dog or whatever.

The Beginnings of Speech

Before the child has any active vocabulary of true words, however, he does try to speak, pointing to something he wants and working his mouth strenuously as though in search of words. Further, the child may give evidence of building a vocabulary prior to speaking. He may point at an object, making an interrogatory sound (in one child, "Buh? Buh?"), and when supplied with a name, point to something else. Then, too, there is the phenomenon known as expressive jargon. Before the child has any words at his disposal, and sometimes for a while after he has begun to use single words, he tries to tell people things in a stream of gibberish which has all the expressive intonations of genuine speech, is accompanied by expressive gestures, and often sounds as though it would make sense if only the child wouldn't go so fast.

All these observations, and others that follow, point to an important principle. The child is not learning merely to speak, or to understand words, or to build up a stock of words—he is learning a whole mode of behavior, the linguistic, which is prior to any particular symbolic acts in which he may engage.

It is not always easy to tell when the child begins to speak. He may produce a wordlike sound in what seems an appropriate circumstance but fail to repeat it, either spontaneously or on demand. What may be a word can consist of a sound that is prominent in the child's babbling, making a distinction difficult; one child, for instance, consistently exclaimed "Bah! Bah!" both at bath time and when about to have a bottle, but he also bah-ed liberally, if less consistently, at other times. The child may produce a standard sound for a given situation, but a sound midway between expressive vocalization and true word; one child, for instance, announced his hunger with a cry of "maamaa-maa," which is of ambiguous linguistic status.

Such obscurities should not lead us to believe that verbalization is continuous with vocalization. In the first place, some children show a very sharp transition from babbling to the use of true words—and sometimes, if the literature is to be credited, to full sentences. Also, even in cases where the boundaries are blurred, there soon emerges behavior which is clearly verbal. It is an accepted tradition that the child's first word is likely to be *mama* or *dada*. These two sounds are ingredients in most babies' babbling, and it is likely that adults hear them as words. In fact, however, the meaningful use of *mama* or *dada* is likely to trail well behind other words, often very unlikely-seeming ones. One child's first word was *fish* (pronounced "heefsh"), applied to a Japanese paper fish that hung on the wall of her room and later generalized to a great variety of other things, not including fish. Another child's first word, along with some other sounds that might have been words, was *banana* ("na,na,na").

Although some children embed real words in a stream of expressive jargon, jargon quickly disappears and the child settles down to speaking in one-word utterances (holophrasis). These early sentences seem to be of three main kinds: interjections, such as *hi*, *bye*, and *no*; denomination, or simply naming objects; and commands ("Eat!" "Milk!" "Up!" "Out!"). Interjections and imperative statements are easily understood as part of the child's affective and pragmatic communication with his surroundings. Denomination, however, which seems a more abstract form of activity, deserves a further word. Some denomination seems purely reflexive—the object elicits its name. Sometimes the child names objects as a way of communicating with adults; he enjoys the adult's pleasure and approval, and he enjoys the very fact of communication. Some of the child's naming activity seems to be a request for verification: "Is this a . . . ?" rather than "This is a. . . ." Finally, the child names things to himself, just as though exercising a skill.

It has been said that the child's initial vocabulary consists of nouns, since objects are the first things to have names. Nouns do predominate in the speech of young children, but the child is perfectly capable of using verbs, adjectives, and adverbs referring to meaningful aspects of his experience. The first adjective used by some children is *hot;* it is not clear, however, whether they use it in reference to a single attribute or as a catch-all term for hot things, such as soup and stoves and radiators. Depending on parental usage, too, it may mean simply "Danger!" At the same time that the child begins to use the words he already knows, he sets about learning new ones. Sometimes he asks, by pointing and inquiring "Whadda?" or simply looking to the adult for an identifying label. But the bulk of his vocabulary is picked up simply by hearing words used in context.

The next step in speaking comes with the combination of words into utterances, first two at a time, then three, and so forth to the point where one can no longer keep track. Some writers have assumed that the increasing complexity of utterances comes about through increasing definition and articulation of jargon-like wholes. In fact, though, the child's first two-word utterances are usually predicative statements painfully pieced together, with the words juxtaposed rather than connected, as "Boy. Running." or "Fly. Bite." (Since our information on language learning comes almost entirely from observations of Western European children, we do not know whether children learning a language of radically different structure, especially one in which noun and predicates form a single unit, would show comparable behavior.) The child at first dispenses wholly with pronouns, copulas, conjunctions, and prepositions. He makes somewhat spotty use of past tenses almost from the beginning, but for the most part relies on the present tense plus context to convey a past reference. Some children have to struggle with the relativism of pronouns, and, echoing other people, call themselves "you" and others "I"; one child at age three, long after she had mastered most pronominal uses, still used "we" to refer collectively to her mother and father: "Are we going out to dinner?" meant "Are Mommy and Daddy going out to dinner?" Other children, however, catch on at once, or at least never use pronouns in reverse. First-person singular pronouns (I, me, my, mine) and the third-person neuter accusative (it) usually appear first, although some children refer to themselves entirely in the third person, as "Baby" or by their given name, into the pre-school years. The plural and possessive forms of nouns are used very soon after speech begins.

It is with copulas and the definite article that one observes something like the differentiation of verbal elements from a syncretic totality. A hint of sibilance at the end of a noun fore-shadows the emerging *is*, a barely perceptible "yuh" prefixed to a noun anticipates *the*. However, the indefinite article, as well as *one, two, this, these, more,* and *another,* all appear earlier as differentiated units. So, too, do *and, too, again,* and a great many prepositions. Needless to say, some frequently recurring word groups are learned as a single word, such as "awgone"; a two-and-a-half-year-old, playing in the kitchen with the pots and pans, asks, "Can I play with this potandpan?" Also, some words come out in syncretic fusions, as in a two-year-old's designation of a well-known dentifrice as "colpaste."

The composing of statements points to the fact that in learn-ing language the child does not merely acquire a stock of words. As Brown and Berko [4] and Ervin [5] have pointed out, the child also learns what adults know as the "rules" of grammar and syntax—rules of flexion for tense and mood and number (and, with pronouns, gender and case), of word order, and, eventually, of constructing compound and complex sentences. He learns the intonations that go with such formal distinctions as declarative-imperative-interrogatory, and also those that go with persiflage, exasperation, fatigue, sympathy, and so forth, all of which are highly conventionalized, as becomes embarrassingly evident when we listen to children aping their parents' ways of speaking.

The child's learning of the rules is by no means flawless. He may initially pick up concretely, for instance, the forms "I bring-I brought." Then, as he begins speaking according to the rules, he shifts to such forms as "I bringed" and even "I broughted." Indeed, affixes may be completely displaced, as in "He pick it ups" (alternatively, "He pick up its") and "I walk homed." In addition to these variations on standard flexions, the child invents flexions of his own, as in "They're fighting with their chother" and "We're going with our chother." Such "errors" are interesting because they show that the child acquires general principles independent of vocabulary and that such learning does not take place by direct imitation. We must stress that what the child learns from other speakers is not ready-made formulations—although he picks up some of these, too—but a way of constructing formulations, a set of schemata. If one tells a two-year-old, "Go ask Mommy for some soap," he does not say to his mother, "Mommy, for some soap" but "Daddy want soap." That is, the child transposes and recombines what he knows to suit his purposes. Indeed, the child of parents each of whom talks to him in a different language not only transposes but translates in carrying messages between them.[6] It is only when a child finds an utterance incomprehensible that he parrots it word for word, as in echolalia or in memorizing advertising jingles, where he incorporates as coda "a product of the Blank Corporation."

Even after he has become a fluent speaker, the child's syntactical arrangements leave something to be desired. It is interesting that adults seldom really hear what a young child is saying. Either they hear an indecipherable garble or they grasp the sense of what the child is saying without actually hearing his utterance. When adults skilled in stenography, including those with considerable experience with children, are asked to record verbatim the speech output of a preschool child, their records, compared to one carefully transcribed from a tape-recording, are in fact reconstructions in adult English. The child's actual verbalizations are fraught with gaps, hesitations, elisions, strange inversions of word order, repetitions, false starts, and irrelevancies that appear from nowhere, often completely changing the sense of what the child is trying to say. Much adult speech, of course, shows the same features, if one is alert to note them.

Some Characteristics of Early Language

Now it is time to turn from the verbal materials that the child has to work with and take note of the way he uses them. In effect, we are interested here in the child's speech as an indicator of his orientation to reality and the way he deals with it verbally. One feature of early speech is the high incidence of

negations, which we shall discuss at greater length in connection with autonomy. Another feature is the frequent confusion
of antonyms—*up-down, open-shut, on-off, wrap-unwrap, like-
don't like*—which suggests that the child grasps the dimension of
space or action or feeling defined by an antonymy before the
polar extremes are clearly differentiated. In this connection, we
must remember that modern languages may designate antonym-
like reciprocal pairs by a single word: in French, *hôte* means
either guest or host, and *apprendre* means either learn or teach;
in English, both landlord and tenant rent an apartment. We
might also note in passing such standard schoolboy locutions as
"I'll learn ya how" and "Borrow me your knife." It is interesting
that the child can use antonyms concretely—"It's not good! It's
bad!"—by the age of three or four years, but not until age six
or seven can he perform the task of supplying antonyms on
demand.[7] (See p. 85.) In the same way, the child can use quite
difficult words appropriately at an early age, but the task of
defining words, as on a vocabulary test, is completely beyond
him until age five or six. Indeed, many children reach school
with no notion that there is such a thing as a verbal element
called a word. A recent study by Asch and Nerlove confirms the
impression that children, and many times adults, use the same
word in different contexts without ever noticing that it is the
same word or a homonym.[8] We should note that the locutions
of toddlers are peppered with verbal tags such as "nevertheless"
or "as a matter of fact" or "don't you agree?" of a purely ornamental character.

Although the toddler has words for objects and their actions,
his vocabulary of attributes is limited largely to tangibles such
as *hot-cold, hard-soft, rough-smooth,* and so forth. *Big* and *little*
appear later, as do *good* and *bad,* usually applied first to foodstuffs. He can readily enough learn the names of shapes that
have an independent identity—heart, star, triangle, and even
individual letters and numbers—but cannot specify the shape
of objects such as a block or a ball. Neither can he draw such
shapes, nor can he until much later fit them into a formboard,
which suggests that he sees them physiognomically, without
seeing how they are composed. He has trouble learning circle

and square as abstract entities because a circle to him means moon, or ball, or face, or the letter "O," while a square means table, or window, or block, or box. However, for this very reason, he can draw them, provided they are named as concrete things. Similarly, he cannot copy a cross if it is called "cross," but he can copy it if it is called "airplane." We should mention, parenthetically, that in copying a parent's drawing the toddler and young preschool child has trouble because he tries to reproduce the adult's arm movements rather than the marks made on the paper. Nor is the toddler very sensitive to what adults would consider marked deformations of shape; for instance, he may call an oval or an ellipse a clock.

The baby's first references to past and future are couched in the present tense, although, as we have suggested, the past-tense forms appear quite early. It is clear that the toddler has vivid recollections of isolated past events, often ones that his parents have altogether forgotten; it is equally clear that his memories lack continuity—indeed, it is usually not before the school years that the past begins to cohere. The toddler likewise has a sense of the future, but it—quite understandably—is even less well articulated than his past. Adults, of course, can pattern their anticipations on precedent. The toddler is likely to anchor all temporally distant events, past or future, with a single term such as "tonight." Words referring to standard intervals of time—*hour, day, year*—or points in time—*last week, yesterday, tomorrow*—crop up soon but without stable meanings. By age two, however, the child is capable of utterances like "I'll put it here so that I can have it after I take my bath," suggesting that he can order his own short-range affairs into workable sequences. And, as is true throughout development, he can understand more complex temporal statements than those he utters. By age three, children usually are aware that there is a correlation between people's age and their physical size; from then until the school years, it is almost impossible for them to disentangle the correlation, so that the bigger of two people must of necessity be the older.

As we have said, *two* enters the child's vocabulary quite early, with the meaning of "more than one." The next stage in enumeration is "one, two, a lot," then "one, two, three, a lot." Notice that counting is distinct from summation. The two-year-old can correctly count four trucks but, when asked how many there are, still says "two." Many children delight in learning the number sequence, and it is quite common to hear a two-year-old counting a collection of things, "1, 2, 3, 4, 5, 6, 7, 8, 9, 10, 11, 12, 16, 9, 1, 20. . . ." The child at first has no notion that in counting there has to be a one-to-one correspondence between successive numbers and things counted, so that he skips both items and numbers and has no compunction about counting the same item repeatedly, so that a collection of five things can last him as high as he wants to count.

Colors, as we said before, are at first firmly embedded in objects. One eighteen-month-old, for instance, called all red motor vehicles, ranging from sports roadsters to trailer trucks, fire engines, but could not reliably distinguish a patch of red from other colors even after considerable instruction. (We might note in passing that he did not at this age identify as fire engines telephone and power company trucks, which also bristled with ladders and other fire-engine-like equipment, although a year later he did.) The child can learn that there is such a thing as color, and the standard color names, before he matches names to actual colors. That is, the question, "What color is that?" is a meaningful one for the toddler, since he examines the object and comes up with a color name, but the wrong one, or the right one only by chance.

Generalization In our fire-engine example, we have touched upon the problem of generalization, together with the related notions of abstraction and categorization. The kind of generalization found in young children and animals is quite different from that involved in formulating, say, the law of gravity on the basis of a number of specific observations, and can probably best be thought of as recognition—recognition not of the same thing encountered again, but of something new resembling in some essential way something already known.[9] From this point of view, generalization is not a mental activity of some sort; it merely states that object B produces in us a reaction very much like that produced by object A. To account for the similarity of response to two objects, we need only invoke some basis of perceptual similarity. We do not need the notions of concept and abstraction. If our response to the new object is to give it a name, then we can say that the name is or represents a concept, but this does not advance us very much. There is such a thing as concept formation, in which we seek out and make explicit some point of similarity shared by two things, which in turn involves the abstraction of common features; but there is no reason to attribute such a process to an eighteen-month-old. Recognition can take place without the individual's having the slightest idea what properties he is responding to. Far from being the product of abstraction, generalization often, as in Pavlovian conditioning experiments, reflects only lack of differentiation.

In general, physiognomic recognition may completely disregard the logical attributes that make things members of a class, even when physiognomic class and logical class coincide. The toddler recognizes a cat by its catness, just as he can tell boys from girls long before he has any idea of the formal, anatomical basis on which they are distinguished. We would suspect that small children's marked aversion for barbers is based on a global resemblance between barbershop and doctor's examining room. Sometimes, of course, the logical determinants of a class may be irrelevant for practical purposes: for the zoologist, the Tasmanian wolf is a marsupial; to the sheepherder, it looks like a wolf, acts like a wolf, and is treated like a wolf. While we may be able to point to a single feature that accounts for an act of recognition by the child, we may also find that other features of the original class representative can equally well serve as a basis for recognition. A toddler, having seen an old-fashioned, shingled, grain-grinding windmill, thereafter applied the name to a large, rambling, shingled house; to a modern, skeletal, water-pumping windmill; to a television antenna; and to a water storage tank.

It should be noted that such deviant generalizations are exceptional and occur most often with objects with which the child has no concrete dealings. However, it appears that attribute-words, such as adjectives and adverbs, may also be generalized in rather unexpected ways. A parent, offering a child a cup of water, is greeted with "Too much! Too much!" and turns to pour some off, thereby provoking a tantrum. It appears that in this case "too much" means "a lot"; in fact, too much is a lot, but, as the two-year-old failed to note, a lot is not always too much. Another two-year-old, trying to reach a plaything on a shelf, says, "That's too heavy for me," meaning, of course, "too high." A few days later, he comments, "This is a heavy hill," this time meaning "steep." Such misconceptions are not restricted to the beginnings of language, however. A five-year-old asks of a display stand, "Is this heavy?" meaning "strong." Another five-year-old, taking leave of a playmate, says, "I'm ashamed to go," meaning "sorry." Such generalizations are obviously related to the confusion of antonyms mentioned earlier, but here the connections between terms are mediated more deviously and egocentrically. Again, we must say that adults are often guilty of peculiar generalizations, as when they treat a crippled person as feeble-minded or shout at a blind person.

To understand the categorization expressed in the toddler's generalization, we must see the different kinds of operations that have been labeled as categorizing or concept formation. The subject is presented with a standard stimulus-object, such as a red triangle, and asked which of two other objects, say a green triangle and a red square, goes with it. If he is asked to explain his choice, the task ceases to be one of perceptual pairing and becomes one of abstraction. The subject can be shown two objects, told they are a pair, and asked to choose a third exemplar of the class from a miscellaneous array. Here the task can be either perceptual or conceptual, depending on the nature of the trait that defines the class. Or the subject can be given two objects, or two words, and asked to say why they form a class. Or he can be given a collection of abstract forms and asked to sort them into classificatory groups. Or the same task can be given using real-life objects, which increases the possible range of solutions. We shall have more to say about such procedures in a later chapter; here we only wish to point out that concept formation can be conceived and can proceed in divers ways.

One important distinction can be made, that between "upward" categorization and "downward" categorization.[10] Downward categorization, which is what we observe in the toddler, means the continued subdivision of poorly defined categories into more precise ones. The toddler must be told that the animal he has called "dog" is not a dog, but a cat, and later that the cat he is pointing to is really a squirrel. He learns to distinguish between cars and trucks, and within cars to distinguish the various makes and body styles. When he is given a new toy truck, he soon learns to test it to see whether it is of the wind-up, friction-motor, or free-rolling type. Note that the verbalization of differences does not have to go beyond providing a new class name. Apparently, the name by itself is enough to communicate to the toddler that he should search for the identifying physiognomy, and he rapidly, often instantaneously, finds it. Note, too, that the toddler hardly ever forgets the new class names he is given. We assume that following such differentiation the previously undifferentiated group still retains a kind of dynamic unity; even though the child cannot make explicit that children and grown-ups belong to the class of human beings, it is quite clear that he sees them collectively as something different from dogs, say, or dolls. Upward categorization is quite different and appears considerably later in development. Upward categorization is the classing together of two things that have never previously been considered the same. Although human beings and cattle are in some ways very different, they share traits that mark them both as mammalian organisms.

It is obvious that the downward categorization of the toddler does not require abstraction, the isolation of a single property from the totality of the object. This is not to say that the toddler's perception may not be dominated by a single property. There is a world of difference, however, between responding to only one aspect of an object because it is the only one that is egocentrically relevant, and an act of abstraction whereby one deliberately seeks out the essential attribute and excludes attributes that might be relevant in other contexts but would simply be distracting in this one. The difference between a primitive and a sophisticated narrowing of attention is exemplified in the case of a person with a long criminal record who is charged with some misdeed. A primitive narrowing would be to see him only in terms of known criminality, while a sophisticated narrowing would be to disregard everything about him except those facts related to the particular crime of which he stands accused.

Studies of concept formation have all too often been carried out by the discrimination method alone. Thus, to see whether the rat can learn the concept of triangularity, one tests to see whether, after suitable training, the rat reliably discriminates between triangles and other forms. The discrimination method needs to be supplemented by the method of equivalent stimuli to determine what else besides triangles may be included in the "concept"—that is, to what other things does the rat react as though they were triangles? It is only through the method of equivalent stimuli that generalizations of the kind we are talking about here show up.

Egocentric Speech. The young child's egocentric orientation is, as we might expect, reflected in his language. We must, however, take partial exception to Piaget's own widely quoted definition of egocentric speech:

> . . . He does not bother to know to whom he is speaking nor whether he is being listened to. He talks either for himself or for the pleasure of associating anyone who happens to be there with the activity of the moment. This talk is ego-centric, partly because the child talks only about himself, but chiefly because he does not attempt to place himself at the point of view of his hearer. Anyone who happens to be there will serve as an audience. . . . He feels no desire to influence his hearer nor to tell him anything. . . .[11]

In all fairness, it should be pointed out that we have quoted the Piaget of thirty years ago, and that he may no longer hold to what he said then. We should note, too, that he is speaking of the behavior of school-age children, far removed from the beginnings of language. Our own observations, however, indicate, first, that the child initially cannot talk to himself, and that it is a step away from egocentrism when he begins to carry on monologues. Second, the child at first is very concerned about whom he is speaking to; he may be unable to talk to strangers or he may welcome them as a new audience for all the things he has already talked about to his familiars. Third, the child at first can speak only to adults or older children, and again we recognize it as an advance when he tries to communicate verbally with his contemporaries. Finally, the child very early comes to adopt three different speech attitudes, depending on his mood of the moment. He may speak only for his own benefit. He may want adult company but require no response other than an occasional murmur. Or he may want to communicate with the adult, in which case he may thrust his face into the adult's and talk nose to nose, and in any case insists that the adult look at him—nor is the adult allowed to close his eyes. We must also note, however, that when the toddler is talking to himself or when he is on display, as in reciting a poem, he may find adult attention very disturbing.

Egocentric speech is characterized, as Piaget says, by failure to take account of the listener's orientation and information and to make sure that he is given all the information necessary to understand what is said. It is almost as though the child assumes that he and his listener are surveying a common landscape from a common vantage point and have identical interests and concerns, so that all he has to do is point to a few key features to make himself understood. It does not seem to occur to the child that the other person might possibly have preoccupations of his own or be ignorant of something that the child takes for granted. It is not that the child is unwilling to make himself clear; he will repeat himself endlessly and even patiently—it is just that he cannot understand where the difficulty in communication lies.

The egocentrism of the child just beginning to talk may not be too evident. In the first place, the child's experience is likely to be completely known to his listener, who is usually a parent or sibling, so that the listener knows the context of what the child says. It is the outsider who is baffled by the toddler's announcement, "I go train bacon and eggs," and who has to have explained to him that the child has taken a train ride to the neighboring town of Beacon, that he has assimilated this name to the far more familiar "bacon," and that out of his older sister's attempts to explain the difference there has developed a family game, of which his statement is the opening move. Second, the parents make a strenuous effort to understand the very young child and cooperate by quizzing him on obscure details and helping him along when he falters. With somewhat older children, parents are likely to be less forbearing, and egocentrism becomes more visible.

It is likely that the young child's habit of interrupting his elders is less a matter of bad manners than of egocentrism, since a conversation that holds no interest for him simply does not exist. But this is only a partial account. The behavior of young children suggests that when they are mobilized to speak, their hearing apparatus is turned off. This notion is compatible with the findings on attention already cited, and would account, too, for the fact that parents find it extremely hard to get through to a child when he is set to produce. Adults, at least ideally, are of course able to maintain a dual mobilization which allows them to hear even when they are speaking.

Verbal Realism   Like egocentrism, primitive realism persists in the child's use of language, specifically in the form of what has been called word realism or symbolic realism. Word realism is sometimes interpreted narrowly to mean that the child thinks of the name as somehow inhering in the thing named, but this is only one of its manifestations. Its central manifestation is in the power that words have over us, and the sense of power over reality that words give us. One of the finest studies of word realism in childhood—and of childhood cognition in general—is a fictional one, *The Innocent Voyage*.[12] For Emily, the book's ten-year-old heroine, an earthquake, having a name, is an awesome, exciting, significant event; whereas a hurricane, unnamed, is merely a storm during which some odd and faintly disturbing things happen. Simone de Beauvoir [13] reports how her early experience refused to take shape without words, and how, having only the simplistic vocabulary that her parents gave her, her experience shaped itself to the words in ways that falsified her experience but that she was helpless to alter. It seems likely that the toddler's insatiable hunger for names reflects the sense of possession and domination of the object that knowing its name gives him.

Word realism can also be seen in euphemism, whereby we disguise an unpleasant or indelicate reality with a neutral or pleasant word; in circumlocution, where we talk all around a touchy topic without ever dealing with it directly; in reification, whereby we treat a hypothetical construct as a substantial thing; in our reactions to fiction, in which our emotions can become implicated almost as thoroughly as in real-life happenings; and in the so-called defense mechanisms. Word realism is apparent in this excerpt from a letter written by a woman to her psychiatrist: "It is interesting how I could not bear to think of my daughter's marriage not working, especially with a baby coming, and how you jumped right in and talked about divorces and custody fights! What is interesting is how relieving it was to have someone put into words this ghastly, dreadful, unspeakable thing and then to find that the world didn't come to an end. . . . What a good idea it was to have the awful threat voiced out in the open."

It is not true that "names will never hurt me." One can flay a person very effectively with words. With words, one can make people blush, one can infuriate them, one can turn their stomachs and make their flesh crawl—with words that need not even describe any factual reality. We can see that word realism works in several ways. First, we can avoid knowledge of a disagreeable reality by refusing to name it, by giving it a name that hides its true nature, or by giving it a name that keeps it neutral and remote. It is permissible for the student of behavior to discuss in detail aberrant forms of sexuality, but he must keep his language cold and clinical and "scientific," avoiding both the blunt graphic terms of common parlance and the subtly provocative language of literary depiction. Second, having given voice to a notion, we find that we have created an entity that now dwells in reality on the same footing as other objects. The list of purely verbal entities which sages and ordinary people have taken seriously—sometimes seriously enough to kill and be killed for them—is almost endless: the ether, phlogiston, the Holy Trinity, consubstantiation and transubstantiation, national honor, memory traces, drives, instincts, covert behavior, percept, personality, and so on. The psychological personification of inanimate objects is a closely related phenomenon, as in the reverence given to national flags. It is to the flag that the school child first pledges allegiance. Hymns are written to "Old Glory" and the "Star-Spangled Banner." There is an intricate code of ritual governing the handling and display of the flag. When demonstrators wish to insult a nation, they defile its flag; and the insult is felt as such by its recipients. Again, the loyalty of the alumnus to his beloved alma mater can be seen as symbolic personification. Third, there is a species of negative word realism: lacking a word (or a formulation) for something, we cannot quite believe in the thing itself. Similarly, when we lose a word, we are paralyzed, and the substitution of verbal wild cards such as whatchamaycallit, whosis, thing, etc., may be so unsatisfactory that we lose interest in a conversation until we have dredged up the missing *mot juste*.

Word realism is not entirely bad, however; it is also valuable because it seems to underlie all verbal communication. Most of education, for instance, and of miseducation as well, consists in learning verbally about things we have never observed and may never observe but which we may have to think about and take account of throughout our lives. Now it is obvious that words in the narrow sense are not always an effective medium of communication and that there are some things that are better demonstrated or described by other symbolic means: mathematical symbols, maps, charts, diagrams, and so forth. But these devices rest on a verbal foundation and become effective only when they have had a first verbal definition. In the same way, all the field trips and audio-visual aids and concrete demonstrations in the world are educationally worthless unless the student is told (or made to say) what he is witnessing, what it means, and how it relates to other things.

Closely allied to word realism, and rooted in it, is word magic. Apart from its frankly primitive manifestations, as in incantations and spells, word magic takes such everyday forms as talking away unpleasant facts, taking refuge in fantasy, making grandiose promises and then feeling so virtuous that any further action becomes superfluous, inventing evidence to win an argument, and, in general, reshaping reality verbally to suit our own desires.

The phenomena of word realism and word magic point to a

curious dominance of language over concrete perceptual reality. For the most important thing about word magic is that a good part of the time it works. To anticipate later discussion, the words of other people and, later, our own formulations give us a stable physical reality which resists further verbal deformation and becomes our primary frame of reference. Even the most relentless verbalizer and student of other people's verbalizations cannot possibly explicate the whole of his experience; he will always know implicitly and schematically far more than he can know explicitly and symbolically. But once he has discovered a few thematizations—verbal formulations of experience—which define in general how things operate, these become the schematic framework against which he tests subsequent experience. There comes a time when the individual is so solidly oriented to an orderly, predictable concrete reality that he can dismiss as "nonsense" or "hot air" verbal formulations that contradict his knowledge. His knowledge, of course, may be erroneous, but that is not the issue here.

Early Logic Virtually from birth, the child builds up schemata of segments of reality based on his concrete concerns and operations, but it is many years before his bits of knowledge are integrated into any sort of orderly system. Until he comes to inhabit the extended spatial and temporal framework we know as adults, governed by principles and values that transcend particular instances and lend coherence to the conceptual flux in which the young child lives, we cannot expect adult rules of logic to apply to the child's thinking. Parents who try to reason with young children often find themselves sinking in a quagmire of rapidly shifting premises, logical inconsistencies, unforeseen implications, word magic, and dissolving obviousness. Told that a toy he wants is too expensive, it follows for the child that his parents must be willing to buy him another, less expensive one. A three-year-old, overhearing his professor father say that he was going to take sabbatical leave, burst into tears; it was some time before his parents could get from him that he had understood his father's remark to mean that he was leaving *him*. The young child has no doubt that a single object can simultaneously be in two widely separated locations. A new adult encountered in the home of other children is almost certain to be classed as parent of those children, even though this may provide them with two or more mothers or fathers. A four-year-old, commenting on how much she liked peaches, observed that it was best to eat them out of doors, since they were so juicy, and besides, "that helps the peaches to grow." It must be noted that the child is neither a passive victim nor a devious exploiter of his way of looking at things; he is constantly in search of a reliable reality and is very much concerned about logical rightness. The four-year-old wrapped up in the role of cowboy cannot go swimming until he has ascertained that cowboys sometimes wear bathing suits as well as cowboy costumes. The four-year-old girl who wants to be a policeman assumes that in the course of growing up she will be transformed into a male; the five-year-old girl with the same ambition, however, wants to be assured that there can be such a thing as a woman policeman.

Principles of Learning Language

Biological and Experiential Readiness

So far, we have been concerned with describing the facts and characteristics of early symbolic behavior. Now it is time to look more closely at the conditions which govern the learning of language. On the side of the organism, we assume that the child must have reached a point of biological maturity or "readiness" before he is able to understand or use language. There are two points to be noted, however. First, babies reared under conditions of emotional and social deprivation suffer a delay or deficit of biological readiness. This leads us to the second, corollary, point, that verbal stimulation prior to the point of readiness may also be influential in laying the psychological groundwork of language. Some observers feel that children who are talked to a great deal in early infancy talk sooner and better than the children of more taciturn parents. This is a hard assertion to verify by empirical test, but it is at any rate compatible with findings that children who are read to a great deal as toddlers and preschool children read more easily and better than those having less experience with the written word. Studies in this area probably suffer from a compounding of variables, since we would expect volume of reading to vary directly with level of symbolic usage of all kinds, but such a compounding does not militate against the general thesis.

An interesting analogy is to be found in the singing of young birds. Finches, among others, do not sing the typical song of their species unless they have been exposed to the singing of adult birds. But such exposure has its effect even when it precedes any actual singing by the young bird.[14] The question whether the baby bird goes through a stage of "passive singing," comparable to the human infant's passive-language stage, will probably have to be left unanswered. We do not yet know very much about such "pre-readinesses" or about the effects of delaying opportunity to learn beyond an assumed critical period. L. K. Frank[15] has proposed that there may be recurring cycles of readiness for various kinds of learning, and that what fails to happen one time may happen the next. Even if such a supposition proved true, there would still remain the problem of possible effects of altering the usual sequence of learning.

Misconceptions about Learning Language

Before going further, let us look at some of the ways the child does not learn language. Theorists have long held that the child in his babbling makes all the sounds known to all the languages of mankind, and that, through selective reinforcement and extinction, he comes to speak in the sounds of his native tongue. This view is expressed and perpetuated by B. F. Skinner in *Verbal Behavior:*

A child acquires verbal behavior when relatively unpatterned vocalizations, selectively reinforced, gradually assume forms which produce appropriate consequences in a given verbal community. In formulating this process we do not need to mention stimuli occurring prior to the behavior to be reinforced. It is difficult, if not impossible, to discover stimuli which evoke specific vocal responses in the young child. There is no stimulus which makes the child say *b* or *ā* or *ē*, as one may make him salivate by placing a lemon drop in his mouth or make his pupils contract by shining a light in his eyes. The raw responses from which verbal behavior is constructed are not "elicited." In order to reinforce a given response we simply wait until it occurs.[16]

Let us see how well this formulation corresponds with the facts. When Skinner speaks of "relatively unpatterned vocalizations," he apparently assumes that the baby emits random clusters of miscellaneous speech sounds. In point of fact, babbling the world over follows a highly stereotyped pattern, and, as sound-spectrographic analysis indicates, is based on a rather narrow repertory of sounds.[17] It should be noted that the earliest phonetic records of infantile vocalizations, apart from technical inadequacies, included every sound emanating from the baby's mouth, whether actual babbles or the accidental effects of crying, sobbing, yawning, belching, hiccoughing, chortling, or whatever. There is a phenomenon of "phonetic drift" during infancy, by which the baby's babbles increasingly take on the intonations, but not the particular speech sounds, of his linguistic community (see p. 88).[18]

One problem that seems not to have occurred to phonetic theorists is why, if the baby has such a fine phonetic endowment, his early pronunciation of the simplest words should be so consistently atrocious, and atrocious in the highly consistent, predictable ways of baby talk. Then there is the matter of selective reinforcement of what the baby does produce. Three things need to be said. First, parents are likely to reinforce the baby's babbling indiscriminately, since most of what he says does not resemble true language anyway. Insofar as this reinforcement has any demonstrable effect, it is in the direction of producing new patterns of babbling rather than of stabilizing the old. Second, research by Rheingold and associates [19] indicates that one can control volume of babbling, at least in the presence of a particular stimulus-person, but there is absolutely no evidence that one can selectively reinforce particular babbles. (There is, however, recent evidence that one can teach animals to emit particular vocal signals as a way of getting reinforcement.[20] This should be no more surprising than that one can teach them to press a lever or exercise any other part-activity, such as stretching the neck. However, if one had to put as much effort into teaching a child individual words, it would take him a lifetime to build a normal vocabulary. In theory, one should be able, by chaining, to teach nontalking animals to utter approximations of true words, but there is no reason to suppose that a dog who could say "beefsteak" would be any closer to human speech than one who simply barked for his dinner.) Third, and here we take up Skinner's "gradually," babbling stops when speech begins—that is, they are discontinuous forms of behavior. Again, there is the matter of "appropriate consequences." Skinner himself points out that the student who, learning French, says *"Donnez-moi le sel, s'il vous plaît,"* is rewarded by *"Très bien dit,"* whereas the Frenchman is rewarded by salt. However, the language of the toddler is not always pragmatic, either, and does not always lead to utilitarian rewards. The child may say "cookie" as a way of getting a cookie, but he may also say "cookie" when he already has a cookie and simply wants to make sure that he knows the word, in which case the parent simply replies, "That's right." Even the imperative usage does not always produce the thing desired, since parents are likely to reply with "No," "Not now," or "Later." Such consequences do not, however, lead to extinction of learning.

When Skinner speaks of "stimuli occurring prior to . . ." he seems to be thinking only in terms of immediate stimulus-response connections. In point of fact, as we saw earlier (p. 34), there are quite a few sounds that one can reliably elicit from the preverbal infant, some of which are sounds that occur spontaneously in his babbling. In general, however, Skinner is right, in that, as we have stated, one cannot get the infant to reproduce *words*. This does not mean, however, that we can disregard prior stimulation. For when the baby does start to speak, he says words that he has heard, and unless he has heard them, he cannot use them. Although saying a word to a child does not, indeed, cause him to speak, it enables him, at some later date, to speak. It would be a risky inference that talking to a child makes no difference to his speaking, and that one has only to wait for the right sounds to occur in the right circumstances in order to reinforce them. Parents would be a long time waiting, and children a long time speaking. What seems to be missing from Skinner's formulation is any recognition of the passive language that precedes active speech and of the contribution of passive learning to active behavior. All in all, Skinner's account is a logical reconstruction of how language learning might possibly occur, but it fails to describe what actually does occur.

It is quite obvious, to anyone who takes the trouble to look, that the child does not piece together words out of phonetic elements, but grasps and utters them globally (which may account for the way he drastically compresses longer words, often to a single syllable). Phonetic elements are logical units, not psychological ones, very useful for the written representation of speech but submerged acoustically and motorically in the Gestalt of the word. Any first-grade teacher knows the difficulty of getting a child to hear the component sounds of words, as he must when learning to read, or, once he has learned to string together phonetic components, to hear the word that they compose.

Reinforcement, Reward, and Feedback We are forced to question not only the notion that it is sounds, rather than meaningful words, that are learned, but also the role of reinforcement in the learning process. For one thing, it is irrelevant to passive language; we do not even know when passive learning occurs, so we cannot very well reinforce its occurrence—we only know that, at some point, it must have occurred. But the same is true of active language: the first word, and the first spontaneous use of any word (that is, saying the word other than in response to prompting by an adult), is the product of prior passive learning. For the child's first unequivocal speech comes not as a product of parental prompting but when, without warning and for no discernible reason, the child one day points to something and says its name. Needless to say, parents are inclined to greet their children's first words, and spontaneous use of new words, with delight and so to reinforce them; but the actual word comes first, indicating that it has already been learned, and the reinforcement comes after. Nor does it help to assume that the first word and new words are only some sounds among many, for they are not; or that reinforcement is necessary to maintenance of the response, since not every word that the child makes a part of his vocabulary receives special reinforcement.

There seems to be even less occasion for reinforcement in the schematic learning of grammatical, syntactical, and stylistic rules, including the expression of affect through intonation, that goes on during the second and third years of life. All in all, it probably makes no better sense to say that speech is selectively reinforced babbling than that writing or drawing is selectively reinforced scribbling. Nor does reinforcement help explain the baby's steady improvement in pronunciation, since parents are likely to think the child's speech cute and to reinforce baby talk rather than clean up his pronunciation.

A further quotation from Skinner may show how enthusiasm for a point of view can lead one away from the facts:

> When [verbal behavior] is emitted in the absence of a listener, it generally goes unreinforced. After repeated reinforcement in the presence, and extinction in the absence, of a listener, the speaker eventually speaks only in the presence of a listener.[21]

This statement is accurate only if one gives a rather special meaning to three terms: *listener, eventually,* and *speak.* Young children talk at least as much to themselves as to other people, and are often stricken dumb by the presence of a responding listener. Eventually, of course—say after two or three years of nonreinforcement, and even active discouragement—spoken monologue tends to disappear. But even when overt monologue has been extinguished, introspective evidence suggests that nonsocial speech continues unabated in the stream of consciousness—indeed, novelists such as Joyce and Faulkner would have us believe that the stream of consciousness is nothing more than a stream of language, an interior monologue.

In general, we cannot take overt extinction as evidence that a form of behavior has been unlearned or forgotten: after all, one may go for years without riding a bicycle or swimming, but such skills can be revived at will, without relearning. Perhaps some of the difficulty comes about because learning theorists do not distinguish enough between behavior and the learning—specifically, the schematization—that underlies behavior. Such schematization can come about through either overt behavior or participative perception. One might say that much of the child's solitary speech is addressed at least to an audience of playthings. While this is so, it is hard to see in what sense a stuffed animal or a doll is a listener, and even harder to see what sorts of reinforcements it provides.

Something akin to reinforcement does seem to be essential, however, in the schematization that takes place through overt behavior, and in the moment-by-moment modifications of behavior that are not generally thought of as learning. But reinforcement in such cases can be thought of as a special instance of feedback, the environmental echoes of our own behavior by which we navigate. The difference is that feedback operates informatively, while reinforcement operates, as far as we can tell, blindly. This does not mean that feedback is necessarily conscious, in the sense of focal. It is only under the most difficult walking conditions—ice, rocks, mud, soft sand—that we become aware of how the ground feeds back to our feet, but the response of ground to foot is still one ingredient in the total orientational frame.[22]

The feedback, informative nature of reinforcement is nicely shown in operant conditioning experiments where the animal is taught to perform some atypical action—one can, for instance, teach a pigeon to bowl—by the method of successive approximations. Such situations resemble a game of twenty questions. In anthropomorphic terms, the conditioned reinforcer serves to signal to the animal, "Yes, you're on the right track," while its absence signals, "No, try something else." Similarly, experiments in verbal conditioning, where the subject is led by selective reinforcements, which often go unnoticed, to increase his usage of some single, often peripheral feature of speech such as plural nouns or statements of opinion, seem to work by feedback rather than by reinforcement as such (see p. 111).

A difficulty with the notion of reinforcement is that it is closely tied to motivation. There is abundant experimental evidence showing that learning occurs in the absence of specific motivation and reinforcement. Everyday experience, too, indicates that neither motivation nor reinforcement is essential to learning— the mindless jingles of television commercials keep gibbering through our heads, but there is no reason to assume that we either want to learn them or find it in any way rewarding to do so. In general, reinforcement theory ignores the fact of learning which sticks with us because it is so irritating rather than because it is satisfying. Nor does it have much to say about activities that are intrinsically satisfying rather than the means to satisfying some need; the young toddler, for instance, may spend prolonged periods dismantling and reassembling a coffee pot, apparently for no other reason than that he enjoys it. The child is not at first motivated to learn language, either for its own sake or for what he can do with it. Later, of course, language may take on positive value for him and further learning may indeed be highly motivated. But in such a case we would say that motivation is a product of reward, rather than its cause. We shall have more to say on this subject in the final chapter.

Finally, reinforcement theory remains ambiguous as to what it is that is being reinforced. On the one hand, it is a particular response that produces an effect and so is reinforced; but it is a whole class of equivalent responses—an operant—that is learned. This distinction is not important when it is a matter of learning to press a lever; whether the animal presses with its paw, its nose, or its tail, the lever gets pressed, the reinforcer gets delivered, and the operant lever-pressing is learned. (We mention only in passing that operants defined by a common locus of application might better be described as place-learning than as response-learning.) But what are we to make of an operant such as antonym-giving, studied by Dallenbach and his co-workers? The six-year-old will ordinarily deny that he knows what an "opposite" is, but when he is told that *big* is the opposite of *little*, he can then go on to give any number of antonyms. Assuming that he is reinforced for saying *black* to *white*, how does this learning generalize so that he says *fat* to *thin* and *over* to *under*? For the particular response *good* is related to the particular response *shallow* only because each is the opposite of something. It would appear that insofar as anything is being reinforced, it must be a schematic relationship which is psychological rather than behavioral.

The Verbal Environment

We have already suggested that passive language is learned in a context of feelings and actions. The salient words are those that coincide with salient objects and gestures. When the adult says, "Come here," he holds out his hands to receive the child. When he says, "Now you give it to me," he reaches out for the toy; and when he says, "Now I'll give it to you," he hands it back. When the baby makes off with the parent's slippers, the adult cries, "Where are my slippers? Bring me back my slippers!" When the parent pretends not to see the baby, he says, "Where's Bobby? Where's Bobby?" and elaborately panto-mimes the business of looking for him; when he finally finds him, he announces, "There he is!" When the adult holds the cup to the baby's lips, he says, "Drink your milk." In effect, we can think of the child's passive vocabulary as the product of simple association. We must remember, however, that the child is learn-ing something more than signal-words—he is acquiring a notion of verbal communication in general.

Further, in keeping with the principle of participation, we assume that words are not simply abstract forms that impinge upon him from without, but that they reverberate in him and arouse him to at least a partial mobilization. For at some point the words he knows cease to belong entirely to the sphere of parental action and become part of his own equipment for behavior. Perhaps more accurately, his practical mobilization toward an object now implicates his vocal cords in a new way, until, one day, out pops the object's name. Such an account lacks elegance, but it seems to be the only one that conforms to the known facts of how children actually begin to speak. The problem is this: We cannot understand how language gets from outside the child to inside unless it is in some way inside from the beginning; we cannot understand how passive language becomes active language unless it is always to some extent active. It is probable that the child's first speech occurs without any intention of speech, but it leads to a discovery in himself of a power of speech, of verbalization, a new style of behaving and of dealing with things. As we have seen, the child's first use of language is rather skimpy, but he almost immediately senses this new tool's power, which, at its highest development, becomes the power to capture the world in a net of symbols, to possess it, to manipulate it in new and wondrous ways, to master it, and to recreate it.

Imitation

It is important to see the role that imitation does and does not play in learning to speak. As we have said, there is no reliable imitation of words until, on the average, early in the second year. (Lewis,[23] however, states that younger babies may develop a stable vocal response to a given word and believes that such a response may be an inaccurate attempt at imitation; assuming Lewis's assertion to be well founded, we would say that the baby is imitating a sound rather than a word.) The baby beginning to speak does reproduce the words he hears, but not, at first, in a direct echo—there may be a considerable lag between hearing the word and using it. Once the child has begun to speak, imitation becomes an important device for learning new words. The parent says, "See the rabbit," and the child echoes the word. Or the parent says, "That's not meat, that's a pea." Or the child points to an anonymous object and the parent supplies its name. But in spite of the substantial amount of learning by imitation, the greater part of the child's vocabulary is learned by simple absorption. In the course of a day one hears the two-year-old say, "I forgot my milk," "I forgot my tractor," "Don't forget, Mummy," and realizes that the child has learned a new word. Ordinarily, the process of learning goes on so fast that one fails to notice single acquisitions. In the learning of grammatical and syntactical rules, as we have said, direct imitation plays an even smaller part, since application of the rules requires that they be transposed to suit speaker and occasion.

Sound Schematization

Imitation may enter into correcting the child's pronunciation; but again, much of the improvement in pronunciation comes about automatically, without benefit of special instruction. We have already mentioned the phenomenon of phonetic drift. We would say that among the various implicit schemata that the child learns is one that defines how words (and utterances) sound in his native tongue. As he comes to know what English (or whatever) is supposed to sound like, words take on greater clarity and stability—no longer do so many syllables get lost or transposed, terminal consonants dropped, and sounds slurred. We must note how this schema, like others, is both sensory and motoric. We cannot say for certain whether the child's early mispronunciations are caused by inability to hear words clearly or by inability to articulate what he has heard. But the behavior of both toddlers and adults confronted with a "difficult" word, trying to say it, apparently in order to hear it clearly, suggests that the problem cannot be defined in terms of sensory versus motor. Our first perception of an object is organismic, participative, and it is only as we mobilize ourselves toward the object that we perceive it perceptually, in all its objective quiddity. To perceive an object objectively, we must in a manner of speaking first become the object. Only with such a formulation can we account for being able to hear a word well enough to reproduce it but not well enough to hear what it sounds like. If, of course, the word conforms to a familiar schema, it is easily heard.

When we listen to a speech in an unfamiliar tongue, such as Russian, we can at first hear its Russian quality, but we cannot pick out any words. As the speech proceeds and we get the "feel" of the language, we begin to detect words that have English cognates. After a while, we can even begin to make out some frequently recurring Russian words. The more remote the language from English, of course, the harder for us to hear. It is interesting to note that skilled mimics can give a very convincing imitation of Russian or French or German or Greek without knowing or using a single word of these languages, simply by aping their enunciatory style. (This process is different from that of imitating a regional accent in English, since one must reproduce not only the characteristic New England or Midwestern or Southern sonorities and rhythms but also the special turns of phrase found in different sections.) When we do begin to pick out foreign words, it is likely that our perceptions are somewhat distorted by our English schema. The anglicization of place names illustrates how we assimilate unfamiliar words to a familiar schema. Just a few of the transformations from the Dutch that have taken place in the New York City area are Arthur Kill from Achter Cul, Flushing from Vlissingen, Brooklyn from Breukelen, and Turtle Bay from Deutel Bogt.[24]

If children pick up foreign accents more easily than adults, it is probably because their incompletely crystallized schema of English interferes less with the new style of behaving. We are at a special phonetic disadvantage in learning a new language when we rely too heavily on the written language, and especially when the new language uses the same alphabet as English but assigns the characters different phonetic values. Adults rely not only on the visual appearance of the word to tell them what it is and what it sounds like but also on formal rules of grammar and syntax, which handicap them severely in learning a new language. If, however, they can put aside their visual and conceptual prejudices for a while, and simply listen and try to repeat, they find themselves absorbing the style of the language. Needless to say, the "logical" approach to language-learning works very well for dead languages or for those one wants only to read for informational purposes. An amusing side-effect of schematization is seen in the behavior of certain travelers abroad, who quite sincerely believe that to make themselves understood they have only to speak their native English, let us say, with, say, a French intonation. (Of course, such a practice might indeed help in communicating with a Frenchman who knew written English but was unfamiliar with the spoken language.)

Parents, knowing that little pitchers have big ears, adopt

various devices for talking over children's heads. Small children seem unmindful of sesquipedalian English or of spelled words, but promptly come alert when parents switch to a foreign tongue or when they insert a foreign word in an English sentence. Already at age two or two and a half children have enough of a sense of how English sounds to be able to detect alien importations.

Verbal Learning Sets

It is apparent that there is a snowball effect in learning language, so that the more the child is able to speak, the more he learns to speak. This effect is analogous to the phenomenon known as learning set. It is as though each linguistic mobilization alters the individual in such a way as to broaden the range of his symbolic capacities. We should signal, too, a contrary phenomenon, which might be called negative learning set. This is exemplified by an experiment by Walter,[25] in which education proved a decided impediment to learning a simple stimulus-response task. Ways of thinking that accompany advanced learning may be inappropriate to lower-level problems, just as it would be inappropriate to use a slide rule to find the product of 4 times 5. This negative effect need not occur if the individual can learn to disband his higher-order mobilizations when action at a lower level is called for. No matter how much intellectual effort, verbalization, and deliberation go into learning to drive a car, driving is best done at a sensorimotor level.

It is clear, however, that some ways of thinking are permanently outgrown, which helps account for the fact that communication between parents and their children is usually less than perfect. We should not, of course, assume that negative transfer, whether of the general kind involved in learning sets or the more circumscribed kind that theorists of learning usually talk about, is necessarily bad. After all, the Hegelian dialectic of thesis-antithesis-synthesis cannot take place unless one finds knowledge in conflict. Developmentally, one has to unlearn a great deal, and one can learn a great deal in the course of unlearning something that one thought one knew.

The amply demonstrated but still incompletely understood phenomenon of learning set, or learning to learn, is essential to a theory of development. Biologically oriented theories, such as those of Piaget and Werner, have suffered from their lack of a theory of learning. Learning theories, on the other hand, have characteristically dealt only with the learning of a single task and have not asked the further question of what difference the learning makes, how the individual is changed as a result of learning something, or what he has learned besides the assigned task. For instance, to the best of our knowledge there have been no studies testing the hypothesis that rats which have been taught complex behavioral chains would learn new chains better than naïve rats. It seems obvious, although psychologists have not always thought so, that meaningful learning is assimilated into the organism's total schematic framework, where, even if it loses its special identity, it still contributes to the individual's general orientation. The value of an education lies only partly in the things we come to know—after all, we forget the greater portion of what we learn—and even more in the kinds of persons it makes us by virtue of our having learned what we have learned, including what we have forgotten.

NOTES

(1) Maurice Merleau-Ponty, *Phénoménologie de la Perception* (Paris: Gallimard, 1945), pp. 324–344.

(2) B. F. Skinner, *Verbal Behavior* (New York: Appleton-Century-Crofts, 1957), pp. 35–51.

(3) *Ibid.*, p. 2.

(4) Roger Brown & Jean Berko, Word association and the acquisition of grammar, *Child Development*, 1960, 31: 1–14; Jean Berko, The child's learning of English morphology, *Word*, 1958, 14: 150–177; Roger Brown, Linguistic determinism and the part of speech, *Journal of Abnormal and Social Psychology*, 1957, 55: 1–5. Note that these authors do not study the origins of speech forms, nor are they concerned with the principles of learning involved.

(5) S. M. Ervin, Grammar and classification, paper given before the American Psychological Association, 1957.

(6) Jules Ronjat, *Le Développement du Langage Observé chez un Enfant Bilingue* (Paris: H. Champion, 1913). It is reported (Michael West, *Bilingualism*, Calcutta: Government of India, Central Publication Branch, 1926) that as an adult the bilingual Louis Ronjat used French (the paternal language) for logical and technical discussions and German for emotive expression and literary discussions, switching languages as the topic of conversation changed.

(7) George Kreezer & K. M. Dallenbach, Learning the relation of opposition, *American Journal of Psychology*, 1929, 41: 432–441. Very bright children may be able to perform this task at age five. See Ralph Robinowitz, Learning the relation of opposition as related to scores on the Wechsler Intelligence Scale for Children, *Journal of Genetic Psychology*, 1956, 88: 25–30.

(8) S. E. Asch & Harriet Nerlove, The development of double function terms in children: An exploratory investigation. In B. Kaplan & S. Wapner, eds., *Perspectives in Psychological Theory* (New York: International Universities Press, 1960), pp. 47–60.

(9) This point has recently been made again. See E. J. Gibson, A re-examination of generalization, *Psychological Review*, 1959, 66: 340–342. We should also recall Wapner's findings on primitive generalization: S. Wapner, The differential effects of cortical injury and retesting on equivalence reactions in the rat, *Psychological Monographs*, 1944, 57, no. 2.

(10) The distinction between upward and downward categorization has been overlooked by Brown and by Bruner and associates: Roger Brown, *Words and Things* (Glencoe: The Free Press, 1958); J. S. Bruner, J. J. Goodnow, & G. A. Austin, *A Study of Thinking* (New York: Wiley, 1956).

(11) Jean Piaget, *Language and Thought of the Child* (New York: Meridian, 1955), p. 32. Quoted by permission of Humanities Press, Inc.

(12) Richard Hughes, *The Innocent Voyage* (New York: Harper, 1929). Also published as *A High Wind in Jamaica*.

(13) Simone de Beauvoir, *Mémoires d'une Jeune Fille Rangée* (Paris: Gallimard, 1958), pp. 20–21.

(14) W. H. Thorpe, *Learning and Instinct in Animals* (London: Methuen, 1956), cited in F. A. Beach, Experimental investigations of species-specific behavior, *American Psychologist*, 1960, 15: 1–18.

(15) Personal communication.

(16) *Verbal Behavior*, p. 31. It is interesting to observe that W. V. O. Quine (*Word and Object*, New York: Wylie, 1960, ch. 3) takes note of the criticisms that have been raised against Skinner's view but nevertheless accepts it as essentially correct and goes on to reason from it.

(17) A. W. Lynip, The use of magnetic devices in the collection and analysis of the preverbal utterances of an infant, *Genetic Psychology Monographs*, 1951, 44: 221–262.

(18) O. C. Irwin. For an extended bibliography of the work of Irwin and his collaborators, see: Dorothea McCarthy, Language development in children, in Leonard Carmichael, *Manual of Child Psychology* (New York: Wiley, 1954), pp. 492–630.

(19) Harriet Rheingold, J. L. Gewirtz, & H. W. Ross, Social conditioning of vocalizations in the infant, *Journal of Comparative and Physiological Psychology*, 1959, 52: 68–73.

(20) Norman Ginsburg, Conditioned vocalization in the budgerigar, *Journal of Comparative and Physiological Psychology*, 1960, 53: 183–186.

(21) *Verbal Behavior*, p. 52.

(22) See: S. Wapner & H. A. Witkin, The role of visual factors in the maintenance of body-balance, *American Journal of Psychology*, 1950, 63: 385–408. It is interesting to note that the series of studies of which this is one anticipates some principles of sensory deprivation.

(23) M. M. Lewis, *How Children Learn to Speak* (New York: Basic Books, 1959).

(24) G. R. Stewart, *Names on the Land* (New York: Random House, 1945).

(25) W. Grey Walter, in: B. Schaffner, ed., *Group Processes* (New York: Josiah Macy, Jr., Foundation, 1959), p. 153.

CHAPTER

4

THE VERBAL ORGANISM

We have in effect posed two polar modes of experience, the preverbal and the verbal. It is clear that when the child first begins to speak, it is merely as a way of extending forms of behavior in which he is already engaged; that is, language is assimilated and subordinated to the child's preverbal orientation. But the ontogenesis of language is interesting because of the opposite tendency, the way language opens up new orientations and new possibilities for learning and for action, dominating and transforming preverbal experience. We must emphasize that language is not just one function among many. One does not speak in the same sense that he walks, or eats, or makes love. Language is an all-pervasive characteristic of the individual, such that he becomes a verbal organism, whose walking, eating, love-making, and the rest are altered in keeping with his symbolic experience.

Language transforms experience first by creating new chan-nels through which the human environment can act on the child. The sounds that formerly brought him only excitement or amusement or fear or irritation now bring him information and instructions as well. Through language one can manipulate the child's behavior, one can shape his objective and subjective reality, and one can, in time, induct him into a purely symbolic realm of past and future, of remote places, of ideal relationships, of hypothetical events, of imaginative literature, of values, of imaginary entities ranging from werewolves to psi-mesons, and of alternative systems of symbolization such as mathematics.

At the same time, the learning of language transforms the individual in such a way that he is enabled to do new things for himself, or to do old things in new ways. Language permits us to deal with things at a distance, to act on them without physically handling them. This action at a distance takes two forms. First, we can act on other people, or on objects through people. This kind of action is not new, although language expresses our wants far more precisely than affective vocalizations or gestures. But action on people is not confined to getting what we want out of them. We can edify or amuse people as well as persuade them, we can apprise them of facts, or flatter them, or delude them with language. Second, we can manipulate symbols in ways impossible with the things they stand for, and so arrive at novel and even creative versions of reality, as in a scientific theory, a work of art, or a joke. Word realism and word magic, although an essential part of the symbolic attitude, can also impede effective verbal action, since it often seems that, in acting on things verbally, we are acting on the things themselves.

The real value of symbolic action, of course, is that we can verbally rearrange situations which in themselves would resist rearrangement, as when we discuss social or political or educational reforms; we can isolate features which in fact cannot be isolated, as when, in criticizing a work of art, we can talk separately about the artist's technical competence and his particular "vision"; we can juxtapose objects and events far separated in time and space, as when we try to relate infantile experience to adult personality, or look for regularities in historical events; we can, if we will, turn the universe symbolically inside out, as, in effect, such innovators as Copernicus and Einstein have done.

The Thematization of Experience

Egocentrism, as we have said, reflects the ambiguous localization of experience, and an important feature of development is the progressive internalization of one's own functioning and feeling, together with the systematization of the outer world. This process is largely a matter of language, and a major change in the child's symbolic functioning occurs when he becomes able to communicate with himself.

It has been noted that certain of the toddler's first denominations and predicative utterances—"Baby crying"—seem to be not so much assertions as requests for confirmation. In effect, the toddler is talking for his own benefit, but he needs another person to mediate and verify his observations and phrasings. Within a few months, however, he is able to talk to himself without an intermediary, and there begins a period of frequent soliloquy, the child giving a running commentary on his own doings. In addition, the child begins to engage in verbal self-direction, telling himself what to do and how to do it [1]—he even, somewhat later, scolds himself for his own misdeeds. Adults also direct themselves verbally, especially when learning a new skill. But although the toddler presumably hears what he is saying, he does not yet answer himself back. The first sign of solitary dialogue comes at about age two and a half or three, in dramatic play, when the child carries on "conversations," speaking now for this character and now for that one. (Here we see another example of how the child acquires a whole class of behavior, not by deliberate instruction or by external reinforcement, but by empathically observing and absorbing the styles of those around him.)

By age three, the child deals very well symbolically with his familiar pragmatic world. By about age four, he begins once more to find his language inadequate to his experience. He is now learning—through accounts by adults and older children, through his travels, through television, through stories—about a great many things which may not fit the established schemata of his existence, his familiar world-picture. He learns about bad men and ghosts and rockets and magic and football and religion and war and surgery and wild animals (some gentle and some fierce). His body boundaries are becoming more stable and by that very fact more vulnerable—perhaps this is the reason for the marked increase in fears, phobias, nightmares, and so forth, around age four, noted by a number of observers. It is apparent that many of the dynamisms of the child's world are being given explicit shape, and these incarnations are often frightening. The conflict between feelings of omnipotence and impotence, and between conservatism—wanting to live in a narrow, safe, familiar groove—and progressivism—wanting to grow, explore, experiment, and be independent (this conflict is called "growth ambivalence")—which dates at least from the toddler's first strivings for "autonomy," likewise becomes more pronounced. The child is becoming increasingly aware of the complexity and inconsistency of adult behavior, and he finds that the world keeps taking away his privileges and making new demands on him as he matures. By the same token, he becomes more aware of past and future, of growth and change, and of temporal relationships in general. Life keeps him off balance, and he is driven to wonder and to ask questions.

It is worth emphasizing that the solution to the child's perplexities lies in *thematizing* them—reducing them to manageable symbolic forms—which is, after all, the goal of the philosopher, the artist, and the scientific theorist. As he thematizes his experience, he reforges the schematic framework within which his existence is oriented. Again, like the nominalistic toddler, the four-year-old cannot undertake the job of thematization single-handed, but needs an adult participant in his dialectic with reality: "Are gorillas fierce?" "What would happen if you fell into the deep water and you couldn't swim?" "When I grow up to be a big man [this from a little girl], will I have a penis like my daddy's?" It can be seen that the child's concerns are still largely (although not exclusively) personal, but that, if only for selfish reasons of orientation, he is trying to decipher and order the world, to classify things and make generalizations. He is still at the stage of phenomenalism and realism and does not yet seek out the systematic links between events. Nevertheless, he is beginning to suspect, to doubt, to sense that things are not always just as they seem.

Just as the toddler acquires confidence in his capacity for denomination and predication and learns to dispense with an adult sounding board, so the older preschool child learns to try answering his own questions. Not that he gives up asking his parents—but his questions come increasingly after an attempt at a formulation of his own, in the form of hypotheses. Also, whereas the toddler's monologues tend to be a verbal parallel of his concrete actions, the preschool child's thoughts are more often detached from the immediate situation and given to things in general—mostly in the form of reveries and fantasies, let it be noted, but also sometimes in an approximation of analytic thought.

It is not until considerably later, usually in adolescence, that the child's interior monologue becomes an interior dialogue. The adolescent's interior dialogues usually postulate a receptive audience which listens admiringly and feeds him cues while he displays his wit and wisdom and deploys a splendid future. In the same way, an adult who has fared badly in a debate may later, in solitude, re-enact the discussion, this time, however, marshaling his arguments with perfect logic and acid clarity, backing them up with brilliantly conceived illustrations and analogies, quoting fluently from the pertinent authorities, and in general dumfounding his opponent. Despite the childish, egotistical nature of much interior dialogue, it is the prototype of dialectical and synthetic thinking. It is the device by which we apprehend our own thoughts, criticize them, revise them, organize them, and make them our own. Until our thoughts have been formulated symbolically, they are only elusive feelings and impulsions to action; once we have said them, no matter how imperfectly, we have objectified and externalized them and can work with them. Obviously, it is not easy to view one's own ideas objectively, since they continue to resonate with feelings and connotations and associations that may be very vivid to their creator but completely hidden from everyone else. Authors are driven to various stratagems to counteract this effect—they can ask someone else to read and criticize a manuscript, or they can set it aside for a while and let it "cool off," after which they can return to it with rather more detachment.

It is impossible to say when the stream of symbolic consciousness takes firm hold, but in many adults—especially those who are described as "verbal"—we find an almost uninterrupted flow of internal verbalization by which the individual orders, integrates, and embroiders his experience as it is happening, in the manner of a critic who writes his review simultaneously with watching a play or reading a book, or of the psychologist who, in the course of an ordinary conversation, finds himself analyzing and classifying the other person's attitudes, motives, defenses, role identifications, style of thought, and so forth. Many people can deal with routine situations while their thoughts are, as the saying goes, miles away—thus, of course, the absent-minded professor.

The Verbal Self

It is clear that thematization deals not only with the environment but also with the child himself. The child's verbal self is at least partially distinct from the schematic self, discussed earlier, that arises out of action and feeling and observation—we have already mentioned how the child can know explicitly that he has two eyes, whereas functionally he experiences himself as a Cyclops. The verbalization of self begins when the child learns the names of body parts—here again, if asked to show his ear, he is at great pains to show first one ear and then the other; but it will be a year before this concrete knowledge of having two ears can be voiced, even though the child will long since have been able to say that he has two cookies. It is interesting, too, that not much before age three can the child correctly answer such questions as "What do you see with?" and "What do you hear with?" The toddler's verbal identity receives a focus when he learns his name—indeed, the proper name seems to retain through life a pregnant importance: note how school-age children write their names on every available surface, how adolescents lovingly practice elegant signatures, how resentful the adult feels if his name is misspelled or mispronounced or forgotten, how when we meet someone who shares our name we feel a thrill either of kinship or of resentment at the usurpation. It is a dogma of salesmanship that one call the client by name as often as possible; what the salesman may not realize is that overdoing this may strike the customer as a desecration, a taking of his name in vain. It is reported that many primitive peoples give their children a real name, known only to the family, and, as a shield against nominal sorcery, a public pseudonym. Many adolescents adopt pseudonyms and nicknames which they feel represent their new true selves more accurately than the names chosen by their parents.

Stages in the Formation of a Thematic Identity

Self-verbalization is closely linked to what is called the "search for identity." In primitive, closed societies the individual's identity is defined from birth by the social role he occupies. In Western societies, by contrast, each member must find his own place in the scheme of things, his own goals and meanings and values, his own functions and roles—in sum, his own unique identity. Even when, in our society, a family offers a child a more or less complete identity—as exemplified in the novels of John P. Marquand, notably *The Late George Apley* [2]—he is likely to repudiate it and go questing, at least temporarily, after his own.

Toddlerhood and Autonomy

Early schemata of the self are founded on practical competences, on control, on the bringing of implicit body experience into awareness, on the pain and pleasure that arise out of action on the environment and the environment's action on the child. For we must bear in mind the inexorable reciprocity of experience: it is always experience of a world vis-à-vis me, and of me vis-à-vis the world.

As the body schema becomes more stable, there arises the experience not only of self in the momentary situation but of self in relation to the world at large. This awareness is expressed in general orientations or attitudes of passivity, mastery, vulnerability, persistence, playfulness, helplessness, deviousness, flexibility, resignation, resistance, and so forth. However, according to Erikson—and the evidence supports him—the child who has in infancy acquired a trustful attitude toward the world will, as a toddler, characteristically develop an attitude of autonomy. Autonomy is sometimes equated with one of its most striking manifestations, negativism—an occasional obstinate resistance to adult commands, requests, questions, and suggestions. Negativism has its antecedents in early infancy: the hungry two-month-old, for instance, may turn his head away and cry angrily when the parent tries to give him a pacifier in lieu of a bottle. Slightly later, the child may vigorously refuse unfamiliar foods or foods that he finds distasteful. Still later, when he has become mobile, he scampers away and hides, or is suddenly very preoccupied with a plaything, when his parents summon him. Such behavior is sometimes whimsical and sometimes in earnest, but even playful negativism shows the child's growing sense of autonomy. Negativism reaches full flower when the child learns, early in his linguistic career, to say No, which he does to every remark which is even faintly interrogatory or imperative in tone. It is interesting that most children use *no* some months in advance of *yes*. The child's verbal No may be quite independent of his actual wants, intentions, and actions, but he seems called upon to assert at least a token autonomy on every possible occasion. The child refuses not only direction and coercion but also help and support—he wants to do it himself. On the other hand, he likes to make his parents do for him things, such as feeding him, of which he is perfectly capable. He wants to control not only himself but others as well.

Autonomy rests upon a schematic, unverbalized self-knowledge. As we have said, the toddler's early active vocabulary refers only to things external to himself. His first self-references are a matter of defining ownership or giving accounts of things he has done or seen—such accounts, let it be remembered, are usually comprehensible only to adults who know the child well or have been present on the particular occasion. It is some time before the toddler makes any attempt to define himself objectively or to give explicit voice to his inner states. He does not say "Hungry," but "Eat" or "Lunch"; if he feels good, he smiles; if he feels bad, he cries or fusses—but in neither case does he say what he feels. If he is eating a favorite foodstuff, he devours it avidly; if a disliked one, he spits it out—but he at first has no way of verbalizing "pleasant" or "unpleasant." He echoes what his parents say about him—"Good boy," "Big boy"—but the words have only affective meaning. Even though he can say quite early whether he is a boy or a girl, the difference is for him strictly a matter of minor externals, such as coiffure. Even a five-year-old, seeing a picture of a nude girl, may insist that it is a boy because "he" has his hair cut like a boy's.

Role-playing begins while self-verbalization is still in a nascent state. The child may strut about, shoulders back and chest outthrust, proclaiming himself to be Superman or Mighty Mouse; or he may drop to all fours and alternate barks with cries of "Dog, dog." It would appear that even the schematic self can be sufficiently stable and conscious to serve as a plaything; we would guess, however, that it is still highly dependent on immediate environmental feedback and would dissolve rapidly if external conditions changed markedly. Again we must remember that the organism cannot function psychologically without its environmental context, as in conditions of sensory deprivation, and that even adults change character markedly from one situation to the next. It is a commonplace that a man may be a tiger in the office and a mouse at home (or vice versa), the life of the party among strangers and a sphinx with his own family.

The Preschool Years

During the preschool years, the child begins to acquire and to apply to himself explicit notions of temperamental differences, tastes and preferences, life goals and life styles, physical attributes, and so forth. Also, he becomes able to talk about his own feeling states—he now not only has feelings about objects but feels his own feelings and knows what they feel like. Of course, like everybody else, the preschool child attends to himself only in times of inactivity, of recollection, and of preparation for action, or when he is at odds with his environment; once he is in action, his self-awareness ceases to be focal and becomes part of the background against which he perceives the figural object with which he is dealing. Unlike adults, the preschool child feels no need to idealize himself verbally, although fear of censure may force him into silence. Even though, at this age, the child is far from able to describe himself in terms of personality traits, there does seem to be a concrete knowledge of himself as a total person, implicit in such chronic attitudes as smugness, anxiety, guilt, self-assurance, strength, and so forth.

The School Years

In children of all ages, the stability of the self-image derives both from pragmatic feedback and from the regard of other people. As long as people view the child with approval, he does not question himself; if others disapprove him, he is made uncomfortable, defensive, and anxious. Or, if he is too long ignored, he may feel the threat of disintegration. The toddler and the preschool child orient themselves to parental affection. So, of course, do school-age children; but, in addition, they measure themselves against the standards of the school and, perhaps more important, of the children's society of which they become a part.

The school child's self-descriptions are largely in terms of his acceptability to his contemporaries, as gauged by his physical characteristics, his competences, his mastery of the tribal ways, and his commitment to the tribal morality (which may differ radically from that of adults). This means that he is becoming skilled in the duplicity that is so important a part of adult functioning, the ability to adapt oneself to the changing demands of different situations and to mask one's true feelings when these conflict with the standards of one's surroundings. We might mention that the school-age child's duplicity may be a peril to empirical research, since he has no qualms about giving misleading answers and telling his age-mates about procedures which he has sworn to keep secret. We might also say that this very gift of duplicity may, in adolescence, be a source of guilt and self-reproach—even while the adolescent is charging the adult world with hypocrisy and insincerity, he senses the seeds growing in himself.

The school-age child has not yet learned to ask, "Who am I?" but can give quite an elaborate answer to "What am I?" He is becoming explicitly aware of some of the peculiarities of his body, as shown by his delight in such stunts as crossing his eyes, testing his patellar reflex, holding his arm pressed against a wall and then, as he steps away, watching the arm rise unbidden, and turning the flow of urine on and off by an act of will. Yet he has only the most rudimentary notion of himself as a person apart from his body, as a consciousness, and as an agent rather than a reagent. If he has been taught that he has a soul, he does not conceive of it as his own vital essence, his psychism, but as some vaporous stuff, vaguely human in shape, that effuses from the body at death. If he imagines the torments of hell, it is not because he sees his sentience trapped in his soul and carried to damnation, but because he imagines his own corporeal self among the flames. Although the school child vehemently disowns his infantile past and talks grandiosely of the future, adult life and its concerns are still wholly remote and essentially meaningless for him.

During the school years, nevertheless, the child becomes increasingly the master of language. Not only does he learn to deal with written language and with quantitative and schematic symbolizations, but he begins to apprehend and exploit the possibilities of language as an abstract sphere: he enjoys puns and *double-entendres*, he is intrigued to discover that foreigners use different words to designate the things he knows, he revels in codes and ciphers, he grasps figures of speech, and, above all, he becomes more proficient at translating his own thoughts and feelings into words.

Adolescence and Adulthood

It is in adolescence that the youngster begins to define himself as a psychological entity different from—and even in conflict with—his body, and explicitly to question his own identity: Do I really exist? Why do I behave the way I do and can I really control my behavior? Why am I so different from everyone else? What do I believe in? Will independence to decide for myself be a blessing or a curse? Whom can I count on? What do people really think of me? What does it all mean?

Needless to say, the adolescent does not spend all his time brooding about such matters. His practical knowledge carries him along very nicely most of the time. But these questions do lurk in the background, ready to assail him in moments of solitude, in moments of confidential intimacy with friends, and whenever reminders occur in the form of failures, temptations, vocational and educational choices, draft calls, and so on. The adolescent is usually able to define at least some of his own salient personality traits, especially those that he worries about —shyness, moodiness, impulsiveness, stinginess, attitudes out of keeping with his sex role, and the like.

While the adolescent's self-esteem continues to be dependent on public opinion, he is beginning, too, to define more abstract, ideal standards to which he compares himself. The adolescent's self-judgments include some which are factually quite accurate, some which are much too harsh, and some which give him rather more credit than he deserves.

Like the adult, the adolescent seeks self-understanding only up to a point. There are some things he would rather not know about, because they conflict with either the standards of the group or his own professed ideals. In addition, to acknowledge some impulses is tantamount to approving them, and approving them to acting on them. In short, a portion of the adolescent's (and adult's) self-knowledge is cast in the form of the "defense mechanisms" mentioned earlier—denial, reaction formation, rationalization, projection, displacement, and so forth. The defense mechanisms work in either of two ways. One can refuse to give a name to a wish, impulse, attitude, or idea, thus denying its existence; or else one can give it a verbal formulation which masks its true nature and so neutralize it. We can see an early defense mechanism in the legalistic quibble of the school-age child: "You said not to hit him. I only gave him a little shove."

However, the use of defense mechanisms in the construction of a stable verbal self-image, including the secondary elaborations by which one integrates partial self-insights, does not seem to occur before the adolescent years.

Lest we seem to have detached the young person and his development too much from environmental conditions, it should be made clear that the normal person cannot sustain a self-image by verbiage alone but must bolster it by some actual accomplishment. Our notions about ourselves are always full of doubts and contradictions and ambiguities. What most of us try to do, more or less consciously, is to find the sort of setting that will evoke and support and reflect back to us a coherent and pleasing self-image. But the behavior we engage in to fortify our self-image is futile unless the environment gives back the proper echoes. Unlike the normal person, the schizophrenic defends his precarious intactness by avoiding any real test of his self-image or else by trying to destroy the surroundings that mirror his behavior in such an intolerable way. The individual in an environment alien or hostile to his style of life may find his behavior and his self-image shifting as he takes on the coloration of his surroundings. In trying to resist the process of adaptation, the individual may be driven to extremes, until he becomes a caricature of what he is trying to stand for—like the legendary British colonial who, to avoid going native, dressed for dinner even in the middle of the jungle and allotted himself a single copy of the *Times* at breakfast each morning.

Language and Consciousness

The use of language both to know ourselves and to guard against too acute a self-knowledge brings us finally to a pair of closely intertwined issues that have been latent in all that we have said. Why does the child work so hard to put everything into words? And how does his progressive thematization of reality manage to alter reality's face? These questions can be reduced to one: Why do symbolic realism and magic work? We cannot answer this question. Symbolic realism is an empirical, descriptive principle, and nothing more. We can say something, however, about the ontogenesis of thematization. We must begin by noting that thematization can take the form of fitting new experiences to established conventions of thought as well as of searching out formulations that do full justice to experience. Which style of thematization the child adopts appears to be a matter of cultural identification. The greater the gulf between the adult's style of conceptualization and the child's, the greater the impulse to symbolic elaboration and mastery—always assuming the primary bond of emotional identification between parent and child.

All human beings, of course, grow up in a setting of artifacts, symbols, and conventions, and, presumably because of their biological constitutions, are both less fit for direct adaptation to nature and better equipped for mediated, artificial adaptations to a largely artificial environment. Some societies, however, exploit their members' cognitive resources more fully than do others, now in the direction of artistic expression, now in the direction of an elaborate metaphysics, now in the direction of techno-logical advance. The adults in a society expect their children to learn to see the world as they themselves do, and children, exception made for failures of identification and for biological deficiencies, set about doing so. In our society, the children of symbol-minded parents quickly pick up styles of analytical, logical, playful, critical language and begin the slow and pain-ful but rewarding venture of working and reworking their experience symbolically until they have achieved rational thought. In so doing, the individual carries a step further the evolutionary internalization of the environment: he internalizes it symbolically and can carry his experience around with him, since every act of thematization increases his ability to recreate, by his own action, any part of his known reality.

Still, we must understand how thematization transforms the appearance of reality. The very act of naming designates an object or an attribute or a relationship as a restricted region of space. But it is in the explication of experience—in saying some-thing about it—that it becomes a part of the schematic frame-work in which we live. In verbalizing reality, we make explicit the properties of and the connections between things, properties and connections which previously were only dynamistically implicit or wholly hidden. Once language has called our attention —has mobilized us—to previously latent features of the landscape, they remain permanently accessible to us. Needless to say, the child does not do all his own thematizing. Adults tell him about things and explain things to him. In addition, they impart typical verbal operations which he takes over and uses for himself: making comparisons, passing judgment, pretending the contrary of what is so, narration, generalizing, exaggeration, wishing, classification, hypothesizing, and so forth.

Thematic learning leads us, of course, not only to facts but to general principles and perspectives. The child is unimpressed by monetary worth, by antiquity, by esthetic values, by high estate, and so forth. The adult may be excessively impressed by all of these. In any event, our way of looking at things shifts, sometimes abruptly and sometimes cumulatively, and the appearance of things shifts accordingly. To the child, the department-store Santa Claus seems a majestic figure compounded of jollity, abundant generosity, stern justice, omniscience and omnipotence, and so on. To the adult, the same Santa Claus looks seedy, meretricious, pathetic, and altogether implausible. Similarly, when the adult pays a sentimental visit, after a long absence, to the scenes of his childhood, he finds that memory and present perception are oddly out of joint. Our present perceptual experience is subordinated to a whole conception of reality, a conception built up out of countless concrete events, verbalizations, and verbalizations about verbalizations, whereby successive environments are woven into a world.

The way that perception changes with knowledge can be illustrated by what happens when we solve a problem. Figure 2 shows a square moat, the same width on all four sides. For purposes of the problem, the moat is infinitely deep. The task is to make a usable bridge across the moat. The *only* materials are two boards, each just shorter than the width of the moat. Once this problem has been solved, the moat will never look the same again.

What we are saying is that full consciousness of reality is possible only to the extent that it has been verbalized. We must remember that realistic-phenomenalistic-dynamistic experience is without depth, without wonder, and without subtlety, and that the world becomes marvelous only as we grasp its complexities. It must not be supposed, however, that we are relegating pre-

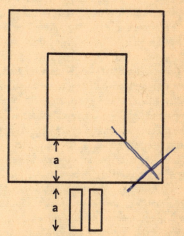

FIGURE 2. *The Moat Problem. See text for description.*

verbal and nonverbal experience to unconsciousness. It is evident that there are many degrees of consciousness, ranging from profound coma to the *satori* of the Zen Buddhist or the epiphany of James Joyce. We can define any behavioral adjustment to stimulation as conscious, whether it be shifting one's position during sleep, or detouring unthinkingly around an obstacle, or absent-mindedly scratching an itch, or solving a difficult problem. We can define not only degrees but kinds of consciousness: the tense vigilance of someone engaged in a perilous undertaking, alertness as when we are paying close and careful attention to an important piece of exposition, receptiveness to esthetic experience—not to mention boredom, apathy, and distraction.

Consciousness can be concentrated on the object, or it can be layered into a simultaneous awareness of object and self. But all behavior implies some sort of consciousness of the object toward which the behavior is directed. The object may be perceived only diffusely—we only half-see the people with whom we share a crowded sidewalk. The background elements in a situation are, by definition, not explicitly perceived, but they play a part in shaping our experience of the situation. For instance, in an experiment by Daniels,[3] the words *club* and *spade* were embedded in a ten-word vocabulary list. These words were never defined as card suits by subjects who had no interest in cards, but were so defined half the time by subjects who were enthusiastic card-players, and every time by card-players interrupted during a card game to serve as subjects. Similarly, as we have seen, the schemata which play so large a part in organizing and integrating experience are not ordinarily conscious. In general, we are aware of ourselves only in terms of the total feeling states that accompany behavior; we know in a general sort of way what we are doing, but hardly at all, except in problematical situations, how we are going about doing it. Least of all do we question our own motives. We do something because we feel like doing it, or avoid doing something because we do not feel like doing it, and not to attain such-and-such logical ends.[4] The question is not so much whether a motive is conscious or unconscious, but in what way it is conscious. To say that an individual is unconsciously motivated is not to say that he feels nothing, but that he has either not examined and identified what he feels or, if he has sensed the illicit nature of his feelings, disguises them to himself in some way. Finally, it does not follow from what we have said that speaking always implies full consciousness or that we are constantly conscious of everything we have ever thematized.

How the notion of consciousness can be confused is illustrated by the notions of "subliminal perception" and "learning without awareness." Subliminal perception implies response to a stimulus exposed too briefly or at too low an intensity to be consciously apprehended. In fact, such an interpretation confuses perceptual threshold and recognition threshold. It is perfectly possible to see something well enough to sense that it is something dangerous or something attractive but not well enough to know what it is. In fact, the subject in a subception experiment perceives *something*, and detects its affective meaning, but without being able to identify it precisely. Here we are reminded of what we said earlier about mobilization and the microgenesis of perception. Similarly, the "awareness" in conditioning without awareness is supposed to be of the reinforcements given and of the experimenter's purpose in giving them.[5] Although such awareness rather often occurs, its absence does not imply that the subject is unconscious. Just as one does not usually take explicit note of the feedback effects of one's actions, the subject does not note the experimenter's behavior in detail but nonetheless feels encouraged to pursue certain trains of thought and discouraged from others. In addition, the subject may show the effect of "unconscious conditioning" not in direct response to reinforcement of the behavior category chosen by the experimenter but because he "interprets" the reinforcements to mean something else—in J. K. Adams' term, he forms a "related hypothesis." Thus, if it is "expressions of opinion" that are being reinforced, the subject may increase his production of such phrases as "*I* think that" or "as far as I'm concerned" either because the experimenter's manner makes him feel defensive or because he feels encouraged to talk about his own views. We might observe, parenthetically, that even the most ostensibly neutral or nondirective psychotherapist steers his client's soliloquies by cues that neither the client nor the therapist may be explicitly aware of—a sudden heightening of interest, a tensing of the body, an increased rate of note-taking, and so forth. The client soon learns, especially if he is in the throes of transference, what sorts of revelations will please his therapist; and it is hardly surprising that orthodox psychoanalysts always discover an unresolved Oedipus complex in their patients, Sullivanians a disturbance of interpersonal relations, Rankians a deficit of will—in Felix

Deutsch's "associative anamnesis" technique, of course, the patient is deliberately steered in this way to what is supposed to be the crux of the problem.

Original and Habitual Formulations

We must draw a distinction, following Merleau-Ponty, between things being said for the first time (in the speaker's own history) and things already said which can be repeated at will. The things people have told us (provided we have accepted them) and the things we have phrased for ourselves become a part of our familiar repertory, the clichés and formulas and habits with which we transact our daily affairs, our stock of habitual language. There is, by contrast, behavior which can be called original speech, ranging from the baby's first utterance to the formulation of a new principle by the scientist or philosopher. For it must be noted that the toddler's apparently banal comment, "Sweater on, Daddy," is at its level a remarkable creative act. It means that the toddler is shifting from unmediated action to contemplation and analysis, he is beginning to give voice to his experience, to take note of variations in his familiar world, to isolate its features and recombine them symbolically. If the reader cherishes the notion that simple description is an easy task, consisting merely in fitting words to the perceived components of a situation, he should try the experiment of presenting a picture to a child and asking him to describe it, or of asking the child to describe yesterday's trip to the zoo. He should be impressed both with the poverty of the description and with the massiveness of the child's achievement in being able to say anything that is not a direct repetition or paraphrase of something he has heard. While the picture or the zoo visit is undoubtedly a rich affective experience for the child, to translate this richness into language requires a detachment he lacks. Far from being a reading off or an enumeration, description is a transformation, even a sublimation from the inert realm of concrete fact to the vital, fluid, subtle, yet somehow rock-solid realm of language.

It is obvious that there are marked individual differences in the tendency to original speech. Everyone must have some gift for it, or very little would ever get said. But for a great many people, the bulk of their experience remains inchoate, at least as far as anything beyond simple cataloguing is concerned. Experience in trying to teach college students to observe and record children's behavior makes it clear that they usually verbalize only the most peripheral and trivial portions of what is available to perception, and miss out on the very things to which they respond affectively and behaviorally in their practical dealings with children. In general, the problem seems to be one of egocentrism. First, the observer is too little aware of his own reaction to what he perceives, and so cannot isolate the features of the child's behavior or manner or appearance responsible for the reaction. Second, the observer cannot see beyond the child's momentary behavior into the pattern of feelings and attitudes and intentions that produce it.

It is likewise obvious that for many people the verbalization of experience must take place retrospectively and that it requires the help of another person. The morning after the big dance, the telephone system is taxed while the matrons and adolescents exchange impressions until the event has been given verbal shape and so can enter into the corpus of their experience. Most people cannot maintain the duality necessary to experience both an event and their own experience of it—which is essentially a verbal matter—simultaneously. Some of the oddities revealed in studies of the psychology of legal testimony may follow from this same tendency to ex post facto verbalization. Similarly, the tendencies to sharpening, leveling, and rationalization found by Bartlett [6] in studies of recall show how experience is verbalized so as to accord with established schemata. At the same time, however, as Strauss [7] has pointed out, our past experience takes on new meanings in the light of more recent events and must be constantly reworked and re-evaluated in accordance with our present outlook, even to the point of repudiating past selves.

As we have observed earlier, of course, there are those people who witness their own experience like critics at a play. A fair number of people compose running autobiographies, often couched in the third person, while virtually everyone dwells at length on the major triumphs and disasters of his life, working them into the verbal fabric of his existence.

It is apparent that the verbalization of experience does not always result in an accurate picture. We have already mentioned the more or less automatic changes that events undergo in being recalled. Also, there is a tendency to reshape events in an image esthetically more satisfying than reality, which is notoriously disorderly and resistant to neat formulations—not in principle, of course, but in the particular case. We have mentioned, too, verbalization as a mechanism of defense that blocks the verbalizer off from his own experience. Verbalization can even act as a defense mechanism by its very accuracy. Every psychotherapist knows clients who can give a perfectly precise account of their own difficulty, its causes, logic, and function, without in the least benefiting from their knowledge. Indeed, the patient's "insight" may be harmful, because he finds his thinking about himself locked in by terms designed as logical, objective categories and not as vehicles of feeling. As a result, he can no longer return to his own experience and begin afresh with his own formulation. Many psychotherapists warn their clients away from the literature of abnormal psychology, but such warnings are not always heeded. It is true, too, that the chronic verbalizer may find himself in a fixed role of spectator, who gains gratification vicariously without ever having to commit himself to action. At its worst, verbalization can degenerate into rumination, where the individual's existence becomes a quagmire of verbiage.

Whatever the dangers of verbalization, it opens up vast possibilities to us. As we grow older, we find that a decreasing proportion of our time is given to direct dealings with objects and an increasing proportion to dealing with objects by way of symbols or even just with symbols themselves. There are certain occupations, such as teaching, writing, advertising, business management, theology, bookkeeping, data processing, and diplomacy, which are almost entirely a matter of symbols. Practitioners in these fields may talk about concrete realities, but they may have little or no personal contact with the realities they talk about. In general, most of us have no hesitation in talking about things of which we have no first-hand knowledge. Furthermore, we can use symbols, as in mathematics, for which there are no objective counterparts. Even when our tongues and our minds are momentarily mute, we are verbal organisms living in a verbal world.

Concrete and Abstract

It is now time to return to the topic of concrete and abstract functioning which we touched upon in discussing generalization. The dichotomy of concrete and abstract has occasioned much controversy, at least partly because people insist on dichotomizing it, whereas in fact we can recognize many forms and degrees of abstractness or concreteness. In general, we would say that sensorimotor functioning is more concrete than perceptually mediated behavior, and that behavior mediated through schematic perception is more concrete than thematically mediated functioning. Behavior dominated by external stimulation (i.e., stimulus-bondage) is more concrete than behavior dominated by the individual's own plans and purposes. Obviously, of course, the individual has to adapt the execution of his plans to environmental circumstances, and it is hardly a mark of advanced cognitive evolution to ride roughshod over one's surroundings; but abstract functioning does require that one be able to define a destination and find one's way to it through a thicket of distractions. Abstract behavior may be addressed either to the present situation or to remote ones. But one can act toward a present concrete situation either concretely or abstractly. Concrete behavior becomes abstract when the present situation is seen in terms of the general, the possible, and the hypothetical, and when covert features as well as overt ones are taken into account—in other words, when one is able to transform the stimulus situation symbolically. It will be seen that this notion of abstraction is not the same as the grammatical one of a noun without a substantial referent, even though there is some overlap. Grammatically defined abstractions are often very concrete, reified constructs with which individuals club each other or which orators brandish aloft as signals to emotion—in short, they operate at the level of word magic. Abstractness does not mean lack of content but content refined to its essentials. Abstractions are rooted in the concrete, but many abstractions can be manipulated independent of specific content. Number, for instance, is not a spontaneous category or a built-in ideal form of thought, but an abstraction from experience. Nevertheless, we can manipulate numbers as though they had an existence of their own.

However, the logic of numbers, like the logic of words, can be misleading. We cannot conclude, because two and two "always" make four, that two quarts of water plus two quarts of alcohol produce four quarts of solution, or that adding together two piles of sand and two piles of sand produces four piles of sand. Things have their own logic, and we must fit our verbal and mathematical formulations to the things, rather than the other way around. In using abstractions, we tend to hypostasis. We find nothing odd, for instance, in saying that five is odd, prime, greater than four and less than six, and so forth—that is, in making five a noun modifiable by adjectives, whereas its "real" status is adjectival rather than nominal, as in "five fingers." As semanticists have pointed out, there is potential danger in the reification of abstractions, just as in the reification of such abstract nouns as *liberty, honor, duty*, and the like. There is the further danger of making irrelevant abstractions. In operant conditioning experiments, for example, adults, children, rats, and pigeons produce highly similar learning curves, from which it might be concluded that learning is a homogeneous process without regard to species or maturity. Such a conclusion would be seriously at variance with findings that show very different patterns of learning in other kinds of learning situations. Skinner has derived a theory of human functioning based on such a narrow range of observations. His theory qua theory is innocuous enough, but from it he deduces, in *Walden Two*,[8] a program of social organization which, if anyone were to apply it literally, might prove calamitous. In general, psychologists show a tendency to confront organisms with tasks that limit the possibilities of behavior, or to confine their observations to a limited portion of what the organism does, and then to draw sweeping conclusions about the organism's limitations.

Abstract thought need not involve the kind of explicit abstraction found in concept-formation tests: a tumbler and a windowpane are both made of glass. It may equally well be concerned with establishing differences, as when one suspects that an opponent's logic depends on using one word in two different senses. It may entail searching for the appropriate formula by which to solve a problem, whether a ready-made one, such as a standard mathematical formula, or some precedent of principle on which to draw. It may involve trying to trace out a causal chain in an intricate tangle of events. It may consist in piecing together two widely separated and perceptually unrelated events —typically, primitive peoples regard gonorrhea as more serious than syphilis, since the early symptoms of syphilis disappear while those of gonorrhea persist, and who is to connect the paresis or blindness of later life with the syphilis of youth? Most fundamentally, however, abstract behavior is a matter of maintaining perspective, of not becoming engulfed in the multitudinous flux of reality. This does not mean lack of commitment, but an integrity which keeps one detached even when committed.

We have spoken of how our conceptualizations are embodied in and transform perceptual reality. We should note that certain perceptual effects—the perceptual "imperatives"—are stubbornly resistant to conceptual transformation. No matter how firmly we believe that the earth revolves on its axis, we *see* the sun rise and set. The many visual illusions likewise persist—although their magnitude is diminished by experience—in spite of what we know about them. If one looks at a stationary spot of light in a dark room, it appears to be moving (the autokinetic effect), and assurances as to its fixity cannot make it stand still. (Its movement pattern can be altered, however, either by direct suggestion or by instructions that tell the subject to report what words the light is tracing.[9]) But a perceptual realm indifferent to conceptualizations has its complement in a conceptual realm which has no perceptual counterparts. Historical reconstructions, the higher reaches of mathematics, theoretical physics, theology, the literature of fantasy and nonsense, and so on, deal with entities no one has ever seen, heard, touched, or tasted except as symbols, and some of which, indeed, defy even schematic depiction. Although our everyday reality represents some sort of merger of abstract and concrete, of perceptual and symbolic, there is also a realm of "pure" abstraction where one can operate without reference to things as we know them directly. Abstract operations may lead to important new principles, some with practical applications, or may become an esoteric game, as in much of present-day philosophy. We have already suggested that abstraction can also be a dangerous game when the theorist derives from abstract principles a program of concrete action which may be grossly inappropriate to reality.

It is obvious, of course, that there can be no truly "pure" abstraction short of vacuum. Abstract operations are operations with symbols (including the "rules" of symbolic combinations) and are possible only because of word realism. The fact that symbols refer only to other symbols does not mean that they are devoid of content, because symbols themselves are real entities with characteristics of their own and can be talked about just as much as shoes and ships and so forth. We shall have more to say on this subject in later chapters.

Developmentally, abstraction is not merely a movement from the particular to the general, from the abundance of the concrete to the austerity of the abstract. It also is the unification and simplification of experience, the reduction of complexity to orderly, manageable principles. So much stress has been laid on development as differentiation, as increase of complexity, that we must emphasize the complement of differentiation, hierarchic integration, by which differentiated perceptions, knowledge, and processes are brought together in new, higher-order patterns which permit simplicity and directness of action. If we speak of integrity of functioning as a mark of maturity, we mean that the mature individual is simpler than the immature. His simplicity, however, is richly textured and tapestried and expresses the harmonious working together of many components.

We must distinguish between normal and pathological concreteness. The child behaves concretely because he is bound to the affective valences of the environment. The child struggles against the pull of the present and tries to dominate reality with language. The brain-damaged patient, by contrast, may find that the world has lost its affective meanings and that he is at the mercy of variations in stimulus intensity. Central to the concreteness of brain damage is a leveling-out of feeling, with a concomitant dissipation of desire, purpose, and control. It is probably not accurate to describe schizophrenic behavior as concrete. Schizophrenic thought, as we shall see later, characteristically mixes levels of reality, but it has access to abstractions and is not confined to the sphere of the concrete.

A somewhat deviant form of abstraction is to be found in jargon (which is akin to but not identical with the special slangs and argots developed by such groups as schoolboys, gangsters, seafarers, railroad men, nurses, and television technicians). Jargon sometimes works in the interests of precision and economy, referring to commonly recurring facts, conditions, principles, and relationships essential to the group that uses it—"dis-saving" and "the discretionary dollar," for instance, although they offend delicate ears, are precise and useful terms for the economist; even more barbarous, but equally precise, is "to accession," which is the procedures by which a library fits a new book into its collection. It is often, however, like the over-ornate speech of many schizophrenics, only a grandiloquent way of giving weight and significance to something quite commonplace, or of advertising one's affiliation with a particular group, and so belongs in the category of word magic.

NOTES

(1) A. R. Luria, The directive function of speech—I: Its development in early childhood, *Word*, 1959, 15: 341–352.

(2) Boston: Little, Brown, 1937.

(3) M. E. Daniels, The effect of value and situational context on word definitions (unpublished manuscript).

(4) This point has been made very effectively by Arthur Pap as regards psychoanalytic notions of unconscious motivation. See: Arthur

Pap, On the empirical interpretation of psychoanalytic concepts, in Sidney Hook, ed., *Psychoanalysis, Scientific Method, and Philosophy* (New York: New York University, 1959), pp. 283–297.

(5) J. K. Adams,, Laboratory studies of behavior without awareness, *Psychological Bulletin*, 1957, 54: 383–405; Leonard Krasner, Studies of the conditioning of verbal behavior, *Psychological Bulletin*, 1958, 55: 148–170.

(6) F. C. Bartlett, Social factors in recall, in T. M. Newcomb & E. L. Hartley, eds., *Readings in Social Psychology* (New York: Holt, 1947), pp. 69–76.

(7) A. A. Strauss, *Mirrors and Masks* (Glencoe, Ill.: The Free Press, 1959), pp. 144–147.

(8) B. F. Skinner, *Walden Two* (New York: Macmillan, 1948). We shall return to Skinner's Utopia in Chapter 8.

(9) Muzafer Sherif, A study of some social factors in perception, *Archives of Psychology*, 1935, no. 187; Allan Rechtschaffen & S. A. Mednick, The autokinetic word technique, *Journal of Abnormal and Social Psychology*, 1955, 51: 346.

PART II

Problems, Issues, and Methods in Language and Cognition

CHAPTER

5

VERBAL AND CONCRETE

REALITY

In Part I we set forth an account of human cognitive development with particular reference to the learning of language and the changes in cognition that it brings. The remainder of this book is devoted to an elaboration of the point of view contained in Part I. It is not our intention to treat all the implications of this point of view, but rather to suggest some lines of thinking and study that emerge from it.

This chapter deals largely with spurious problems—problems created by habitual ways of thinking about language. So solid are the habits, however, and so widely debated the problems, that we are forced to begin by treating these problems as though they existed.

We begin with two realities. On the one hand, we have the concrete world of objects deployed in space, changing in time, and bound together by physical, psychological, and logical relationships. On the other hand, we have the reality of language. Language is real not only because utterances have a perceptible existence and can produce measurable effects in human beings, but also in the subtler ways we have described. One can leave concrete reality only by dying, but it is possible to keep it in the background while operating primarily in a world of symbols, without any sense of being shut off from reality. Indeed, we are so steeped in language that we fail to notice that it is different from nonverbal reality; a recent book [1] devoted to nonverbal communication includes as examples traffic markers, posters, and symbols having highly conventionalized meanings—the hitchhiker's upraised thumb, after all, is as verbal as a spoken request for a ride.

Reference and Meaning

It is obvious that these two realities are not independent of each other. Since we assume that physical reality is going to go on existing whether or not anybody ever says anything, it is treated as the basic reality. Linguistic reality is assumed to refer to concrete reality in the manner of a map or a catalogue. Such a formulation makes sense, though, only if we think of language as a static collection of verbal labels, and language in this meaning does not exist except in dictionaries. Dictionaries are not a source of supply for speech, but a tabulation of things already said. Language treated not as elements but as an accumulation of utterances conforms even less to the notion of reference, since we can make meaningful statements which are factually untrue, which are nonsensical (but still meaningful), which deal with hypothetical rather than actual situations, or which may even postulate the absence or nonexistence of something.

Even when we deal with true factual statements, the exact correspondence between statement and fact is rather hard to understand. Let us take the utterance "Helen went to Chicago last week to visit her mother." We first notice that the statement is a highly condensed version of the actual event, that it omits a good deal. It does not say why Helen chose this time to visit her mother, what mode of transportation she used, what she saw or did along the way, where she stayed while in Chicago, what she and her mother talked about, whether Helen is still in Chicago or has now returned. Considered simply by itself, it omits these details. If, however, we assume our statement to be a real utterance by somebody to somebody, we see that it says a great deal more than at first appears. Since both speaker and listener presumably know Helen, they know from what point her trip originated. The listener may know that Helen's mother has been ill, or that Helen has been having domestic or financial difficulties, and so be able to divine the reason for the trip. He may know that Helen cannot drive a car and dislikes flying, which strongly suggests that she took the train. He is likely to know whether Helen has returned, especially if she happens to be in the room when the statement is made. If the utterance was provoked by the question, "Where's Helen? I haven't seen her lately," then it implies that she is still away. It is obvious, then, that an utterance draws much of its meaning from the context in which it is uttered and from the corpus of information common to speaker and listener. Written utterances, of course, must be made more elaborate than spoken ones, to compensate for the lack of concrete common context and the nonverbal props—gestures, expressions, intonations—available to the speaker.

It is because they are spoken utterances uprooted from their vital contexts that literal transcriptions of primitive literature seem obscure and require so much reworking before they make sense to the European reader. We cannot be sure whether the scholars who "edit" such passages into acceptable English always do an accurate job, but it is certain that a purely literal translation does even less justice to the original. Consider the following line, rendered literally, from an American Indian chant:

Hearken! Wherefore; the man stood, he gave a far-sounding cry traveling to reach—Hearken!—the abode of the lesser gods—Hearken!—seated up yonder in the heavens.

In the free translation this line is rendered:

Hearken! And whence, think ye, was borne/ Unto these men courage to dare,/ Strength to endure hardship and war?/ Mark well my words, as I reveal/ How the gods help man's feebleness,/ The leader of these warriors was a man/ Given to prayer. Oft he went forth/ Seeking a place no one could find./ There would he stand, and lift his voice/ Fraught with desire, that he might be/ Invincible, a bulwark 'gainst all foes/ Threatening his tribe, causing them fear./ Nighttime and day this cry sped on,/ Traveling far, seeking to reach—/ Hearken! those places far above—/ Hearken! within the circle vast/ Where sit the gods, watching o'er men.[2]

A sentence has form as well as content, but the correspondence between the structure of a sentence and the structure of the described reality is no more satisfactory than that between its constituent words and the facts represented. There are, to be sure, some correspondences. Grammatical flexions of number, tense, case, and so forth represent characteristics of situations; but they by no means exhaust these characteristics. Other features of the described reality have their counterpart in certain syntactical, logical, and stylistic features of the utterance, but these follow linguistic rules and disregard the concrete order of things. In any event, an utterance is linear, while the thing it describes may have any number of dimensions. Nor does the temporal sequence of words in an utterance in any way reflect the temporal sequence of represented events. We must even question the notion that a statement is an act of predication, since the grammatical subject of an utterance need not be its logical subject; indeed, most statements can be cast in a variety of ways without altering their factual meaning.

There are two problems here. First, there is the problem of determining the rules by which we "codify" concrete reality in saying something about it. Second, there is the problem of defining meaning—a necessary task if we are to distinguish between meaningful and meaningless utterances.

It appears, however, that there are no rules for codifying reality—or none that anybody has so far discovered. There are only rules for making statements. That is, these rules say nothing about the relationship of words to things, but only about the relationship of words to other words—they are rules of composition rather than of description. This is not to say that an utterance cannot describe a reality. But it does so not by standing as a direct or analogical model of the reality but by calling the listener's attention to the reality. The rules of composition, then, become rules of communication, the system of verbal gestures by which a speaker points out a reality to a listener. Needless to say, the reality to which an utterance points can be an imaginary or an abstract reality as well as a concrete one. We have, in effect, a dual determination: the structure of reality determines what is to be said—that is, the "idea" to be expressed—while the "rules" of the language determine how it is to be said.

It is in trying to decipher the semantics of utterances detached from their behavioral contexts that students of meaning have gone astray. Instead of asking what a statement, considered as an objective entity, means, we might better ask what this individual means (or intends) when he says thus-and-so, *and* what this statement uttered by so-and-so means to this listener. It is obvious that we have removed meaning from the level of the word to that of the utterance. Words do not have meanings, but functions. The "meanings" assigned to words by dictionaries are abstractions drawn from the ways words function in various contexts. It is true that a single word can constitute an utterance, as in "Yes," "Why?" "Never," and so forth; but again the meaning of the one-word utterance comes from its behavioral context. By itself, the utterance "Wood" does not make much sense; as an answer to the question "What is your house built of?" it is perfectly coherent. We must also, of course, grant status as utterances to nods, gestures, grunts, grimaces, and whatever other devices people use in communicating with each other. We must draw a distinction, however, between conventional *signs*, which have a single fixed meaning regardless of context, and *symbols*, which convey information and vary in meaning according to context. In some cases, of course, an utterance can be both sign and symbol: a forefinger against the lips has the sign-value "Quiet!" but it can also convey that the signaler wants to surprise somebody, that the person to whom it is addressed was about to say something dangerous, that there is something important to be heard that would be drowned out by speech, and so forth. We are saying here that what has long been treated as a logical problem is in fact a psychological one, that the problem of meaning is the problem of how meaningful utterances come to be uttered by a speaker and comprehended by a listener.

From the listener's point of view, the meaning of an utterance can be defined in terms of the changes it brings about in his relationship to the speaker, to the immediate situation, and to the universe at large. The change may be one of feeling, of action, or of knowledge. Notice, however, that a statement can have meaning for an individual even when he does not understand its meaning; he may be puzzled by it, or made uneasy, or irritated, or even amused without quite knowing whence his amusement comes. As Empson [3] has pointed out, an utterance tells us several things simultaneously. Not only does it designate a reality, it also says something about the speaker, about his attitude toward what he is talking about, about the situation of speaker and listener, and about his feelings toward the listener. It may also say some things the speaker would rather leave unsaid. As Brown [4] points out, the propagandist who wishes to present himself as an unbiased source of information is liable to betray his bias by using the special vocabulary of the faction to which he belongs—the Communist speaks of the People's Democracies, the anti-Communist of the Satellite Nations. In addition, every utterance betrays to some degree what kind of person the speaker is. All these "dimensions" of an utterance may be expressed not only in the speaker's choice of words but also in his manner, his facial expression, his gestures, his intonations, his stresses, and so forth.

Just as the speaker says many more things than the bare factual content of his utterance, so the listener can respond multifariously. He may, for instance, comply with a request, at the same time resenting the tone of voice in which it was made, planning or fantasying revenge, and being amused at himself for taking a slight so seriously. In the same way, we may be revolted by the cheap sentimentality or contrived dénouement of a television drama yet find our eyes smarting with tears or our viscera gripped by excitement; we usually recognize flattery as specious, but we cannot help feeling a warm glow toward the flatterer.

There is still a gap in our account. We have referred to the objective or logical content of an utterance—what it says—without defining how this content is apprehended. It is apparent that we perceive the sense of an utterance without explicitly attending to the words in which it is couched. But how is this sense represented to us? The notion has been proposed and opposed that words conjure up images of the objects they stand for. There are some people who experience strong images in response to language. Such imagery may be pictorial or may occur in a relatively specialized dimension, as with the colors that some people visualize in association with sounds. Imagery of this sort is rather rare among adults, however, and so cannot be taken as the norm.[5] Part of the difficulty in the quest for images may be that, in the visuocentric way of human beings, researchers have been preoccupied with visual images, to the neglect of tactual, olfactory, auditory, and somesthetic ones. Certainly language produces feeling-states, whether the relatively indescribable ones such as the feeling of sudden comprehension or of excitement, or the better-defined ones such as hunger, lust, disgust, rage, and so forth. But language arouses us to feeling and action not through the intermediary of an associated image or collection of images but directly, by virtue of being meaningful in and of itself. There is a complication, however. Even though the utterance serves as the direct, unmediated stimulus to behavior, the behavior is not addressed to the words that evoke it: we do not try to eat the words that make our mouth water, or to strike the words that make us angry (but woe to the messenger who brings ill tidings!). Words orient us, not to themselves, but to a realm of action, whether actual, potential, or purely symbolic. Ordinarily, an utterance is transparent: one sees through it to the reality it designates. There are, of course, exceptions. A strained or garbled message draws attention to itself. Poetic language is at least semi-opaque: we are asked to attend to the poem as an object and only secondarily to the reality glimpsed through the words, just as the nonrepresentational painting is itself an esthetic object created out of visual materials. Oratory, too, while sometimes seeming to be representational, is often only a study in crude literary symbolism.

It is easy enough to see how an utterance can orient us to a segment of concrete reality. But what does it mean to say that an utterance orients us to any other sphere of reality? What does behavior point to if not the real world? Not, as we have seen, an imaginal world, nor yet a world of words. We are, of course, concretely oriented to the source of the utterance—the person who says it or the book in which we read it. But if I am arguing with somebody about American foreign policy, I am behaving only partly toward my opponent and partly toward the topic of discussion. How, then, does the "topic of discussion" exist for us? It can only exist as schemata, mine and my opponent's. When my opponent speaks, he is verbalizing a portion of the schematic framework within which he orders his life. Or, to speak phenomenologically, the topic of discussion exists concretely in the uprush of feelings, and the corresponding changes of body state, that come when the subject is mentioned. In a matter where a person has no first-hand experience, his schemata are the residue of all the relevant verbalizations that he has met and made. If he has thought out his position carefully beforehand, his utterances flow out easily as habitual speech. Otherwise, he is forced to translate his feelings into words. He mobilizes himself to speak and his feelings take vocal shape. I, listening, put on his schema and, finding it uncomfortable, try to find words to express its lack of congruence with my own. In other words, my reaction to a statement as true or false, correct or incorrect, inspired or foolish, is contained in the schematic—and therefore affective—arousal it produces. In short, the nonmaterial realms to which language may direct us lie in the schemata of speaker and listener. When a topic is defined, the disputants are mobilized toward each other in such a way that their knowledge of the topic is ready at hand. As they talk, they live—by participation—each other's thoughts. It is not enough to say that a particular set of response habits comes into play, since the disputants are likely to say things they have never said before, or to say old things in new ways and in new combinations. What happens in fact is that one person begins to thematize his attitudes, and the other chimes in with elaborations, corrections, objections, or alternative thematizations.

It should not be supposed that the individual, in thematizing his knowledge or comprehending an utterance, experiences his schemata directly. Schematic arousal is mobilization to action and it is the direction of movement, the intention, that is experienced. But like many inner states, these tend to be absorbed into exteroceptive experience, so that they have no identity of their own. Indeed, there are many inner states, and particularly those that express meaning, which we can experience only as Christopher Robin experiences the bears, lurking just out of sight but ready to pounce. That is, they can be experienced, but never figurally—the only way one can feel them is by not paying attention to them. Thus, although "knowledge" and "understanding" and so forth may objectively be localized in body states, phenomenologically they have no locus—they merely exist.

The situation is similar when we read a story for entertainment. The story creates its own schemata, and we, having surrendered to it, participate in the action set forth. Again, the action and our participation in it have no phenomenological locus—they exist only in the realm of feeling. If we are in a critical mood, of course, we may dismiss a story as false to reality. Usually, however, we are willing to accept the particular reality created by the story, and to accept it as real. Needless to say, a fictional account of a gunfight would pale into insignificance if cops and robbers were to start shooting at each other across the room; but in the absence of such standards of comparison, the fiction dominates reality.

When we read a work of nonfiction, the sense may at first elude us. If we persevere, we find ourselves adapting to the author's style, orienting ourselves to his particular symbolic reality, and his meaning begins to take shape. The unfamiliar words become meaningful, and the familiar words used in unfamiliar ways make sense. It may be some time, of course, perhaps long after we have finished his book, before the total pattern and coherence of the author's thought becomes clear. Also, it may be that the book produces the proper mobilizations as long as we are reading it, but that these collapse as soon as we turn away, just as we can follow step by step an intricate mathematical demonstration but be totally unable to reproduce it ourselves. Sometimes we find, either in a flash of insight or gradually as time goes by, that a book has opened up a whole new perspective on reality, that it has effected a basic change in our ways of being mobilized to reality, that it has given us new powers of speech and of perception.

We have raised here the problem of communication. Skinner [6] solves this problem handily by denying that there is any such thing. We must, however, face the stubborn fact that people do communicate facts, skills, ideas, attitudes, and values to other people. If one takes the notion of information transfer too literally, as though bits of energy or matter were being moved from place to place, it makes no sense. But if we think of an item of knowledge as a pragmatic or affective or symbolic mobilization toward reality, then we can certainly induce such mobilizations in others. When we are instructing someone, of course, we take account of what he already knows. In teaching the child arithmetic, for instance, the teacher begins by demonstrating to the child how much "natural" arithmetic he already implicitly knows. She can then go on to formalize and extend his knowledge and, hopefully, teach the techniques of mathematical thinking. Considering that speaker and listener operate within different contexts of knowledge, of course, a message may be something very different for receiver and sender. Collections of students' boners contain only the more picturesque specimens of what confronts every teacher reading examination papers—one student, for instance, gleaned from a course in child development that "children are either Oral, Anal, or Gentile."

Linguistic Determinism

We have mentioned that symbols and symbolic combinations may have a logic of their own at variance with the logic of concrete reality. This fact has been generalized by Whorf [7] in the doctrine of linguistic determinism, which says that the structure of perception and thought is dictated by the structure of the language one speaks. Thus, what are usually described as cultural differences in behavior would become linguistic differences, and the language would be the incarnation of the culture.

Now it is true that most non-European languages have characteristics quite different from those of Standard Average European (Whorf's collective term), and that the thought processes of preliterate people may be very different from our own. Many non-European languages, for instance, lack subsumptive categories—the classical example is that Eskimo has no word for snow, although it has words for crust snow, powder snow, granular snow, and many other types of snow that the white man might never think to notice. The Hopi use the same words to refer to both time and distance, almost as though, according to Whorf, they had anticipated Einstein's concept of space-time. It is interesting to note, parenthetically, that the dances by which bees signal the location of nectar to other members of the hive use the same patterns to indicate either that the nectar is a long way off or that it will require great effort to get there because of terrain or adverse winds.[8] Nouns in Navaho have a classificatory stem based on geometric shape, so that things which for us would be exemplars of a single category—as a rifle and a pistol are both firearms—might, because of their different shape, belong to two distinct categories in Navaho. In Hopi, again, things that we name as nouns may be named as verbs or participles.

Empirical tests of the Whorf hypothesis, designed to see whether the primitive's thought processes actually reflect the structure of his language, yield equivocal results.[9] The sorting tests so often used in cross-cultural studies are, of course, remote from the subjects' everyday activities, and it is probably not safe to generalize even unambiguous findings. Such tests do indicate, however, that when a primitive color name embraces colors that to the European are markedly different, colors are grouped by name rather than by "objective" color. The question arises whether such colors are perceptually as well as nominally equivalent. A test of equivalence of unlike colors would be to discover how the subject generalizes rewarded or punished color stimuli. Certainly if a two-year-old is given two candies, identical except that one is light brown and one dark brown, he calls them both brown; but if he is asked whether they are the same or different, he replies without hesitation that they are different.

Osgood and his associates have attempted to test the Whorf hypothesis by obtaining semantic differential scalings (see p. 184 ff.) of equivalent terms in different languages.[10] Such studies suggest that, contrary to the Whorf hypothesis, there is good agreement between cultures about the meanings of words. Certain reservations must be noted, however: the semantic differential assesses the connotative value of a term, not the denotative; in spite of generally good agreement between cultures, there are some decided discrepancies in scalings; and, even assuming exact logical equivalence of terms, we have no way of comparing the use made of terms in actual utterances by the speakers of an alien tongue. However, it is easy to find instances in the behavior of children where they are not bound by their vocabularies. A five-year-old, describing his drawing of a horse, lacks the word *stirrups* but is able to include "the things where you put your feet." A six-year-old, taking the picture-completion subtest of the Wechsler scale, refers to the missing comb tooth as "prong," and to the missing antennae on the fly as "the things that stick out in front."

Although the notion that language influences our awareness of reality is basic to this book, it is doubtful whether the connection is as direct as Whorf saw it. Most fundamentally, the Whorfian view is preoccupied with words to the neglect of utterances, although the notion of word meanings must have been derived from their role in utterances. A culture cannot so easily be reduced to the vocabulary of its language. The values and practices of a culture, when they are made explicit, are embodied in precepts and didactic statements, not in single words. But, as Kluckhohn [11] has pointed out, a culture contains, in addition to explicit beliefs and values, many implicit, unverbalized elements which nevertheless affect perception and behavior. Such implicit elements may be carried in the affective connotations of terms: Americans take it for granted that marriage must be founded on love, and are shocked at the idea of arranged marriages; we view cannibalism as vile, even though we are not explicitly instructed to that effect. Other things are so completely taken for granted that it never occurs to us to mention them:

Americans simply do not think of insects as food—or did not, prior to the recent fad for freakish hors d'oeuvres from the Orient. Silence, too, can speak volumes on a subject: witness how attitudes of prudery can be communicated by avoiding any mention of sex. There is a further difficulty in assuming that any language is a homogeneous whole. Technically, the French peasant and the Parisian intellectual both speak French, but they draw on very different stocks of words, use the same words in different ways, observe different rules of composition, and are culturally very dissimilar. Whorf is guilty also of confusing etymological and psychological fact. Just because a word has a metaphorical origin, one cannot conclude that metaphorical connotations still cling to it. Metaphors die rapidly and come to mean simply and literally what they mean. Brown [12] uses the example of *strait-laced:* nowadays, the term means simply morally strict, and although it may carry images of a person who holds himself stiffly upright, it has wholly lost its metaphorical sense of tightly corseted.

In general, as we have said before, few words stand in a neat one-to-one relationship with referents, and we cannot conclude that because people apply the same word to two different things, the two things are equated in thought—no one is likely to confuse a dinner table and a table of contents; just because I speak of *my* arm and *my* office, one should not suppose that I see both in the same relationship to me. Similarly, one cannot derive the experience of an object from the grammatical part of speech to which its label is assigned. Just because the Hopi use a verb where we use a noun, one cannot conclude that the Hopi respond to the active properties of the object and we to the static ones. We need a way of finding out whether logically defined parts of speech correspond to classes of experience. Attempts to define such correspondences in European languages have not been very satisfactory,[13] and we are inclined to subscribe to the functional view, which defines part of speech by the role the word plays in a sentence, rather than by what it stands for.[14] Finally, if language binds us as completely as Whorf seems to imply, it is hard to see how anybody ever says anything new or different. People keep inventing new concepts and new symbols and reporting on previously unreported experiences, which seems out of the question for a linguistically determined system.

The Whorf hypothesis probably makes sense best when we lack ready-made forms with which to describe an event and so are forced to an original formulation. If such a formulation is beyond our powers, we may be unable to assimilate an experience and as a result either lose it or be forced to live with an uncomfortable, undigested lump of knowledge. Sometimes ready-made formulations offer an approximate fit and we accept these rather than make the effort required for a more precise statement, with a consequent blurring, distortion, or falsification of experience. It is this process that Simone de Beauvoir recalls and complains of (see p. 74). It is also what happens, of course, when people talk in clichés and platitudes.

Whorf's thinking has had a considerable influence on the movement known as general semantics, which is especially concerned with verbal usage that falsifies or seriously distorts concrete reality. Although the adherents of general semantics have often done a good job of demonstrating how linguistic logic can blind us to empirical fact, their general hostility to language is based, as we have said, on the erroneous assumption that we can grasp concrete reality independent of language. Developmentally, it is clear that one comes to terms with reality only through a continuing dialectic in which language plays an intimate and indispensable role, and which orients us schematically to a multi-dimensional universe infinitely broader and more variegated than anything that can be known perceptually and at first hand.

The semanticist, of course, can attack language only with language, and to talk about language he must invent a meta-language, and the harder he struggles to escape from the web of language, the more thoroughly enmeshed he finds himself. For all his appeals to empiricism, the semanticist, like the logician, is devoted to rational analysis of a kind which may generate endless pseudo-problems without ever solving actual ones.

Culture

We have said that a considerable part of our knowledge about reality is given to us vicariously, through language, through other people. This is another way of saying that our knowledge of reality is culturally defined. Even when we think in solitude, we think in the way we have learned as members of a culture. If we are creative innovators, if we discover novel facts or arrive at unprecedented formulations—if, indeed, we call our own culture into question, it is as a result of cultural learning. A culture is not simply a way of doing things, a set of practices, an outer coating for a biologically given human nature. A human being can be a human being only because other people have taught him, directly and indirectly, explicitly and implicitly, how to be human and what the important characteristics of the world, human and nonhuman, are that he is going to have to live with. We must emphasize, following Merleau-Ponty, that in man everything is natural and everything is artificial, and that culture is as natural to man as his metabolic functions. Something of the same idea has been expressed by Hebb,[15] who, discussing the relative contributions of heredity and environment to behavior, states that behavior is 100 percent hereditary and 100 percent the product of environment.

Most basically, a culture is a conception of reality and how it works. The structure of a culture is elaborated and made manifest in tribal lore and legend, in aphorisms, in practices, in rituals, in emotional reactions, in patterns of social organization, in personal style, and so forth. In any culture, rituals and institutions lose their original meanings, or once-functional practices survive as rituals, so that it is not easy to derive the psychological life of a people directly from cultural forms. As in the study of children, the only satisfactory way to study cultural psychology is by observing people's reactions to everyday situations, the way they describe and reason about things, what things they talk about and with whom, and what things they do not or cannot talk about. Unfortunately, the psychologist interested in cultural differences is at a disadvantage, since anthropology is not a branch of psychology and the material collected by anthropologists does not always lend itself to psychological analysis.

The first point to be made is that it is a form of verbal shorthand to say that people perceive a culturally defined reality. All human beings live in and respond to the same concrete reality. They differ, however, according to cultural and individual backgrounds, in the perspective they have on reality, in the values they find in various features of reality, in the features of reality which to them are prominent or obscure (i.e., in figure-ground organization), in their sensitivity to the multitudinous possible attributes of reality, and in the connections which they establish between objects, particularly the degree to which explicit causal chains supplant implicit dynamic connections. They differ, too, in the feeling tones with which they endow reality—one could probably describe cultures according to Hippocrates' humoral types (choleric, phlegmatic, etc.) as well as Nietzsche's Apollonian-Dionysian distinction.

People differ, both individually and culturally, in their orientations of mastery or passivity, of fatalism or self-assertion. Cultures differ in the extent to which they foster ego-differentiation, autonomy, and individuality. We should note that Western peoples, for all their professed devotion to individualism, show considerable ambivalence in this area, as demonstrated in the periodic hounding of political, economic, artistic, philosophical, and other heretics. Nor should we suppose that our professed rationalism is a guarantee against prejudice, bigotry, obtuseness, stupidity, pettiness, and dishonesty, even among scholars and scientists. Cultures differ in their structural homogeneity and heterogeneity. In a primitive society, virtually everyone shares the same basic assumptions about reality, whereas in advanced societies there can be profound divisions on the most basic issues without destroying the integrity of the total culture—or perhaps it would be more accurate to say that what we describe as a single culture is really a collection of closely related cultures.

What we are saying is that we are all born into the sphere of primitive experience, with very similar (although by no means identical) capacities for learning, and that our cultural experience develops our capacities in various ways. The more primitive culture institutionalizes, stabilizes, and elaborates our earlier forms of experience, whereas the more advanced culture tends to transform them and replace them with new forms. Let us emphasize that we are talking here about cultural differences, not racial ones. It is our assumption that people of non-European origin brought up as Europeans are not, as a group, at any biological disadvantage in assimilating European ways of thought. It is not merely assumed, but taken as demonstrated, that we Europeans are capable of psychologically primitive behavior, collectively and as individuals. It must be remembered that all cultures are ways of being human, and that for all the diversity of behavior that exists in different parts of the world, human biological constitution sets limits on diversity. Furthermore, it almost seems that the human constitution demands certain kinds of expression, since all cultures operate through language, all have codified family systems, and all have a metaphysics and a theory of tribal origins.

As nearly as we can tell from published reports, the child in a primitive society is inducted into full membership far more rapidly than the Western child, for whom the burden of learning is far greater, both in terms of the amount of information and number of skills to be acquired and in terms of the gap between adult conceptions of reality and those which he develops out of his own experience. The full assimilation of a verbalized and hence systematized primitive world view appears to act as a serious impediment to learning of the kind we demand of our children. It would follow that beyond a certain point in development—Chauchard [16] proposes age seven as the upper limit—the primitive child could no longer be transplanted to Western society and given a full Western education. The scholastic difficulties of Puerto Rican and recently urbanized Negro children may be at least as much a product of alien acculturation as of the miserable social conditions in which such children often live. Although primitive peoples can learn Western technical skills, such learning is often of a purely pragmatic kind and does not entail any alteration of basic outlook. The Westernization of "backward" countries is a painful affair, and during the transition period people's ideas may be a bizarre conglomeration of primitive and sophisticated, as seen in Lord's study [17] of superstitions in educated Ethiopians and in the report that the late Prime Minister of Ceylon, an Oxford graduate, always consulted an astrologer before making important decisions of state. An account by Anthony West [18] of the cultural ambivalence of a modern Japanese beautifully and tragically illustrates the same point. Still more serious is the disintegration of a culture without opportunity to assimilate a new culture. In certain American Indian tribes the breakdown of the old ways is accompanied by decay in even the most "basic" forms of behavior, such as parent-child relationships.[19]

It has been suggested that cognitive differences between primitive and Westerner—and between child and adult—are to be accounted for in terms of the primitive's ignorance of the facts known to the European. Although it is true that the primitive—as well as the child—is comparatively ignorant, this is an incomplete explanation. First, we must take note of ignorance at the level of principles as well as of facts. The primitive may know perfectly well how to raise a crop, but he does not know it in the same way that a Western agricultural expert knows it. Furthermore, one might make a case for saying that the primitive knows too much—that he knows things which are factually untrue, and operates according to principles that the Westerner cannot take seriously. Thus, what to the European are purely utilitarian operations may, for the primitive, be bound up with seemingly extraneous moral, emotional, and mystical considerations. In sum, a primitive culture is not an incomplete culture but a highly organized one which positively resists the intrusion of new and conflicting knowledge and ideas.

A major distinction between primitive and advanced cultures is that the former are "closed" and the latter "open." That is, the primitive culture is static; it contains no gaps or ambiguities or mysteries; everything is accounted for; everything is preordained according to fixed principles, so that change can come about only very slowly and gradually. As Barnett [20] has pointed out, a modification of traditional practice, as in a dance step or style of ornamentation, which appears daring and radical to the primitive may be all but imperceptible to the European. If change is introduced too abruptly, as by Western intervention or by a natural disaster, there is danger of complete cultural collapse. European culture, by contrast, includes knowledge of ignorance and ambiguity, as well as susceptibility to rapid change. Needless to say, there is not the same readiness for change at all strata and in all segments of European society, as seen in the difficulty with which people take a realistic attitude toward social problems—currently, such things as inadequacies in our educational system; the threat (or actuality) of overpopulation with respect not only to food but also such other natural resources as water, energy supplies, and outdoor recreational space; and the turbulence of nationalist movements in backward areas. However unready we may be for change, we recognize its rapidity; social chroniclers are kept busy devising names for the "eras" and "generations" that succeed each other with giddy regularity. Along with increasing mastery of the physical world, there has been decreasing certainty with respect to our total grasp on reality, and with respect to human nature and ethical and moral values. We do not even know whether the ambiguities raised by modern ways of thinking are ambiguities of fact—whether, that is, reality is so constituted that no single set of coherent principles will ever be able to describe it—or ambiguities of conceptualization, and, if the latter, whether man is simply not equal to the task of conceptualizing the universe whole or simply has not yet found the proper cognitive tools.

If characterizations of modern youth—from delinquent to cool cat to beatnik to easygoing privatist—have any validity, it is as children of ambiguity. Deliberate attempts to bring up children in an atmosphere of relativism are probably misguided. For reasons of moral, emotional, and intellectual growth—insofar as these can be separated—it probably works better to hold children to a stable set of standards, meanwhile giving them an education that will enable them, later on, to work out a personal orientation. This is not to say that parents should feign adherence to a set of values in which they do not believe, but rather that they should not hesitate to assert values in which they do believe, even when they do not always live up to them. It seems better to have a child resist and rebel against parental values and, in contesting them, be obliged to think about them, than to assimilate them passively and without emotional involvement. If one really wants a child to decide for himself rather than merely drift with the moral current, one must give him something solid to work with, either as a bastion which he defends against the heresies he encounters or one that he assails from the standpoint of the heresies he has adopted.

It seems paradoxical that the moral and cognitive ambiguity of Western societies should go hand in hand with a remarkable stability and predictability of the physical environment. But the very concepts which lend order to the physical world also call into question, directly or indirectly, our assumptions about our human situation, and we have not yet found the right formulas by which we can situate man in the natural order and still account for his special human capacities for feeling, knowing, wanting, and self-direction. Directly, scientific knowledge challenges established beliefs and values. Indirectly, it provides us with a huge array of facts and a perspective on the terrestrial future that we must somehow arrange in a rational pattern for action. It must be remembered, too, that the European's technological modes of thought rest on empathic and dynamic functioning, so that his generally stable reality is full of pulsations which, given the proper conditions, can still take shape as ghosts, hobgoblins, monsters, and messages traveling through extrasensory channels.

It is evident that culture is essential to human development. Culture is an inevitable component of the human organism, since cultural transmission is involved in every act of child care, but it is also an obligatory one. The human child, even following the stage of infantile helplessness, is not built for animal existence. The human being can come to terms with reality only via a learned—that is, culturally imparted—orientation. The cultural orientation which an individual acquires may strike us as unsound, or even pathological, but the most profound pathology of all is that which expresses a failure of cultural identification. What is usually spoken of as emotional deprivation in childhood is only partly that. Solid emotional attachment between parent and child provides a stability of experience which permits the child to explore his surroundings and form a set of basic pragmatic schematizations. Note, however, that the child's physical surroundings vary from culture to culture—the environment that the Balinese baby explores is very different from that to which a middle-class, urban European child is exposed. At least as important, bonds of affection between parent and child make communication possible. Discipline, for instance, is useless or destructive when parent and child do not love each other; given strong affection, even rather harsh discipline does not impair the child's functioning.

What the parent communicates to the child is not a culture, but simply an account of how things are, how they operate, and how one deals with them. Seen from without, the parent's account of reality is a culturally biased one, but for the parent—and, eventually, the child—it is simply reality. It is only the most highly educated Europeans who have any sense of "having" a culture. People everywhere are quick to admit that their neighbors—the people in the next village, the next valley, the next nation—have a culture, in that they entertain some bizarre notions and engage in some outlandish practices; but *our* experience of reality is always just that—reality.

We should stress that something analogous to cultural learning goes on in a number of animal species.[21] We have already mentioned the phenomenon of imprinting and the fact that the characteristic song of some bird species has to be learned. There is evidence that cage-reared animals, ranging from white rats to chimpanzees, are defective by comparison with animals reared under stimulating conditions. This point is strikingly supported by Smith's finding that Lashley's laws of "mass action" and "equipotentiality" of brain functioning hold for cage-reared rats but not for those raised in a free and stimulating environment.[22] The notion has been voiced that most of the generalizations about animal behavior have been drawn from studies of sick animals. We know that "natural enemies," such as cats and mice, reared together from birth never develop enmity. Human-reared animals develop characteristics quite unlike those of their naturally reared fellows. Scott [23] points out, for instance, that a sheep raised in human company develops most unsheeplike behavior, such as solitary independence. Furthermore, as Liddell has shown, such an animal is disqualified for life with his fellows: he does not know how to get along with them, and they in turn reject him as an alien. [24] Some human-reared animals even try to mate with human beings rather than with members of their own species. It is quite commonplace that domestic cat mothers house-train their young. We do not know very much about whether predatory animals train their young to hunt, but what looks like such teaching has been observed in, for instance, bears and foxes.

There seem to be two different patterns of unusual acculturation in animals. In the more primitive—and less plastic—species, the fundamental behavior appears to remain much the same but is directed toward new objects. In higher species reared by human beings, by contrast, there seems to be a genuine transformation of behavior such that the animal becomes capable of forms of thought and action and feeling closed to his normally reared fellows. As in human cultural learning, we must assume a great deal of nonspecific learning, a more general orientation to reality that emerges from the totality of the animal's experience. [25] In the animal's normal existence, the right things usually happen to him at the right time, and his development proceeds so regularly that it seems to be the product of innate dispositions. When we look closer, however, we see that the young animal's conditions of life shape his development, and that a different pattern of events can lead to quite a different pattern of development.

NOTES

(1) Jurgen Ruesch & Weldon Kees, *Non-verbal Communication* (Berkeley: University of California, 1956).

(2) Nellie Barnes, American Indian verse, *Bulletin of the University of Kansas*, 1921, 22, no. 18, pp. 33–34.

(3) William Empson, *The Structure of Complex Words* (Norfolk, Conn.: New Directions, 1951).

(4) Roger Brown, *Words and Things* (Glencoe, Ill.: The Free Press, 1958), ch. 9.

(5) The actual incidence of imagery is hard to determine, since no one technique has yet been found that elicits adequate reports from all subjects. See Ian Oswald, Number-forms and kindred visual images, *Journal of General Psychology*, 1960, 63: 81–88.

(6) *Verbal Behavior* (New York: Appleton-Century-Crofts, 1957), pp. 10, 44, 82, 152, 364.

(7) B. L. Whorf, *Language, Thought, and Reality* (New York: Wiley, 1956).

(8) Karl von Frisch, *Bees, Their Vision, Chemical Senses, and Language* (Ithaca: Cornell, 1950).

(9) *Words and Things*, ch. 7.

(10) See, e.g., C. E. Osgood, The cross-cultural generality of visual-verbal synesthetic tendencies, *Behavioral Science*, 1960, 5: 146–149.

(11) Clyde Kluckhohn, *Mirror for Man* (New York: Whittlesey House, 1949), pp. 33–37.

(12) *Words and Things*, p. 142.

(13) J. Marouzeau, Analyse syntaxique et analyse psychologique, *Journal de Psychologie Normale et Pathologique*, 1950, 43: 34–36.

(14) E. Buyssens, La conception fonctionelle des faits linguistiques, *Journal de Psychologie Normale et Pathologique*, 1950, 43: 37–53.

(15) D. O. Hebb, Heredity and environment in mammalian behaviour, *British Journal of Animal Behaviour*, 1953, 1: 43–47.

(16) Paul Chauchard, *Le Langage et la Pensée* (Paris: Presses Universitaires de France, 1956), p. 38.

(17) Edith Lord, The impact of education on nonscientific beliefs in Ethiopia, *Journal of Social Psychology*, 1958, 47: 339–354.

(18) Anthony West, Our far-flung correspondents: The stranger, *New Yorker*, May 16, 1959, 109–129.

(19) Aleta Brownlee, The American Indian child, *Children*, 1958, 5: 55–60.

(20) H. G. Barnett, *Innovation* (New York: McGraw-Hill, 1953).

(21) F. A. Beach & Julian Jaynes, Effects of early experience upon the behavior of animals, *Psychological Bulletin*, 1954, 51: 239–263.

(22) C. J. Smith, Mass action and early environment in the rat, *Journal of Comparative and Physiological Psychology*, 1959, 52: 154–156. Analogous findings are promised in a forthcoming report: David Krech, M. R. Rosenzweig, E. L. Bennett, and B. Krueckel, Effects of environmental complexity and training on brain chemistry, *Journal of Comparative and Physiological Psychology*, in press. See also the various accounts of human-reared chimpanzees, e.g.: Cathy Hayes, *The Ape in Our House* (New York: Harper, 1951).

(23) J. P. Scott, *Animal Behavior* (Chicago: The University of Chicago Press, 1958), p. 180.

(24) A summary of the Cornell findings on early experience in sheep and goats is given in A. U. Moore, Studies on the formation of the mother-neonate bond in sheep and goat. Paper given before the American Psychological Association, 1960.

(25) See: T. C. Schneirla, Instinctive behavior, maturation—Experience and development, in B. Kaplan & S. Wapner, eds., *Perspectives in Psychological Theory* (New York: International Universities Press, 1960), pp. 303–334. We might also quote a comment by Denenberg & Bell: "We should also like to point out that such a subtle environmental factor as transporting a mouse from its nest to the shock apparatus and back (0.0 ma) is sufficient to modify its learning scores when it is an adult. The mechanisms that bring about these behavioral changes are not known." (V. H. Denenberg & R. W. Bell, Critical periods for effects of infantile experience on adult learning, *Science*, 1960, 131: 227–228.)

CHAPTER

6

LANGUAGE AND THINKING

In this chapter, we shall be concerned with a variety of activities which can be grouped together loosely as "thinking." Our particular concern is with the relation of language to thought. We shall also have a few words to say on the psychopathology of language and thinking.

Verbal and Nonverbal Thinking

One can find proponents of, and evidence for, two distinct views of the relationship between language and thinking.[1] One school says that thinking consists of verbalization, that the thought and the words in which it is expressed are one and the same thing. The other says that thought takes shape independent of language and that language is merely the vehicle, the container of an already accomplished thought. This division of schools, let it be noted, cuts across theoretical orientations. For instance, the notion of the identity of language and thought is embraced by both Merleau-Ponty, who is concerned with language as the medium of full consciousness, and by behaviorists who, in reducing thought to subvocal speech, seek to abolish consciousness as an element in behavior.

If thinking is a wholly verbal activity, only human beings past infancy should be able to think. Yet it is perfectly clear, if only from the problem-solving behavior of chimpanzees, that animals think. They can even think and plan ahead, as shown in an account of the chimpanzee who, whenever a new visitor came to the primate laboratory, got a mouthful of water and waited innocently until the visitor came near his cage, when he would give him a thorough spraying. Introspective accounts of creative thinking, such as those of mathematical thinking by Hadamard [2] and Poincaré,[3] suggest that much thinking, and sometimes the most fruitful kind, goes on unconsciously and apparently wordlessly. We all know the kind of experience described by St. Augustine: "When you do not ask me, I know; when you ask me, I do not know," indicating that though words may fail us, thought does not. There is abundant evidence that some types of human concept formation can take place without verbalization.

In the face of such evidence, how can it make any sense to say that language is necessary to thought? We must begin by abandoning all-or-none formulations. There are many different kinds of activities that are grouped together under the rubric of thinking, and we must distinguish those kinds which seem contingent on language. As a further step, we must try to determine how language contributes to the thinking in which it does play a part.

Let us first stress that in keeping with the principle of intentionality, all thinking, like all behavior, is in essence dialectical. *Dialectical* does not always mean verbal: communication between organism and environment can take place at the automatic level of perceptual feedback, at the more conscious level of concrete exploration, as when the baby pokes at an insect and watches to see what happens, and so on up to the full-fledged Socratic dialogue or creative soliloquy.

We can identify two rather different kinds of problem-solving dialectic. The first is the systematic analysis and classification of a problem, illustrated by Inhelder and Piaget's accounts [4] of the discovery of physical principles by adolescents. The second is the intuitive hypothesis, the flash of insight, followed by a dialectical test of its soundness. We leave out of account, of course, the blind guessing and the magical solutions by individuals for whom the problem is intrinsically insoluble. It would appear, then, that all except habitual action either is or entails thinking. We cannot even exclude behavior which looks like an escape from thinking, as when someone answers a rational argument with a punch on the jaw, since such an action implies that the actor is trying to resolve a problematical situation. We can, however, exclude pure experiencing, where no effort is made to comprehend or analyze the source of stimulation, as when we give ourselves up to a spectacle or a piece of music.

Although thinking may in general be thought of as problem solving, we should not assume that it is motivated only by barriers to action. Much thinking has no other motivation than simple curiosity. We can pose as a principle that novel objects and situations, in the absence of negative valences, invite us to know them. Even when something is frightening or repellent, we may still hover ambivalently about in "horrified fascination." The six-month-old, fearfully hiding his face from a stranger, nevertheless steals quick glances at the source of his fright; if the stranger holds aloof, the baby in a few minutes' time studies him carefully and may even make overtures of friendship. Thinking may also be in response to a purely abstract perplexity of no great practical consequence, as in basic research. Needless to say, thinking of this sort occurs only at a stage of development where one's schematization of reality is systematic enough for irregularities and gaps in the system to become evident. We can say that all thinking is motivated in the sense that the individual is made uncomfortable by the presence of an unclassified object or by awareness of an esthetic imperfection in his knowledge. Such a conception would make thinking a homeostatic function, but does not imply that it is necessarily motivated in terms of serving some transcendant end. Learning is objectively beneficial to the child, but he does not learn for the sake of the benefits, of which he may subjectively know nothing.

Although it seems safe to say that thinking ordinarily produces learning, learning need not entail thinking. Most of the early schematization of space, the learning of passive language, and the empathic absorption of behavioral styles can be regarded as incidental by-products of action. A fair amount even of academic learning, particularly of skills, may be acquired passively, without intention to learn. It seems certain that many of our values must be learned without thinking. But these un-thought-about learnings ineluctably shape our thought since they provide an implicit framework of what is possible or impossible, desirable or undesirable.

Varieties of Thinking

Let us look now at some of the varieties of behavior that are called thinking. Certainly reverie, fantasy, free association, and reminiscing are forms of thinking, but they belong to Maier's category [5] of undirected thinking and, however interesting, need not detain us. We have already mentioned one of the earliest and most pervasive kinds of thinking, that of coming to know a new object, whether a novel instance of a known category or a wholly unprecedented sort of object. This kind of learning seems to puzzle reinforcement theorists, since the learning that takes place may be completely "internal"—although behaviorally demonstrable—and the pattern of reinforcement obscure. Certainly the baby's explorations of new objects can be very overt and active, and it is easy to understand how feedback from the object defines it cognitively. In the same way, visual exploration, with its accompanying somatic mobilizations, provides ample opportunity for feedback. The knowing of an object can be at several levels. The baby merely wants to know what it is like, how it behaves, what it can do to or for him and what he can do with it. At a higher level, there is the impulse to crude classification in naming the object. Later, there is the more disinterested question of what the object is for, what function it serves. Still later, higher-order problems of classification become paramount.

Yet another kind of thinking is decision making, ranging from the laboratory rat's hesitation at a choice point in a maze to the national leader's pondering whether to send troops into another country. Closely involved in decision making—insofar as it is a matter of thought rather than impulse—is the process of making predictions, of extrapolating from the present situation the consequences of pursuing various courses of action, including inaction. Prediction, of course, is a special case of the kind of thinking that looks for patterning in events or groups of events and tries to sort out the causal links or detect the prime movers. Sometimes thinking is a matter of finding a problem, as in trouble shooting, rather than of solving one. Thinking can take the form of making something, whether a utilitarian object, or a whimsy, or a work of art or philosophy. Sometimes thinking is a matter of applying a familiar formula, as when we multiply two numbers; sometimes it is a matter of reconstructing a forgotten formula; and sometimes a matter of inventing a formula, as in the problem of adding a long string of successive integers. A formula, of course, is a guide to action and tells us how to behave or how to dispose ourselves with regard to the materials of the problem. Note that the formula need not be an explicit one, as in a mathematical formula or a principle of physics, but can be a habitual way of acting, a behavioral cliché or stereotype, that falls into place as soon as the object is classified. If the stranger on our doorstep turns out to be a salesman, we react one way; if a panhandler, another; if a lost wayfarer, yet another. Thus, the identification of the object and the finding of the formula may be two parts of the same behavior. Yet another variety of thinking is that of description, of saying what something is like, for one's own benefit or that of a listener. Sometimes the goal of thinking is to clear out the situational underbrush that camouflages the essentials or distracts attention from them. And, of course, thinking is involved in the business of classifying things, of putting them into pigeonholes, or of constructing the pigeonholes into which to put them.

Processes of Thinking

The first distinction we must draw is between perceptual thinking, addressed to an immediate concrete situation, and nonperceptual, addressed to remote or hypothetical ones. Perceptual thinking can take the form either of overt action toward the situation or of a verbal attack on it. Overt action can be guided by directly and naïvely given perceptual information, as when a dog detours around a screen to get food; by relational schemata of the kind that can be acquired through concrete experience, as when the ape uses a stick as an extension of his arm or piles boxes to reach a lure hung out of reach; or by relational schemata of a kind that are necessarily a product of thematization, as when a repairman systematically hunts out the source of failure in a television set. Let us note that schemata which rest on verbalization do not always require such explicit thematization of a procedure as the repairman's trouble-shooting program. It has repeatedly been shown, for instance, that hearing children do better than preverbal deaf children on intellectual tasks such as concept formation. In a study by Vincent,[6] however, it was found that the superiority of the normal children was not attributable to explicit verbalization of the problem and its solution. It appears, rather, that verbalization in general leads to an articulation of reality whereby the solution becomes self-evident without further analysis. That is, symbolic thinking does not always imply verbalization. Of course, a problematical present situation may call for verbal analysis before we know how to proceed concretely.

Nonperceptual thinking is obviously grounded in symbolization. Here again, however, thinking can take place schematically, without explicit verbalization. Consider the following problem: We have two metal balls identical in size, weight, and surface appearance. One of the balls, however, is made of a denser metal than the other and has a hollow center to compensate for the difference in density. How, without damaging the balls in any way, can we tell which is which? A physicist or engineer already *knows* the answer to this problem even though he has never before been asked it, and gives the solution in the same way that one gives the time of day. Those less versed in physics may find the problem wholly impenetrable and may have to have pointed out to them the similarity between the hollow sphere seen in cross-section and a flywheel. Even though one knows the principle of the flywheel, this is of no help unless he sees the hollow ball as a member of the flywheel class.

Symbolic thinking, by contrast with schematic nonperceptual thinking, involves explicit analysis of a situation, with a view to diagnosing it, depicting it, or reconstituting it. Note, however, that a problem can be solved at various levels of specificity or generality. For instance, a river is flowing at one mile per hour. A man in a boat drops his hat into the water and then travels upstream at a constant rate of two miles an hour for one hour, turns and starts downstream at the same speed. How long does it take him to reach his hat? It is quite easy to discover arithmetically that it will take him one hour. The subject may not notice, however, that the speed of the current, being first negative and then positive, cancels out, or, even if he does, that any other rate of flow could be substituted without changing the answer. Even if the subject reaches this point, he may still not arrive at the general principle: When two bodies are moving relative to the same medium, any movement of the medium as a whole can be disregarded.

When the solution of a problem or an inductive principle occurs to us, we first become aware of it as a somatic tension which moves us toward expression. The expression may begin as "Aha!" or "Eureka!," but it cannot stop there. Our insight is of no value—and may be a spurious one—until it has been thematized and given a concrete, detached existence. For it cannot be supposed that the tension we feel signals the existence of a "thought" for which we must now find the symbolic counterpart. It represents, rather, a shift in perspective by which the elements in the problem come to stand in a new relationship to each other and we, reciprocally, begin to mobilize ourselves toward the problem in a new way. If our dialogue with the problem situation has been successful, our beginning mobilization will culminate in a concrete or verbal solution—or one that proceeds by verbal self-instruction as to the actual moves to be made. Spearman's work [7] on the "eduction" of relationships, and the more recent work of Bruner and associates,[8] suggests that one is most likely to go beyond the solution of an immediate problem to the formulation of a general principle when confronted with a succession of problems alike in principle but different in details, as with Katona's matchstick problems.[9] In terms of educational practice, we do not know whether it is more beneficial, after posing a problem or group of problems, to give the principle by which they are to be solved or to let students work out principles on their own. Since one can marshal irrefutable arguments in support of both positions, it would seem that the answer—which will probably turn out not to be a simple one—must be found empirically. It is certain, however, that too great a reliance on the individual's powers of spontaneous formulation would require him to recapitulate singlehanded the history of human thought, which might prove burdensome.

The different levels at which one may comprehend a situation brings up the "fallacy of the implicit." It has been concluded, for instance, that because the principle of evolution was strongly implicit in the work of forerunners of Darwin and Wallace, these early workers should be given the credit for its discovery. However, a principle cannot be said to have been discovered until it has been explicitly enunciated. We find this expressed by C. Northcote Parkinson, formulator of "Parkinson's Law":

> What has still further increased the impact of this discovery is the fact that I had crystallized a thought which existed, half-formed, in the minds of half my readers. Many could say, "That is something I have felt for years," while realizing that the idea was one they had never expressed in words. My work has thus had the effect of saying what many people had been longing to say, giving form to a concept that was at once somehow familiar and yet completely new.[10]

The dimension of perceptual-nonperceptual actually has a middle term, the imaginal. Some individuals—especially, it would seem, children and primitive adults—have a pronounced capacity for eidetic recall. Bartlett,[11] for example, having heard of the remarkable memory of the Swazi tribesmen, asked the Swazi herdsman of a farm to tell him about a herd of cattle purchased a year before. With only two minor errors, the herdsman described all eleven animals, with the distinctive markings of each, its purchase price, and the name of the seller. While his account was obviously verbal, his recollection seems to have been imaginal. Children, too, often have highly vivid recollections of people, places, and events, including details that adults have forgotten or never noticed in the first place. Although eidetic recall is rather different from problem-solving thinking, thinking in eidetic images is sometimes found in mathematical problem-solving and in musical and artistic composition. It is, however, clumsy by comparison with symbolic thinking. The eidetic image tends to cohere too tightly as a unit so that it cannot be taken apart and shifted around with as much freedom as verbal elements. In addition, it resists organization into essential and trivial features—the child's memory for details is to be attributed not to his acute powers of observation but to the lack of articulation in his experiencing. The Western adult, by contrast, recalls the essential gist of things, represented in a pulse of awareness that we assume to correspond to a vestigial somatic mobilization.

It might appear at first glance that schematic representations such as models, charts, diagrams, and the like also fall between pictorial imagery and symbolic thought. In fact, as we said earlier, such devices are highly sophisticated means for objectifying conceptual schemata and making abstract thought more manageably concrete. They are founded on thematization and are taught linguistically. It is questionable that any but the most gifted children ever spontaneously discover schematic representation for themselves. Indeed, even in college it is a rare student who, reporting to the class, ever uses the blackboard to diagram difficult material. Similarly, supervisors of student research must constantly remind their charges that data can be presented in tabular and graphic form.

So far, we have been talking about essentially conscious problem solving, even though, obviously, conscious thought relies on schematic arrangements which are not themselves conscious. But what are we to make of the "unconscious" sort of problem solving described by Poincaré, Hadamard, and others? Their descriptions, and introspective evidence generally, indicate that problems sometimes have to "incubate" underground and that during the incubation period a problem may, as it were, solve itself. This is not, however, a complete account. As Hadamard recognizes, there are many degrees of consciousness—he follows William James in speaking of "fringe consciousness"—and the choice is not simply between focal consciousness and oblivion. The developed human organism is not limited to doing one thing at a time. We can subdivide ourselves among several activities or, when engaged in a single activity, be engaged at several levels. We can, for instance, carry on a conversation and, while attending chiefly to the main topic, also think things about the person we are talking to (perhaps deploring a wasted talent, or being amused by the clicking of his false teeth or some odd mannerism), pursue inwardly some tangential ideas suggested by the conversation, and even worry about some personal concern such as debts, an impending operation, or a falling-out with a friend. Whether we do all these things simultaneously or in rapid alternation would be difficult to determine, but we can do them all rather successfully. Furthermore, we do not have to guide all our activities consciously. Over and above habit patterns and situational cues that tell us when to do what, we can more or less consciously program our activities ahead, so that we do the right things at the right times without having to stop and think at each transition point.

Implicit in the foregoing is that both the various things we attend to and the behavioral "mechanisms" by which we deal with them are organized in a shifting pattern of figure and ground. Thus, we can work on a problem with a peripheral automatism while our main attention is directed elsewhere. We know that our ruminations on a problem that is bothering us are never wholly unconscious. Apart from the fact that we periodically bring the problem out into the clear light of consciousness to have a fresh look at it, we feel occasional twinges which, if we stop to notice them, we recognize as twinges of thought focused about the problem, in the same way that we intermittently sense a persistent anxiety prowling in the background. If a problem lies in familiar cognitive territory, then our thinking about it may be almost entirely schematic, with only an occasional impulse to thematization.

The problem here is of who or what it is that thinks. It seems quite clear that it is not nervous systems or language or response sets or schemata that think, but organisms. As we said in the last chapter, environmental events do not automatically evoke symbolic formulations or problem solutions, except when these have already been worked out and are available as habits—habits, let it be stressed, of a very general kind, since it is not particular neuromuscular sequences or even particular acts that are habitual, but kinds of activity. New situations and problems require new symbolic or pragmatic mobilizations which may be anything but easy to come by. It is true that established formulas may seduce us into misclassifying a situation, or may seriously interfere with attempts at description. Similarly, individuals highly practiced in verbal formulation may find the task of describing something new greatly facilitated—verbalization, as we have said, seems to be one of the highly general skills that develop out of many particular acts. But none of this is to say that thought is linguistically determined, save in the negative sense: those whose verbal resources are limited are at a disadvantage in symbolic problem solving. If the individual thinks in clichés, or allows the connotations of words to dominate their denotative meaning, or deals in empty reifications, or is satisfied with words that obscure the facts, then his thinking is linguistically determined. If, on the other hand, he systematically checks his formulations against empirical fact, then it is not.

We must note in passing, too, that the problem situation itself contributes greatly to the ease or difficulty with which a problem is detected or solved.[12] Essential clues may be hidden or camouflaged, or distractions may keep the organism away from the locus of solution. The propagandist takes pains to conceal the biased logic of his appeal so as to impede ready refutation. The child or the ape who can use a stick to retrieve a lure as long as the stick is in position for use may not be able to solve the problem when the stick lies at right angles to the path to the object. The problem of finding principles of problem presentation deserves far more attention than it has received. This is a problem in both basic and applied educational research. Should we, for example, as with teaching machines, program material in such a way that the student moves by easy steps, with a minimum of obfuscation, or is it better to leave material in its illogical natural state and try to teach the student to find his own order, his own thematizations?

Mental Structures

At this point, we must attack the notion that thought resides in any sort of "structure" or "faculty" or "mechanism," even though these terms may be useful metaphors. Thought resides merely in the knowledge of how things are and the consideration of how they might be. But our knowledge has no locus and no shape. It exists only latently, in our concrete surroundings and in our capacities for action, by word or deed; it exists in the way we hold ourselves, in our feeling states, in our attitudes, in our orientation to the future. Experience leaves its traces on our bodies: it lines our faces and hunches our shoulders and corrodes our viscera and circulatory systems. But it does not provide us with mental furniture or logical compartments or sorting devices. This is not to deny the organism its psychological properties— the general quality of sentience, and the particular range of sensitivities through which it apprehends the environment; the capacity for change that is called learning; the capacity for schematizing reality; and needs, urges, wants, and motives. But these are not autonomous properties; they have meaning only in the context of the person in communication with objects, real or fancied. Whatever mental structures the organism has are *ad hoc*, arising from its mobilization to deal with a particular situation and patterned after the situation itself. If the human organism has a capacity or a property that is entitled to be called mind, it is the practice of talking to itself, ruminating, recalling, anticipating, planning, worrying, playing verbal games, solving problems, ordering experience—in short, the practice of constructing an utterance, an edifice of symbols, and then reacting to it as object. And this, of course, is what we call thinking.

Psychopathology of Language and Thought

We suggested earlier (see p. 118) that one source of symbolic opacity is psychological disturbance—neurosis, psychosis, organic psychosis, organic deficit. Neurosis does not ordinarily imply cognitive impairment, but only preoccupation with personal concerns and conflicts—or with defenses against them—such that the individual cannot properly give his attention to the usual pursuits of life. Although the neurotic usually reveals himself in his style, there are no features of symbolization that can be labeled as typically neurotic. Many schizophrenics, by contrast, not only express bizarre ideas but express them bizarrely. Let it be noted that while bizarre forms of expression go hand in hand with bizarre ideation, bizarre ideation is often found with no accompanying disturbance of the individual's powers of formulation.

The behavior of one patient well known to the author illustrates abnormal ideation given coherent expression. The patient's attachment to the author seems to have originated in the circumstance that both their surnames began with *Ch*. From the beginning, however, Mr. Ch attributed rather heroic qualities to the author, perhaps because of the ecclesiastical overtones of his name. In addition, however, *Church* both begins and ends with *ch*, which are the third and eighth letters of the alphabet; and so the word can be written 38UR38. This was at the time of the Korean War, when the 38th parallel was much in the news, and here were two 38's in parallel. It should be said that Mr. Ch attached great significance to parallels and symmetries of every sort, and made the Greek letter *pi* a keystone of his philosophy. The character *pi* resembles a bridge (π) and therefore, in Mr. Ch's view, was capable of uniting all manner of antitheses. Since 38UR38 is *ur* flanked by two 38's, it can also be rendered UR238, which was close enough to the symbol for uranium to convince Mr. Ch that the author was imbued with atomic energy. And since *Church* contains two *h*'s, it contains H^2, or heavy hydrogen, or the makings of a hydrogen bomb as well.

Mr. Ch had no trouble with verbal functioning. He presented his ideas clearly, patiently, and at rather tiresome length. (His letters to high government officials, it must be admitted, sometimes became incoherent.) It is rather different with the speech of some psychotics. There exist many learned analyses of schizophrenic speech, but they can be reduced to a relatively few descriptive statements. Some of the recorded features of schizophrenic speech are the following: word salad, an incoherent jumble of real words which, to judge by vocal inflections, is meant to make sense—and seems to do so to the schizophrenic himself—but which, like the toddler's expressive jargon, tantalizingly refuses to jell; asyndetic speech, in which juxtaposition of more or less related terms takes the place of normal linkages; metonymy, the use of an idiosyncratic approximation (Cameron gives "I have menu three times a day" [13]) or of a personal idiom which the listener must translate; alien intrusions of disturbing ideas or extraneous associations; defective generalization; and neologisms (invented words), often a fusion of two related words, as in "steam-sails" or "grismal." It often appears, as we have said, that the schizophrenic's oddities of speech represent a striving after "significance," an attempt to give verbal-magical importance to a factually bleak and vacant existence. Such a striving may be expressed directly in what is called "pseudo-profundity." We would suspect that a similar tendency is at work in the "speaking in tongues" practiced in some religious congregations.

The manic patient, too, in the course of a "flight of ideas" may produce neologisms and odd phrasings, but these often have a creative ring quite lacking in schizophrenic language.[14] The problem of the manic seems to be neither that of a reality shot through with baffling or malevolent forces nor of an unstable cognitive organization. Rather, the manic feels possessed by unmanageable rage or elation—or sometimes both. He may be swept into violent action, or his feelings may come out as speech. It is reported that some periodically manic individuals have learned to turn their manic episodes to good account, accomplishing prodigies of work while possessed.

It would take us too far afield to discuss all the subtle complexities of language disturbances associated with functional and organic disorders, including the problems of clearly differentiating functional from organic. Let us instead repeat the generalization offered earlier, to the effect that the speech disorders associated with organic brain damage reflect a loss of affective contact between individual and environment—it is as though, figuratively, brain damage had raised the patient's threshold of affective meaning. The significance and importance of things becomes blurred for the brain-damaged individual. Even though he may be fully cognizant of events, he cannot become involved, he cannot care. He can no longer easily mobilize himself to action, he loses much of his initiative and surrenders control to the stimulus situation or to random impulse. His emotions are shallower and more labile than before.

We must hedge these assertions about with reservations, if only because the effects of tissue loss are so unpredictable. Damage in the same area of the brain may have very different effects in different individuals, or no discernible effect at all. Even removal of an entire cerebral hemisphere need not be psychologically devastating, although, needless to say, there are always some psychological consequences.[15] As Teuber [16] has pointed out, we must distinguish between immediate, acute effects of brain damage and long-range, chronic ones; over a period of time there is often very good recovery from brain injury. We cannot assume that serious loss of function, including aphasia, necessarily implies a dissolution of feeling or a loss of symbolic capacity. Some brain-damaged individuals can be seen struggling hard to function normally and show great anguish over their disability. One patient, hemiplegic and unable to utter a word, labor as he might, developed a quite effective gestural system, including gestures indicating that he wished the doctors would cut off and discard the useless right half of his body.

Goldstein [17] has proposed that the speech of both schizophrenics and brain-damaged individuals can be characterized as concrete. But where, in some cases of brain damage, capacities for categorical thought, for gratuitous, nonfunctional action, and for concern with spatially and temporally remote events seem to have been abolished, the schizophrenic by contrast confuses diverse levels of reality, both abstract and concrete. The schizophrenic is not incapable of abstract thought, but abstracts and synthesizes and generalizes in a way that we recognize as insane. There is the further question whether the behavioral effects of brain damage and schizophrenia are to be regarded as regressive. This problem is largely academic. Insofar as behavior has qualities of dynamism, realism, egocentrism, and so forth, it can be described as primitive. Whether such primitivity represents a deterioration or is merely an elaboration of lifelong patterns is a question of fact that is not easily answered, since we seldom have a chance to study a person's functioning until after it breaks down. The organic may be unable to perform some intellectual operations, such as imagining what a form would look like reflected in a mirror or rotated 180°, which are beyond the scope of a young child, but it is quite clear that the source of the inability in the two cases is quite different. Similarly, the schizophrenic moved by panic or rage or perversity may behave and reason quite childishly, but in his more lucid moments his behavior may be indistinguishable from anyone else's.

NOTES

(1) Géza Révész, ed., *Thinking and Speaking* (Amsterdam: North-Holland Publishing Co., 1954).

(2) J. Hadamard, *Psychology of Invention in the Mathematical Field* (Princeton: Princeton University Press, 1949).

(3) H. Poincaré, *Science et Méthode* (Paris: Flammarion, 1908).

(4) Bärbel Inhelder & Jean Piaget, *The Growth of Logical Thinking* (New York: Basic Books, 1958).

(5) N. R. F. Maier, Reasoning in humans: I. On direction, *Journal of Comparative Psychology*, 1930, 10: 115–143.

(6) M. Vincent, Sur le rôle du langage à un niveau élémentaire de pensée abstraite, *Enfance*, 1957, 4: 443–464.

(7) C. E. Spearman, *Creative Mind* (New York: Appleton, 1931).

(8) J. S. Bruner, Going beyond the information given, in *Contemporary Approaches to Cognition* (Cambridge: Harvard, 1957), pp. 41–69.

(9) George Katona, *Organizing and Memorizing* (New York: Columbia, 1940).

(10) C. N. Parkinson, His law transforms Parkinson, *New York Times Magazine*, July 10, 1960, p. 58.

(11) F. C. Bartlett, Social factors in recall, in T. M. Newcomb & E. L. Hartley, eds., *Readings in Social Psychology* (New York: Holt, 1947), pp. 69–76.

(12) C. P. Duncan, Recent research on human problem solving, *Psychological Bulletin*, 1959, 56: 397–429, esp. pp. 407–412. See also: Martin Scheerer & M. D. Huling, Cognitive embeddedness in problem-solving: A theoretical and experimental analysis, in B. Kaplan & S. Wapner, eds., *Perspectives in Psychological Theory* (New York: International Universities Press, 1960), pp. 256–302.

(13) Norman Cameron, Experimental analysis of schizophrenic thinking, in J. S. Kasanin, ed., *Language and Thought in Schizophrenia* (Berkeley: University of California, 1944), pp. 50–64.

(14) For an autobiographical account of a manic episode, see: Carlton Brown, *Brainstorm* (New York: Farrar & Rinehart, 1944).

(15) Jan Bruell & G. W. Albee, Higher intellectual functions in a patient with hemispherectomy. Paper given before the American Psychological Association, 1957.

(16) See, for instance: Josephine Semmes, Sidney Weinstein, Lila Ghent, & H. L. Teuber, *Somatosensory Changes after Penetrating Brain Wounds in Man* (Cambridge: Harvard, 1960).

(17) Kurt Goldstein, Methodological approach to the study of schizophrenic thought disorder, in J. S. Kasanin, ed., *Language and Thought in Schizophrenia* (Berkeley: University of California, 1944), pp. 17–39.

CHAPTER

7

THE STUDY OF COGNITIVE

FUNCTIONING

In this chapter, we shall deal with some methods and problems in the study of cognitive functioning, ranging from intelligence testing to standardized experimental procedures to the analysis of style and content. A discussion of methods is included because of their inherent interest, because they suggest lines of research, and because they call forth elaborations of the present point of view. It may be appropriate to stress that the author's methodological bias is toward observation of children's behavior in everyday situations, and whenever possible, repeated observations of the same individuals.

Intelligence

A favorite topic of psychological investigation is the definition and evaluation of an elusive human property known as intelligence. Let us propose as a first crude definition that intelligence is the ability to operate effectively with symbols. As we shall see, this simple definition covers a host of complexities that beset those who want to think about and assess and predict intelligence. We know that sound thinking is predicated on knowledge. We also know, however, that a vast store of factual knowledge does not guarantee intelligent behavior. For knowledge to be usable, it must somehow be organized, it must be bound together in terms of principles that can be applied to problems or that can serve as models when new principles have to be found.

Thus, a definition of intelligence must include capacity for learning in general, for learning at the level of principles, and for the symbolic elaboration of experience. It is likewise clear that effective intelligence requires various personal qualities—those most often mentioned are sensibility, sympathy, balance, flexibility, humor, detachment, drive, and the capacity for self-criticism. These suggest certain parallels with the normal course of ontogenesis to which we shall return later. Yet another trait that seems relevant is "tolerance of ambiguity," or resistance to premature closure, to jumping to conclusions. Here, however, we meet a difficulty. For it seems typical of the creative person, whom we might assume to be the most intelligent of all, that he is very intolerant of ambiguity—which may account for the hypotheses he produces and the theories he spins. The difference may be that in less intelligent people, dynamistic connections or ready-made formulations cover up ambiguities and keep them from awareness, while the more intelligent and creative individual both recognizes the ambiguity and treats his hypotheses as hypotheses rather than as facts.

Intelligence is assessed—for reasons that will become evident, we prefer not to follow the common usage of "measured"—via tests of factual knowledge, reasoning, memory, word knowledge, arithmetic, spatial visualization, knowledge of social conventions, and a number of similar tasks. In other words, an intelligence test samples the total possible universe of cognitive functioning. Some samplings, as on the Wechsler scales, seem to be based on the test maker's intuitions about what is central to intelligence. Others are derived more systematically, often from a theory of factors. A factor in intelligence is revealed by the high intercorrelations among certain tasks, making for a "cluster," and the low correlation or lack of correlation between this cluster and others. The factor is named on the basis of whatever common property distinguishes the tasks within a cluster. Some factor theorists, following Spearman, stress the G-factor—general, unspecialized intelligence—while others are concerned with the importance of narrower factors such as spatial ability, numerical skills, verbal skills, memory, and so forth. The number of factors contributing to intelligence varies widely from author to author,[1] and the suspicion has been voiced that factor analysis is a technique for finding exactly what one put into a test in the first place.

Although it might seem, in principle, that the problem of appropriate sampling would be a vital one, in practice it seems less important, since intelligence tests that sample different areas and kinds of functioning correlate rather well with each other and with academic achievement, which they were originally meant to predict. There appear to be two main reasons that intelligence test scores are less than perfect predictors of academic performance. First, academic success is based on both intellectual factors and nonintellectual ones, such as personal charm, emotional stability, and strong motivation—we shall say nothing here of the standards by which teachers evaluate academic work. Second, intelligence test items, if they are to permit rapid, unequivocal, numerical scoring, must have right or wrong answers. This means that a test cannot include questions of the type, "Discuss problems of school integration," which would have to be graded on a qualitative scale of creative-original-good-uninspired-feeble, without reference to right or wrong.

Some intelligence test tasks call for verbal responses, whereas others require the manipulation of concrete materials. Tests designed for use with infants and young children—often called developmental scales rather than intelligence tests—are of necessity more heavily weighted with performance items than with verbal ones. Infant scales are in effect little more than tests of physical well-being and rate of maturation, although they are often used, as by adoption agencies, to predict eventual intellectual status. Such tests may well be useful in detecting gross organic defect, but otherwise have little predictive value. It is worth stressing, however, that different kinds of tests are used to measure intelligence at different ages—one does not ask an adult to string beads or cut paper, nor does one ask a toddler to solve syllogisms—so that although the numerical IQ may remain fairly stable over the life span, the functioning it stands for changes radically. For this reason, it makes little sense to compare individuals of different ages in terms of IQ. Although a five-year-old and a thirty-year-old may both have an IQ of 100, it does not follow that they are equally intelligent. The five-year-old probably cannot read or write, cross the street unattended, or take account of a future more than a few days distant. The adult has a family and a job; he has opinions about local, national, and world affairs; he can drive a car; he saves money to give his children a start in life; he understands and respects other people's feelings; and his honesty—with a few trifling exceptions—is beyond question. An intelligence quotient is a relative measure stating where an individual stands relative to others his own age and predicting, subject to considerable variability, where he will stand relative to his contemporaries in later life. It does not say "how much" intelligence a person has.

The utility of intelligence tests is further impaired by the fact that they stop introducing new tests at the level of early adulthood. In consequence, mental growth curves seem to show an arrest of intellectual growth in young adulthood and a decline setting in soon after. Although it is apparent that we become less proficient at certain intellectual operations as we become older, it is equally apparent, as Bayley [2] has pointed out, that we become more proficient at others. If only for the sake of logical consistency, testmakers should devise still further instruments that test the special capacities of later adulthood—tests of wisdom, of being able to judge matters in temporal perspective, of decision making, of tolerance for ambiguity, and so forth. Much has been made of the fact that those individuals who make creative contributions to art or science do so early in their careers; less note has been taken of the writers and philosophers who reach full stature only well along in life, and of the artists and scientists who continue to be original and productive well after the first flush of youth has passed. It is undoubtedly and unfortunately true that many individuals become fixed in their ways of thinking quite early in life, but the exceptions demonstrate that early arrest is by no means a developmental imperative.

A further difficulty is that although we assume intelligence to be determined by innate constitutional properties (which are carefully left unspecified), we have no way of measuring it except ex post facto, by the use that has been made of it. If we assume that a group of people have had equal opportunities for intellectual development, then those who have profited the most from their opportunities should be the most intelligent. As critics of intelligence testing have pointed out, however, the assumption of equality of opportunity is a shaky one—the Navaho child or the child of a bayou-dweller has an opportunity to learn a great many things, but they are different in kind from the things that a child from a well-to-do, northeastern suburban family is exposed to and assimilates, and the difference shows up clearly in intelligence test performance. Some authors, to correct for the biases in standard intelligence tests, have developed what are known as "culture-free" or "culture-fair" tests, consisting for the most part of perceptual tasks. Although such tests reduce the disparity between the scores of children from well-favored and from ill-favored environments, they by no means eliminate it.[3] This finding should not surprise us, since our perceptual sensitivities, as we have said, are susceptible to cultural influences. That is, our upbringing makes us aware of perceptible—but not automatically given—properties and relationships in the environment. In addition, children from middle-class homes acquire a general orientation and attitude toward intellectual activities and achievements, including the skill in test taking that is known as "test wisdom," that is denied to children from intellectually less stimulating backgrounds. Test wisdom, of course, can be considered a special case of learning to learn.

Here we encounter yet another paradox. For if middle-class children excel in the kind of intelligence that shows up on intelligence tests and in school learning, there can be no doubt that the primitive or the lower-class child excels in practical intelligence as measured by ability to fend for oneself—what we might call "shrewdness." It is apparent that life in a tribal or lower-class milieu demands minimal symbolic proficiency of the kind necessary for academic achievement. It is only in adult life that the middle-class child's training pays off in utilitarian skills, when the things he is called upon to do practically have to be mediated symbolically. In Western societies, the number of occupations is steadily shrinking in which symbolic intelligence does not play an important part. Even the farm hand nowadays works in an atmosphere of programs of crop rotation, of chemical fertilizers, pesticides, and disinfectants, of elaborate machines, and of modern cost accounting.

There is no reason to believe that any society has a monopoly on the organic constitutional factors which permit the development of intelligence, but it seems clear that the range of developed intelligence is far narrower in primitive societies than in our own. Otherwise stated, moderate mental deficiency is not likely to be a handicap to the primitive, and potentially superior gifts are likely to go unnoticed. Most discussions of group differences in intelligence are exercises in reification, as though intelligence were a thing or a substance rather than a property of behavior. As of now, we know next to nothing of the biological correlates of intelligence. We know, of course, about the gross malformations and the metabolic disturbances associated with various kinds of mental defect such as mongolism and cretinism. We know that there are slight but consistent sex differences in the patterning of intellectual performance, but until boys and girls are given identical upbringings we cannot safely attribute these differences to biological differences. There may also be some reliable differences associated with congenital differences of temperament, tempo, and sensory dominance, and with somatotypes of the sort studied by Sheldon.[4] What we know about genius points more to a correlation with environmental factors than with any known constitutional traits. Until geneticists, physical anthropologists, and physiologists can supply us with more precise information, we shall probably do well to entertain the working hypothesis that all physically normal children are capable of learning to function at an advanced intellectual level.[5] Here again we must add the proviso that cultural identifications seem to be established very early in life, so that by the time children reach school they may already be immutably committed to particular patterns of cognitive development. It must be said, too, that although intelligence tests and the intuitive judgments of those who know a child well can often provide a rather accurate prediction of eventual intellectual status, we still have no reliable means of distinguishing between simple precocity—an early flowering of gifts that may not endure —and the precocity that portends extremely advanced development; nor have we discovered ways of recognizing the "slow starter" who will, in due time, go on to high levels of achievement.

Cutting across the matter of "amount" of intelligence is that of the different ways in which intelligence is manifested. These varieties have yet to be systematized, but they are suggested by factorial studies; by the patternings correlated with constitutional factors of sex, temperament, and body build; by value types of the sort embodied in the Allport-Vernon-Lindzey scale;[6] and by interest patterns, both of the sort studied via occupational interest inventories and those revealed in recreational preferences. In line with what we have already said, we would suspect that such patternings or specializations of intelligence are probably dependent on cultural identifications rather than on differences in innate intellectual endowment. Nevertheless, we are badly in need of more information on the subtle role of individual temperament in the assimilation of cultural values and concepts.

These organizations of intelligence should not be confused with talents, highly specialized abilities that are independent of general intelligence.[7] Thus, it is possible to be a competent mathematician, musician, or artist without being particularly intelligent. Needless to say, genius in these fields demands a goodly seasoning of intelligence; the talented individual of lesser intelligence spends himself in trivial or, at the extreme, foolish occupations such as those of the *idiot savant* who prides himself on his ability to memorize telephone directories.[8] Probably the main basis for a talent is a capacity for vivid eidetic imagery. Certainly the "lightning calculators" work with eidetic images, sometimes translating mathematical terms into human representatives who act out the operations necessary to a solution. Here again we must note that eidetic images need not be visual, but can also be auditory, somesthetic, or, conceivably, gustatory or olfactory. If talents are founded in eidetic imagery, it makes good sense that they should appear early in life, whereas superior intelligence, premonitory manifestations aside, takes a long time to mature. It is interesting, though, that artistic talent flowers somewhat later than musical or mathematical talent. One hears fairly often about the musical or mathematical child prodigy, but there is no record of noteworthy accomplishment in painting at an age prior to adolescence—although, obviously, some children show great promise as artists. At first glance, one might suppose that pictorial representation would follow especially easily from eidetic imagery, so that the child would be a better depicter of reality than the adolescent or adult. But it is likely that the child's eidetic image, like the objects around him, is too solidly three-dimensional and constant and so resists two-dimensional representation. We must remember that painting involves the application of logically derived rules of transposition from three to two dimensions, quite apart from the esthetic "principles" that artists supposedly observe. Also, current notions of painting make it less a matter of depiction than of symbolic statement, placing it even further beyond the child's scope.

Other abilities which we sometimes loosely refer to as talents —for example, unusual facility in learning languages, literary gifts, and genius in such fields as administration, finance, or philosophy—are in actuality specialized ways of being intelligent, and so mature comparatively late.

It will be apparent by now that we have moved in the direction of equating high intelligence with advanced cognitive development as expressed in ego-differentiation, the schematic stratification and integration of reality, flexibility of action, and, along with and dominating all the other characteristics that set off the mature from the immature organism, proficiency in the manipulation of symbols. Western man is moving in the direction of taking conscious control over his own collective destiny, and he is going to need every bit of intelligence—and, insofar as it is different, wisdom—that he can muster, not only in devising and executing policies but in arriving at a framework of values and morals within which thinking about social problems must take place.

Tests of Verbal Functioning

Intelligence tests do two things. They test for passive knowledge, the residue of experience, and they test for the ability to perform various kinds of cognitive operations—to think. Those tests are most interesting, and show the most consistent developmental changes, which ask the subject to operate upon language itself. Let us now look at some of the devices—many of which have been incorporated into intelligence tests—that invite the subject to give direct or indirect expression to his understanding of symbols. In the course of the discussion we shall propose some elaborations, modifications, and extensions that may reveal new information about symbolic behavior and development. We shall begin with the most widely used instrument of all, the vocabulary test.

Vocabulary Tests

Perhaps the best single instrument for estimating intelligence is a test of word knowledge. Not all such tests call for an act of definition on the part of the subject. Some are tests of passive vocabulary which ask the subject to ˙select an object or an action or an attribute from an array of pictures; others simply require that the subject supply the name for a pictured object. Even in the case of tests where subjects must supply a definition of the words, it is not always clear whether he is being tested for knowledge of the word or for skill in definition. This ambiguity, to which we shall return in a moment, is only one of the weaknesses to be found in the usual vocabulary tests. For instance, the words used in a test are supposedly ordered on a scale of increasing difficulty. The standard of difficulty, however, as Stoddard [9] has pointed out, is not empirically determined conceptual difficulty or abstractness, but rarity of usage. Thus, words like *contumely, traduce,* and *logorrhea* are difficult in the sense that they are unfamiliar to most people, but they do not stand for anything beyond the comprehension of the average person. Tests so constructed may inadvertently penalize the intelligent person who has no taste for purely ornamental words, and reward the less intelligent seeker after the esoteric. Such tests do have the clinical virtue, however, that they often bring into sharp relief compulsive tendencies, and especially those associated with homosexuality.

A suitably constructed vocabulary test could be made to yield several scores. If the words were indeed arranged in ascending order of conceptual difficulty, then a score based on number of words known would be meaningful. A straightforward test of word knowledge, as opposed to skill at definition, could use pictorial materials for concrete terms and various sentence contexts, to be judged as appropriate or inappropriate, for abstract ones. But a developmentally oriented vocabulary test would place great stress on style of definition, which changes strikingly with age.

Before age five or six, children seem virtually incapable of defining words at all, even though they obviously have large vocabularies which they use very effectively for everyday purposes. Indeed, there is reason to suspect that young children may have no notion that there is such a linguistic unit as a word. The child's first definitions of words with object referents are ordinarily in terms of functions: *bicycle*—"You can ride it"; *apple* —"You eat it"; *diamond*—"It sparkles." We can see in such definitions hints of the egocentric, concrete, action-bound way in which young children apprehend reality and of the difficulty they have in communicating their own experience to others. At first, verbs and adjectives are likely to be given contextual definitions: *hit*—"Ya hit 'em! Bang!"; *strong*—"He's real strong! Like Superman." It is apparent that young children find it hard to think about predicates apart from the objects of which they are predicates. We can see, too, that word definition is an inherently ambiguous task. It may call for the description or classification of a phenomenal object, action, property, event, or situation, or for the explication of a hypothetical construct (such as *atom*), or for the explanation of an abstract relationship (e.g., *surplus*), or it may focus attention on the word itself and how it is used. However, it is only after the child has moved from action and context definitions through object definitions—"A bicycle is something you ride on," "Run is like you walk very fast," "Strong is you can do things that are very hard, like picking up something heavy"—that he becomes able to deal with words as symbols, rather than only with the things they stand for. Word analysis of this kind is, of course, rather different from the variety of contextual response sometimes found in children: *nonsense*—"That's what my mother says when I ask for something that costs a lot of money." Still later, the individual can deal with words which serve as operators, words with little in the way of constant content but which are functional units in the construction of utterances: *but, through, of, whether,* and so forth. Mature definitions of nouns are usually of two kinds, classifications (*donkey*—"a beast of burden") and synonyms. Although synonyms are perfectly satisfactory as definitions, they may provide too easy an escape from the task, for which reason vocabulary tests might do well to omit words with more or less exact synonyms. Needless to say, classification responses need not be in terms of formal categories, such as *chair*—"furniture," but can equally well stress functional features, as in *microscope*—"a device for magnifying very small things." We must also note the rare occurrence of nonclassifying descriptive definitions, as in *bicycle*—"It has two wheels, and pedals, and a thing you steer with." Adult definitions of verbs and adjectives also take the form of synonyms or, failing a synonym, of paraphrase, as in *different*—"not the same."

Besides scores for variety of words known, abstractness of words known, and maturity of style of definition, one could also assign scores for the number of meanings given for each word. Obviously, most words are homonyms, in the sense either of having a number of related meanings or of having the same physical shape as an unrelated word. A test scoring the number of senses given would have to depart from the usual one in telling the subject to give as many meanings as possible, since most normal adult subjects give only one. In the case of most homonyms, one sense is usually, in Empson's term,[10] the "head meaning," the one that occurs spontaneously to most people. For instance, few people define *head* in the sense of "head of state," and even fewer as an adjective or a verb. The multiple-meanings approach demands not only that the subject know more meanings but that he be more flexible in his thinking, much as in the functional-fixedness technique, which requires that the subject think of all the things one can do with, for instance, a piece of paper.[11] It might occasionally, however, be hard to tell mature flexibility from immature lability. It appears that children's word knowledge is not so neatly organized as adults' into head meanings and secondary meanings, so that they tend more often than adults to offer alternative definitions or to waver between two possibilities. We assume, however, that adults could find more meanings than would ordinarily occur to children.

An additional scoring might be assigned for figurative uses, which we would expect to increase with age. Let us recall the findings by Asch and Nerlove on age changes in the use of "double-function" terms (i.e., quasi-metaphors which describe people in terms of sensory qualities such as warm and cold), showing that when older children begin to understand and use such terms, they do not realize that they are using the same word in two senses. This seems to be generally true of early language. When an old word appears afresh in a new context, it is not recognized as being the "same," even though the child has no trouble understanding it.

A variation on the multiple-meanings technique would be to construct word lists forming contexts that would enhance one sense at the expense of others. The combination "umpire-pitch-diamond-batter" is not likely to bring to mind tarry substances, precious stones, and cake mix. Such a test would place special demands on the subject's powers of abstraction.

We should acknowledge that in speaking of "meanings" we have departed from our own usage in the last chapter, where meaning was assigned to utterances in which words serve subordinate functions. The present usage is simply for convenience. In effect, a test of word meaning asks the subject to abstract a common core from the functions that a word serves in various contexts. Note that "meaning" in this sense overlaps with the notion of "concept," in that the meaning of a referential term corresponds to the common property of the things it refers to.

Concept-Formation Tests

We have already mentioned, apropos of discussions of generalization and abstraction, concept formation and the various ways of testing it. Here we shall say something more about developmental changes in this area.

Many intelligence tests include subtests which require the subject to specify the way two things (or classes) differ from each other or resemble each other. These are developmentally distinct tasks, and the ability to specify differences is prior to the ability to specify similarities. Again, we must note that the ability to specify either differences or similarities comes later than the ability to react to them. The young preschool child, for instance, labels books and magazines each with their proper appellation, but he cannot say what the distinction is. On a concrete sorting task, he may classify things in the same way as an adult but be unable to make explicit the principle of grouping. But note that sorting tests entail recognition of both similarities and differences: the animals go together because they are like each other and because they are different from the plants.

Let us recall that there are several different processes which psychologists have grouped under the common label of concept formation (see p. 70). There is discrimination among things which have no particular similarity to begin with. There is "generalization"—the recognition of something novel as the equivalent of something already known. There is discrimination between things which at first look alike but then are seen to be somehow different. We assume that following such downward categorization, the once-equivalent things still retain a kind of affective kinship, so that cat and dog, man and woman, bird and airplane, robin and pigeon, could be said to belong to globally apprehended higher-order categories. Again, there is the finding of similarities among things that were never experienced as equivalent. There is true generalization, the formulation of a general principle abstracted from a number of particular events or instances. And there is the formation of ideal categories for large-scale classification, as in biological taxonomy. It is clear that upward categorization of perceptually dissimilar things is necessarily a symbolic operation, while downward categorization can take place at the perceptual level.

The most common test of upward categorization is that in which the subject is presented with two words and asked to say in what way they are alike. As with children's word definitions, we see that there is a developmental progression from contextual to formal. Contextual responses are exemplified by: *dog-cat*— "The dog chases the cat"; *apple-peach*—"You eat them both." There are two rather common sorts of categorization intermediate between contextual and formal. First, there is categorization dominated by logically peripheral similarities: *cat-mouse*—"They both have whiskers (or tails, or four feet)." Second, older children (age nine and up) and adults may offer solutions which indicate recognition of the justice of the proposed category but inability to find the right phrasing. Adults of limited education, for instance, asked why a poem and a statue are alike, may say, "Well, they're sort of the same," or "They're both things that people make," or "They're both the same thing, sort of," or "They're ways of saying something somebody wants to say." One also encounters categorizations in which the principle is strongly implicit but cannot quite be made explicit, as in "A pound is a measure of weight, and a yard is a measure of length." We must note something of a developmental paradox, however. On some tests of concept formation, such as those included in the Wechsler scales, supposedly arranged in order of increasing difficulty, it is by no means uncommon to find that a child does better on the intermediate-level tasks (*wine-beer, piano-violin, pound-yard*) than on the "easier" ones. It may be that those things the child knows concretely and at first hand are less easily conceptualized than those things that he knows at a distance and that may first have been presented to him symbolically. We should note that the formal categorizations of both children and adults tend to be overinclusive, but properly so.

It is more appropriate to say that a horse and a cow are both animals than that they are domesticated quadrupedal mammalian herbivores.

Some people—we have no way of knowing how many—spontaneously discover the process of concept formation and the principle that the same object can be categorized in numerous ways, yielding a many-dimensioned logical network—or system of interpenetrating networks—of relationships forming a conceptual space. Others—we suspect that they are an overwhelming majority—seem to form concepts only schematically and pragmatically. Many, but not all, such individuals can make their conceptualizations explicit when asked to on a concept-formation test.

Concept-formation tasks can also be presented as arithmetic problems, of the form "6 apples + 6 oranges = ?" College students often resist such problems, on the grounds that one cannot add unlikes, and remain skeptical even after it is pointed out that one can in fact put six apples and six oranges into a basket which will then contain twelve pieces of fruit. However, once a student has done a series of such problems, including the item "7 cows + 2 horses = ?", he can easily be induced to say that 9 animals − 2 horses = 7 cows—or, from more sophisticated students, 7 animals—even though the problem is possible only if it specifies that the nine animals include two or more horses. Needless to say, tasks of this sort can be expanded to include any number of items.

One final point needs to be made on the subject of verbal similarities tasks. The terms are reacted to on the basis of their symbolic values and not of their "objective" auditory or visual properties. This point has been demonstrated by Sigel,[12] and is analogous to Gibson's observation [13] that drawings are virtually never seen as marks on paper. Similarly, in the Stroop color-word interference test, where color names are printed in colors at variance with the colors named, it is the meaning (once the subject has learned to read) that interferes with perception of the colors in which the words are printed, and not the other way around.[14] In sum, barring ignorance or pathology, meaning is dominant over objective form.

Object-Classification Tests

So far, we have been talking about procedures in which the subject is presented with two or more words, told that they constitute a logical group, and invited to say why. A somewhat different task takes the form of showing the subject a miscellaneous array of objects (or words) and inviting him to sort them into groups. The objects can be abstract forms, as in the Hanfmann-Kasanin test, or "realistic" objects, as in the Goldstein-Scheerer test.

The "correct" classification of abstract blocks is in terms of such physical properties as size, shape, or color. Preschool children are usually oblivious to the requirement of systematic classification and resort to such devices as choosing two big blocks and a number of smaller ones to represent a family. At a somewhat higher level of abstractness, children may group blocks in chains, where block B goes with block A because they are the same color, C with B because they are the same size, and so forth. Another intermediate-level kind of grouping is the cluster, where each block is related to one key block in terms of some property, but the peripheral blocks are miscellaneously related to each other.

As we might guess, the earliest approach to sorting realistic objects is contextual—the objects belong together because they occur together in real-life situations. Thus, a pipe and a hat may go together because they belong to the same person. It is sometimes difficult to score a grouping: are knife, fork, and spoon placed together as instances of the category "silverware," or because they belong together on the dinner table? Sometimes, of course, the subject will reveal the basis of his grouping by arranging the silver as though for a place setting; or he may betray an ambiguity of intention by vacillating over whether to add a mock lamb chop to his grouping. Older children and adults, urged to group the objects in as many different ways as possible, can often go on to classifications in terms of color, material, shape, and even more obscure properties, such as resonance. It is obvious that tests which require the sorting of realistic objects differ from those using abstract forms in that the principles for the various groups of realistic objects need not be related—that is, these things go together because they are all foodstuffs, these because they have to do with writing, and so forth—while the set of abstract forms must be classified according to dimensions applicable to all the objects. In other words, the abstract forms, even when grouped, still belong to the total set from which they were drawn.

Although object-sorting tests are often referred to as concept-formation tests, they become so only when the subject is required to make explicit the basis for his groupings. Even the relatively difficult Hanfmann-Kasanin test can be solved in a way analogous to downward categorization, where the subject reports simply that the blocks in each group look as though they belong together. Indeed, a great many people can solve the task and specify only that they were using "size," without making explicit that the objects are sorted along the two independent dimensions of height and width.

Classification tests clearly show some individual and developmental differences in ability to form and utilize systematic schemata, but they provide little scope for originality, except of the pathological kind observed by Hanfmann and Kasanin.[15] Conceptualization of the real world, by contrast, where things are related in such a multiplicity of patterns, allows many more opportunities for original symbolic arrangements, creative as well as pathological or primitive. Although, as we have said, concept formation of the kind called for on concept-formation tests is found in real life, the more usual kind of concept formation consists in thematic analysis and elaboration—of levels of reality, of functional connections, of values and preferences, and of possible courses of action.

Analogies

A test which combines word knowledge and abstract schematization of relationships is the analogies test, of the form, "Food is to stomach as air is to ———?" Analogies can be very easy, as in, "Boys grow up to be men, and girls grow up to be ———?", or as hard as the ingenuity of the test maker permits. Some of the relationships that can be utilized in the construction of analogies items are part-whole, antonymy, cause-effect, super-ordination-subordination, or properties of the symbols as objects, as in "quack:pack::sack:————?" It is apparent that some analogies tasks set up their own schemata for completion, whereas others call for considerable digging to find the hidden schema. Just as many individuals discover for themselves the formal model for concept formation, so too do they discover the formal relationships which form the framework of analogies.

Empson [16] has pointed out the kinship between analogy and metaphor. There is a difference, however, easily recognized subjectively but difficult to make explicit. Empson's distinction seems to be that analogies compare things in terms of formal similarities between objective attributes, as in the "saddle" of a mountain or the "leg" of a table, whereas metaphors compare them in terms of properties that produce personal reverberations in us. Thus, analogies would be concepts based on partial equivalence, while metaphors would be generalizations expressing a more nearly total equivalence. Historically, some analogies may have begun as metaphors but have survived only as dead metaphors of the kind mentioned earlier. Empson also adds a fourth term to the array "analogy-dead metaphor-metaphor." This is the notion of equation, or the simultaneous use of a word in two senses, one of which may be metaphorical. An example of equation can be seen in the stand of the medical profession that since illness is the province of the physician, only physicians are qualified to treat, or supervise the treatment of, mental illness. Here we can see how the metaphorical "mental illness," or even "psychopathology," is equated to the somatic conditions treated by doctors. (It must be stressed in passing that certain behavioral disturbances originate in or produce somatic pathology which only the physician is qualified to diagnose and treat.) Equations may represent genuine ideational confusion of a rather primitive kind, similar to hypostasis, or a calculated effort to convey a point of view. The use of the term *concept* by students of thinking probably represents an equation of the first sort. In the latter case, of course, equation resembles argument by analogy.

Within this group of operations we must also find room for punning, which is the use of a term simultaneously in two senses, one of which may be metaphorical, just as in equation, but with awareness of the duality. The pun, of course, is fundamental to the humor of school children, as exemplified by the classic riddles: What has four legs and flies? What is black and white and re(a)d all over? Why does the chicken cross the road? Why does the fireman wear red suspenders? It is worth noting that in the last two examples the joke revolves about a subtle shift in the meaning of the nonsubstantive "why." We must also add the notion of "magical participation," a genuine identity of logically discrete elements of thought, as represented in the primitive's identification with the totem of his tribe or clan, in causal explanations in terms of transfer of qualities (as in old wives' tales of prenatal influence), in sympathetic magic, such as torture inflicted on an effigy or on body wastes, in equivalences established on the basis of peripheral features, as when the child frightened by a rabbit "generalizes" his fear to a white fur muff, and so forth. Finally, we must include the group of phenomena, first pointed out by Freud, which we call symbolism, as in dream images or the blocking of thoughts which symbolize repressed material. In sum, analogy, dead metaphor, magical participation, and unconscious symbolism express unitary schematic mobilizations, while puns express dual or multiple ones. Those equations which are persuasive devices, rather than confusions, represent a dual orientation on the part of the speaker and, in intention, a unitary one on the part of the listener.

The Word-Context Test

An ingenious device for studying the understanding of words is Werner and Kaplan's word-context test.[17] The subject is given a nonsense word used in a variety of sentences and is asked to guess its meaning. This technique is especially good for getting subjects to think out loud. Among the many immaturities to be found in young children's translations of the test words are a tendency to see the word as meaning whatever it seems to mean in each context without detecting any central core of meaning, or to combine several incompatible hypotheses into a syncretic amalgam; to take the word to mean the sentence it is in or the clause or phrase of which it is a part; to translate the word as meaning itself (*"hudray* means to hudray"); and to arrive at idiosyncratic meanings that have no visible connection with the various contexts.

Unfortunately, the test suffers from structural weaknesses which may introduce hidden variables and make interpretation difficult. The nonsense words have strong phonetic-symbolic physiognomies ("corplum," "prignatus") which may be distracting. They are inconsistently inflected, now adding final -*s* or -*ed* and now not—the test instructions describe them as foreign words, so that they are not logically required to follow the flexional rules of English, but this disguise may itself be one more unnecessary complication. They are not consistent as to part of speech—"soldeve," for instance, is used both as a verb and as an adjective. They are neither at a constant level of abstraction nor neatly graded along the concrete-abstract dimension. That the words have no synonyms in English (or, to the best of our knowledge, in any other language) may not be a serious drawback, since the subject is thus induced to state his solution at some length, but certain of the words seem to lack any coherent core of meaning. These criticisms are not fatal, but possibly relevant factors should be controlled. Properly refined, however, the word-context method could prove a highly valuable instrument for the study of thinking.

Interpretation of Proverbs

Bühler [18] was able to make accessible the phenomenology of comprehension and reformulation by presenting subjects with metaphorically phrased maxims and aphorisms whose meanings are not immediately obvious but become clear after a brief interval. This technique, however, cannot be used with children. A similar task, the interpretation of common proverbs, works quite well with children as young as eight.[19] Younger children typically misunderstand the instruction to give the meaning of the proverb, and treat it instead as an assertion to be agreed with or disagreed with, to be contested or validated, or as a test of information, as a riddle, and so forth. Nevertheless, it is quite a simple matter to discern what meaning the proverb has for the children. Children younger than eight completely miss the metaphorical sense of the proverb, and somewhat older children grasp it only globally and physiognomically; not before adolescence does one find responses which treat the situation in the proverb as a concrete analogue of a general relationship. An interesting sort of response that turns up often in the interpretations of eight- and nine-year-olds is the one that treats the proverb not as an assertion but as a designation, as though it described a particular person, situation, or event, like a story synopsis or a picture caption: *Out of sight, out of mind*—"Well, there's this person and he can't see very good and he's sort of crazy like."

There are interesting developmental changes in the way children phrase their interpretation of a proverb. Younger children typically reveal their understanding only in the way they react to the problem—"that's right, because . . ."; (in response to *Don't cry over spilt milk*) "What *do* you do?"— while slightly older ones elaborate on the proverb as given without any attempt at rephrasing it—*You can't teach an old dog new tricks* "cuz he's so old and slow." Older children and adults undertake to paraphrase the proverb, to restate it in other words.[20] Early attempts at actual interpretation err in the direction of either overspecificity, in that the proverb is taken to refer to too narrow a range of phenomena, or underspecificity, in that the limits of applicability are left undefined. Underspecificity, or vagueness, persists much later than does overspecificity.

It will be noted that we have shifted from methods that deal with single words to those that deal with utterances. One advantage of using utterances is that they often reveal characteristics of the meanings of single words that would otherwise not be apparent. For instance, in the proverb "Absence makes the heart grow fonder," most adults treat fondness as a reciprocal relationship: both the person who leaves and the person who stays behind miss each other. For school children up to age eleven or twelve, however, fondness is one-sided: either the person who has gone away misses those he has left, *or* those who have stayed behind miss the departed one. This assertion is complicated by the tendency of many school-age children to take "absence" in the restricted sense of absence from school, with resulting connotations either of illness, in which case "fonder" represents a pathological condition, or liberation, in which case "fonder" implies joy.

Here we come up against a general feature of utterances: a two-sided relationship is generally expressed in terms of only one side, as when a three-year-old says "My mouth is behind my scarf" instead of "My scarf is over my mouth." By rights, one would expect a developmental conventionalization as regards which pole of the relationship becomes focal: one ordinarily says that "My shoes are too small" rather than "My feet are too big." Yet incomplete paragraphs permitting a phrasing of either sort elicit from college students and educated adults as many of one sort as of the other. Some relationships, of course, stabilize quite early. The child says, "The book is on the table," never "The table is under the book."

The Line-Schematization Technique

A device for studying some of the structural and connotational features of an utterance is Werner and Kaplan's line-schematization technique. The subject is asked to draw a line representing a statement such as a proverb and then to explain why the line matches the statement. Preliminary findings support the notion that experienced meanings include schematic images aroused by the utterance. It is also possible to use the line-schematization method for personality description, and it is helpful for students who initially find themselves inarticulate when asked to describe someone they know.

The Semantic Differential

Yet another technique of obscure theoretical significance but of considerable empirical promise is Osgood's semantic differential. This method requires the subject to scale words on several adjectival dimensions, such as *hot-cold, hard-soft, heavy-light*. The resulting "profile" of scalings is taken to represent the word's meaning. Perhaps the most interesting finding of the technique is its feasibility—we must point again to the use of intersensory metaphors. (For some words, however, the scales become literal: a boulder, as Brown points out, *is* both heavy and hard.[21]) Recent studies by Osgood and his collaborators, as we have said (p. 134), test the Whorf hypothesis by comparing the scalings of equivalent words in different cultural-linguistic settings.

One must remain skeptical about the semantic differential's claim to be a measure of meaning. Like the line-schematization technique, the semantic differential captures some portion of the connotative meaning of a word. But it is difficult to believe that the ten standard dimensions (grouped into three factors: evaluation, potency, and activity) exhaust all the major possibilities, or that it is sound to use the same set of dimensions for all words. Again, it seems likely that responses on the semantic differential are to the head meanings of words, and quite different patterns might show up if one were to present words in different contexts. Like most other tests of meaning, the semantic differential deals with single words rather than utterances. Furthermore, there are two faults to be found with the use of antonymic dimensions. First, some descriptive terms that might prove useful do not fall on any antonymic scale and can only be treated as present or absent; what, for instance, is the opposite of *tinny*, or *brittle*, or *iridescent*? Second, certain antonyms found on the scale are not antonyms at all. Sweet and sour are simply different positions on the taste tetrahedron. Red and green are complements rather than antonyms, and on a test of opposites they do not reliably elicit each other. College students, given an antonym test that includes color names, react all over the spectrum, not to mention the "shadow spectrum" of grays and browns.

We must point out the similarity between the semantic differential and Asch's trait scales couched in sensory metaphors (or, as Asch calls them, double-function terms).[22] Fitted out with suitable dimensions, the semantic differential might prove useful for the description of persons and of the things people do and make, such as works of art.

To the best of our knowledge, there has so far been no attempt to obtain semantic differential ratings from children, although it seems a promising field of exploration.

The Word Association Test

Jung's word association technique is widely known as both a psychodiagnostic instrument and an experimental tool. The subject is asked to respond to each of a series of stimulus words with the first word that occurs to him. A delay in responding or an unusual association, particularly to words touching on areas deemed to be emotionally sensitive, is thought to have diagnostic significance. Word associations are not so idiosyncratic as to preclude group comparisons, including developmental ones. Children are likely to give contextual responses, of the form "mother—cooks," or *Klang* (as in "fable—feeble") or rhyming responses. Adults, by contrast, are likely to respond in terms of formally related words such as antonyms, synonyms, logical coordinates or subordinates, and so forth. One cannot always be sure, of course, of the classification of a response, as we mentioned when speaking of concept-formation tests. "Chair—table," for instance, can be seen as a pairing of coordinates or as a contextual response. Brown and Berko [23] point to an alternative classification in terms of agreement of part of speech: children are far more likely than adults to respond, for instance, to a noun with an adjective or a verb. Again, we must point to the similarity of developmental changes observed in word associations to those seen both in concept-formation tasks and in semantic generalization. In Riess's now-classic study [24] of the generalization of responses conditioned to words, young children tended to generalize to homophones, somewhat older children to antonyms, and the oldest subjects to synonyms.

Certain stimulus-words have a marked tendency to evoke fairly fixed responses: *black* calls forth its antonym *white,* and *fight* the contextual *angry.* Many common associations seem to be unidirectional: *black* evokes *white,* but *white* does not evoke *black.* A recent case study by Jenkins and Schaefer [25] suggests that individuals who give many high-frequency associations tend to have a decidedly prosaic, conforming, unimaginative orientation to reality, whereas highly idiosyncratic associations reflect maladjustment, but perhaps in some cases maladjustment of a potentially creative sort.

Although some common associations, such as *black—white,* can be accounted for by frequency of joint occurrence, this is not a sufficient general principle, as shown by the developmental shift from contextual to formal associative links.

It is tempting to think of an individual's vocabulary as an intricately connected multidimensional constellation in which some connective bonds are more easily activated than others, but so static a conception hardly accords with the way words rise up from nowhere to fulfill a schematic, expressive intention. Such a conception also leads us to look for storage units and memory banks in the central nervous system, and neurological evidence, in spite of Penfield's provocative findings,[26] will not support such a notion. Certainly there is no evidence that loss of a particular section of the brain leads to the loss of particular information, leaving other information intact. The rationale of prefrontal lobotomy, for instance, is that it severs connections with the "future-oriented" portion of the brain and so reduces inhibitions and anxiety. But some patients are made more inhibited and more anxious by prefrontal lobotomy, and there is no evidence that lobotomized patients have any better or any worse foresight than unoperated controls or individuals damaged in other brain regions. In general, it appears that direct stimulation of the brain which has behavioral consequences works by setting in train a total organismic mobilization out of which feelings, attitudes, memories, and action emerge. This, of course, is the way we would picture word association, or any other associative event, including Marcel Proust's masterpiece.

We have already mentioned Riess's study of semantic conditioning and generalization. Other studies in this area show that generalization takes place from word to referent and vice versa, and to categorically and contextually related stimuli. It might be worth finding out whether there is also generalization from a word to its associates on a word association test.

Analysis of Extended Verbal Productions

We have been speaking largely of verbal responses to artificial experimental tasks. It is obvious that our chief interest is in symbolic communication as it occurs in real life, in the service of the individual's own goals and wants and impulses and whims. But analysis of real-life verbalizations is a study both of the linguistic product and, through it, of the person who produced it. Here we are approaching what is known in literary criticism as stylistic analysis and in psychiatry and clinical psychology as psychodiagnosis—for, while the clinician provokes a number of the client's utterances by asking him questions and thrusting inkblots upon him, he also gives him an opportunity to talk freely and sizes him up on the basis of what he says and how he says it. Logically—but not psychologically—distinct from and complementary to stylistic analysis are the social psychologist's tool of content analysis and the logician's tool of semantic analysis.

Verbal Indicators of Personal Style

Stylistic analysis of literary works is of only tangential psychological interest, since most published writings have undergone considerable reworking that takes them far from the realm of spontaneous utterance. Nevertheless, one can generally derive from literary works some notion of the author's personal qualities, attitudes, and values.

Of more relevance are attempts to define objectively what personal style is and how it is revealed. Classic studies by Allport and Vernon,[27] Sanford,[28] Wolff,[29] Arnheim,[30] and others indicate that there is such a thing, but it has so far eluded its pursuers. Skilled critics and clinicians often do a brilliant job of catching an individual style, but this is not the same as setting forth an explicit theory of style. Some of the objective indicators of verbal style are: the type-token ratio (variety of words compared to number of words); [31] complexity of sentence structure; length of sentences; use of imagery and figures of speech; tendencies to repetition, perseveration, circumlocution, allusiveness, circumstantiality, and the like; emphasis on logical or affective relationships; the Avq (adjective-verb quotient,[32] presumably indicative of whether the individual is more concerned with analysis and contemplation—adjectives—or with action—verbs other than copulas); and the Flesch count of reading difficulty.[33] Although such measures are obviously pertinent, they are by no means complete and suffer—perhaps inevitably—from atomism. More recent studies attempt to deal with differences in "cognitive style," defined chiefly in terms of leveling or sharpening tendencies as described by Bartlett (see p. 113).[34] These tendencies suggest a further typology in terms of preferred defense mechanisms, and, by extension, in terms of diagnostic categories—which is indeed how a great many people describe their friends nowadays.

With reference to spoken language, vocal quality independent of what is being said can convey much about a person's style. One has only to think of such properties as stridency or mellifluence, strain or relaxation, changes of pitch or timbre, flatness or expressiveness, fluency or fragmentation of output, blocking, the dominance of such affective qualities as irony, gentleness, warmth, or whimsicality, and intimations of affectation, role-playing, or insincerity. The individual's speech also tends to proclaim his group affiliations, his socio-economic status and general cultural background, and all that these tell us about him. We must also take account of how speech is patterned rhythmically and melodically, how sounds and stresses and tempi shape an utterance. Here we can think of the speech patterns of various national groups—the Irish or the Italians, for instance. And, of course, we must not overlook the obvious dimension of taciturn-garrulous.

At the level of structural organization, we find individual differences in the tendency to garble word sequences, to leave sentences unfinished (whether by hopping from idea to idea or by letting sentences trail off), to be sidetracked onto tangents and onto tangents of tangents, and to try to tell things wrong end to. Some people compose their utterances before speaking, others improvise as they go.

Choice of words may be biased toward Latinisms or Anglo-Saxonisms, toward the esoteric or the commonplace, toward the abstract or the concrete. One may speak largely in clichés and platitudes, or be forever straining after vivid turns of speech, or insist always on the *mot juste*. Vocabulary preferences betray not only stylistic bents but also social and political and economic orientations. We have already mentioned how certain stock phrasings enter the vocabularies of particular groups and how the user of such catchwords reveals, perhaps unwittingly, his ideological affiliations.

Although we can discuss stylistic indicators one by one, it is obvious that our perception of style is of a person speaking. As we have said, it is ordinarily the "content" of behavior that stands forth in a transparent container of objectively more substantial acts. Although the perfect stylist is the invisible one who allows the listener or reader to look right through him to the subject matter of his discourse, our means of expression always have some degree of opacity. It is only the most banal statements in the most neutral situations that ever attain transparency. As soon as we try to describe a new phenomenon, a new relationship, a new way of looking at something, our medium thickens and becomes prominent. Indeed, much of the innovator's time is taken up with means of expression rather than with what is being expressed. It is not quite accurate, for instance, to say that one can write about writing but cannot paint about painting. The many artistic innovations of the last century are as much statements about the medium as about any subject matter. It is this very reversal, this making form dominant over content, that puts people off and makes them complain of the "lunacy" of modern art, just as they are likely to find lunacy in opaque verbal statements, whether these be the pronouncements of an Einstein or of a schizophrenic.

Conventional statements, whether in the arts, the sciences, or everyday affairs, are for the common observer styleless, although the critic, the logician, and the diagnostician can detect stylistics everywhere. Needless to say, modern preoccupation with form is not restricted to the creator; whole schools of criticism, literary and logical, are concerned primarily with the analysis of form, having only a limited concern for content.

Analysis of Thinking

Content analysis was first designed for the study of persuasive communications such as advertising and propaganda. It sought to make clear the attitudes and actions that a message was meant to induce and the persuasive devices employed to that end. Recent work by Hovland and his associates [35] has gone much further in studying empirically the composition of messages to see which ones work and under what conditions. Content analysis shades into logical analysis, whereby one seeks to make explicit the premises and the inferential chains in a piece of reasoning, with special attention to the inclusion and omission of evidence, the weighting of arguments by extraneous values, and the intentional or unintentional occurrence of various "fallacies."

Analysis of thinking in terms of developmental psychology proceeds rather differently. We are less concerned with the actual operations of thinking, which we have described as a dialectic resulting in a symbolic-affective mobilization to a problem—a dialectic which need not flow in the smooth, orderly sequences of a digital computer but can proceed by fits and starts and jumps and convulsions—than with the cognitive composition of the reality being thought about. But every time we talk about cognitive reality, we are also by necessity talking about the individual and his orientation to the world. Thus, a developmental analysis of thinking is inevitably addressed *ad hominem.* Certain of the categories of analysis of the developmental psychologist correspond approximately to those of the logician; we have already mentioned the parallel between verbal realism and hypostasis, and our use of level or order of reality is akin to the logician's level of discourse. To the best of our knowledge, however, the logician has no categories corresponding to dynamism, phenomenalism, egocentrism, participation, and so forth; nor does logic easily take account of an individual's ability or inability to deal with abstractions without losing sight of the stubborn, often disorderly, concrete realities underlying them. Like the psychoanalyst, the developmental psychologist looks for the logic of unreason and is not content merely to classify an argument as irrational. Again, the logician is concerned with the form of arguments. The developmental psychologist is more concerned with the orientational starting point and with the finished conclusion than with the validity of the route that is followed. For, in fact, the dialectical progression of thought often begins with a total intuitive leap to a conclusion. If the intuition is tried and found wanting, it is modified or abandoned in favor of another. When the intuition "feels right," one sets about integrating it verbally with the perceived situation and with the schematic framework from which the intuition sprang. In the process, either the concrete situation or the individual's assumptions may have to be reformulated. Indeed, it is often only after our intuitive judgments have emerged that we can discover what the assumptions were that produced them. It is in this sense that thinking is often a matter of trial and error, but of directed rather than random trial and error. We must also note that much of the thinking that follows an act of intuition is probably aimed at justifying the intuition rather than testing it. Unlike the student of ideal forms, the student of behavior takes into account that any given premise or group of premises exists in a larger cognitive context that determines which implications, if any, are going to stand out.

The developmental analysis of thought is a more general form of the psychodiagnosis that seeks to define what threats the world holds for the individual, how competent he feels to deal with threats and what actual methods he uses, what his attitude is to past and future, and what learnings and what environmental rearrangements will allow him to function optimally. It is interesting to note that cognitively oriented psychiatrists have begun to question the notion of psychopathological states as autonomous entities indifferent to factual reality, and to study modifications in pathological behavior consequent on modifications of the milieu. Rashkis [36] has pointed out how pathogenic circumstances can produce psychotic ideation which may persist even after removal from the situation but which subsides when the patient is encouraged, in a protective setting, to discuss the pathogenic circumstances realistically and at a distance. This sort of formulation obviously does not apply to individuals who have developed in a lifelong pattern of characterological pathology and who simply no longer have access to what we think of as standard reality.

NOTES

(1) For instance, J. P. Guilford (Morphological model for human intelligence, *Science*, 1960, 131: 1318) proposes 55 distinct dimensions.

(2) Nancy Bayley, On the growth of intelligence, *American Psychologist*, 1955, 10: 805–818.

(3) See, for instance: Henry Angelino & C. L. Shedd, An initial report of a validation study of the Davis-Eells tests of general intelligence or problem-solving ability, *Journal of Psychology*, 1955, 40: 35–38; D. I. Marquart & L. L. Bailey, An evaluation of *The Culture-Free Test* of intelligence, *Journal of Genetic Psychology*, 1955, 86: 353–358.

(4) W. H. Sheldon, with the collaboration of S. S. Stevens & W. B. Tucker, *The Varieties of Human Physique* (New York: Harper, 1940); with the collaboration of S. S. Stevens, *The Varieties of Temperament*, 1942.

(5) Note, however, the startling finding by Yacorzynski and associates that traumatic birth conditions are related to a wider range of intellectual attainment, both upward and downward from the mean, than normal birth conditions. (G. K. Yacorzynski & B. E. Tucker, What price intelligence? *American Psychologist*, 1960, 15: 201–203.)

(6) W. F. Dukes, Psychological studies of values, *Psychological Bulletin*, 1955, 52: 24–50.

(7) H. A. Carroll, *Genius in the Making* (New York: McGraw-Hill, 1940), pp. 186–205.

(8) See, for instance: Martin Scheerer, Eva Rothman, & Kurt Goldstein, A case of "idiot savant:" An experimental study of personality organization, *Psychological Monographs*, 1945, 58, no. 4.

(9) G. D. Stoddard, *The Meaning of Intelligence* (New York: Macmillan, 1943).

(10) *The Structure of Complex Words* (Norfolk, Conn.: New Directions, 1951).

(11) Karl Duncker, On problem-solving, *Psychological Monographs*, 1945, 58, no. 5, Part III. See also: Scheerer & Huling, *supra*.

(12) I. E. Sigel, The dominance of meaning, *Journal of Genetic Psychology*, 1954, 85: 201–207.

(13) J. J. Gibson, What is a form? *Psychological Review*, 1951, 58: 403–412.

(14) See, for instance: P. E. Comalli, S. Wapner, & H. Werner, Interference effects of Stroop color-word test in children, adults, and aged. Paper given before the Eastern Psychological Association, 1960.

(15) Eugenia Hanfmann, Analysis of the thinking disorder in a case of schizophrenia, *Archives of Neurology and Psychiatry*, 1939, 41: 568–579; Eugenia Hanfmann & J. S. Kasanin, *Conceptual Thinking in Schizophrenia* (New York: Nervous and Mental Disease Publishing Co., 1942).

(16) *Op. cit.*

(17) H. Werner & Edith Kaplan, The acquisition of word meanings, *Monographs of the Society for Research in Child Development*, 1950, 15, no. 1.

(18) Karl Bühler, On thought connections, in David Rapaport, *Organization and Pathology of Thought* (New York: Columbia University, 1951), pp. 39–57.

(19) Claudia Richardson & Joseph Church, A developmental analysis of proverb interpretations, *Journal of Genetic Psychology*, 1959, 94: 169–179. See bibliography.

(20) The extent to which the individual undertakes to reformulate the proverb has been designated "degree of dominance" over his own verbal functioning. Due to a misunderstanding, for which the present writer must take responsibility, "degree of dominance" has been interpreted by D. R. Gorham (Verbal abstraction in psychiatric illness, paper given before the 16th International Congress of Psychology, 1960) to mean aggressiveness.

(21) For critical reviews see: Roger Brown, Is a boulder sweet or sour? *Contemporary Psychology*, 1958, 3: 113–115; Harold Gulliksen, How to make meaning more meaningful, *ibid.*, 115–119.

(22) S. E. Asch, On the use of metaphor in the description of persons, in H. Werner, ed., *On Expressive Language* (Worcester: Clark University, 1955), pp. 29–38.

(23) Roger Brown & Jean Berko, Word association and the acquisition of grammar, *Child Development*, 1960, 31: 1–14.

(24) B. F. Riess, Genetic changes in semantic conditioning, *Journal of Experimental Psychology*, 1946, 36: 143–152.

(25) J. J. Jenkins & Marjorie Schaefer, Word association phenomena at the individual level: A pair of case studies, in J. J. Jenkins, ed., *Associative Processes in Verbal Behavior: A Report of the Minnesota Conference* (University of Minnesota, Department of Psychology, 1959), pp. 26–43.

(26) Wilder Penfield & Lamar Roberts, *Speech and Brain Mechanisms* (Princeton: Princeton University, 1959). For a detailed, searching review, see: E. H. Lenneberg, *Language*, 1960, 36: 97–112.

(27) G. W. Allport & P. E. Vernon, *Studies in Expressive Movement* (New York: Macmillan, 1933).

(28) F. H. Sanford, Speech and personality: A comparative case study, *Character and Personality*, 1942, 10: 169–198.

(29) Werner Wolff, *The Expression of Personality* (New York: Harper, 1943).

(30) Rudolf Arnheim, Experimentell-psychologische Untersuchungen zum Ausdrucksproblem, *Psychologische Forschung*, 1928, 11: 1–132. See also: C. W. Huntley, Judgments of self based upon records of expressive behavior, *Journal of Abnormal and Social Psychology*, 1940, 35: 398–427.

(31) Wendell Johnson, Studies in language behavior: I. A program of research, *Psychological Monographs*, 1944, 56, no. 1.

(32) D. P. Boder, The adjective-verb quotient: A contribution to the psychology of language, *Psychological Record*, 1940, 22: 310–343.

(33) R. Flesch, A new readability yardstick, *Journal of Applied Psychology*, 1948, 32: 221–233.

(34) Riley Gardner, P. S. Holzman, G. S. Klein, Harriet Linton, & D. P. Spence, Cognitive control, *Psychological Issues*, 1959, 1, no. 4; Leonard Berkowitz, Leveling tendencies and the complexity-simplicity dimension, *Journal of Personality*, 1957, 25: 743–751. Jerome Kagan (Styles of conceptualization: Their significance for intellective and personality variables; paper given before the American Psychological Association, 1960) describes styles of concept formation which correspond closely to our developmental types of (a) contextual groupings, (b) groupings based on logically peripheral similarities, and (c) groupings in terms of essential formal attributes.

(35) C. I. Hovland, I. L. Janis, & H. H. Kelley, *Communication and Persuasion* (New Haven: Yale, 1953).

(36) H. A. Rashkis, Cognitive restructuring: Why research is therapy, *A.M.A. Archives of General Psychiatry*, 1960, 2: 612–621.

8

EPILOGUE: COGNITIVE

DEVELOPMENT AND GENERAL

PSYCHOLOGY

It is evident that we are seeking not simply a psychology of cognitive development but also a cognitive-developmental psychology. A complete account of human behavior and development must deal with what people do, how they do it, why they do it, and how they feel about what they do. Our focus so far has been chiefly on the *how* of behavior, on the orientation to reality that enables the individual to do what he does. Sometimes, of course, the *how* of behavior is also the *what*, since the individual spends a considerable portion of his time just finding out about and trying to make sense of reality.

It would be a vain enterprise for us to try to catalogue the content of human behavior. It is enough to note that the pattern of interests, concerns, preoccupations, and activities changes with age and with social evolution, and that there are certain obvious contrasts between primitive and advanced societies. Of more immediate importance is an understanding of how problems of emotion and motivation look from a cognitive viewpoint. Let

us say at once that our treatment of these subjects will be
sketchy, since we do not want to depart too far from our central
theme, since much of what we have to say is in any case strongly
implicit in what has already been said, and, finally, since so
many other writers are currently expressing similar—although
not necessarily identical—notions. Having said a word about
emotion and motivation, we shall end with an attempt to show
some similarities and differences between the present view and
those held by other authors.

Emotion

We have been at some pains to point out that human knowledge is not merely a matter of pragmatics; it is also a matter of
values and hence of feelings. Indeed, our knowledge about
objects, the meanings they have for us, has a dual representation,
first in the perceived properties of the objects themselves and
second in the feelings they arouse. In primitive, unmediated
behavior, feelings are epiphenomenal: they arise out of and
surround our interaction with objects but they cannot be said to
cause it. As the individual becomes able to detach himself from
objects, to respond mediately, and as his emotions come to be
localized as resident within himself and to take on identifying
feeling qualities, he becomes able to consult both the situation
and his own feelings for clues to action.

We must pause here to note that talk of emotion has been
freighted with reification, as though an emotion were some sort
of somatic or psychic entity within the organism. It should
be clear that the named emotions—anger, fear, joy, ecstasy,
and so on—are abstractions from the totality of experience,
categories of phenomenologically similar feeling states. Even
here we must not be misled by semantics. We may with all
propriety say that "I love my wife" and "I love my dog," but it
should not be supposed that these two "loves" are identical. Felt
emotions are merely an expression of the valuative component
in our mobilizations toward situations. Our mobilizations are
seldom simple and straightforward; as we see someone we know

approaching us on the street, we prepare to greet him, perhaps with a formal "Good afternoon" or with a less formal "Hi," perhaps with a quick handshake or perhaps in expectation of a few minutes' conversation. But just as we prepare to do certain things, we prepare, sometimes consciously, not to do others. We assume an air of hurried importance lest we be cornered by a bore, we resolve not to be drawn into a discussion of certain sensitive matters, we brace ourselves not to recoil from the too-intimate embrace with which so-and-so is sure to greet us. Again, our mobilizations are not simply for some kind of abstractly utilitarian action but express our anticipation of pleasure or pain, boredom or excitement, sympathy or impatience, and all the other kinds of feelings that go with all the other kinds of objects with which we interact and with all the ways we have of inter-acting with them. A total vocabulary of feelings can distinguish some very subtle nuances indeed. We might suspect, in line with our general thesis, that the individual's capacity for knowing and containing and controlling his feelings depends on his verbal resources for thematizing them. Similarly, one cannot but suspect that those who speak of feeling states only in gross terms or hackneyed figures lead somewhat banal emotional lives. In this connection, we must recall what was said earlier (p. 105) about the verbalization of feelings and defense mechanisms.

We should note in passing that culture has its say in emotional development. For one thing, it defines the value of emotional experience—we have only to contrast the Stoic and Epicurean orientations, the Spartan and the Athenian. Second, the culture dictates what objects are reacted to at all and what feelings are to be attached to those objects that are assigned cultural recognition. Third, it defines how feelings are to be expressed; while babies all over the world cry and smile and cringe and reach out, the more subtle gradations of grief, anger, contempt, rejoicing, and so forth, vary widely from culture to culture—in China, for instance, according to Klineberg,[1] anger is shown by opening wide the eyes. What we cannot know is whether logical equivalence of the situations to which people react—bereavement, for instance—points to equivalence of feeling despite differences in forms of expression, or whether differences in expression represent differences in feeling quality. This problem is complicated by conventional devices not only for expressing feelings but for masking them. It is further complicated by the fact that equivalent feelings may be valued either positively or negatively in different cultures. Warlike peoples, for instance, seem to take pleasure in anger, while the more pacific person avoids it. Within our own society there are numerous people who profess that they really enjoy a good cry. Marked cultural differences have been demonstrated also in reactions to what we would consider painful stimuli.[2] In any event, it seems to be within the range of human possibilities to experience something as both pleasant and unpleasant, not in the two-layered manner of bitter-sweet experiences but as a unitary feeling state.

We have been talking about only one dimension of emotion, the spectrum of specific qualities that distinguish one "emotion" from another, the feelings that embody the meaning of an object or event. We must note a second dimension, that of intensity or degree of arousal, as described by Dumas.[3] (The present scheme, however, differs in some particulars from that proposed by Dumas.) Not all our behavior is emotionally toned: we say of some objects and situations that they are neutral, that we can deal with them dispassionately or automatically. This is not completely accurate, since a wholly neutral object would presumably have no perceptual or behavioral existence at all; even the most routinized of activities usually are accompanied by feeble flickers of feeling, if only of the kind that keeps all our body parts located with respect to each other and the body located in space and time. At a level of arousal beyond that of the matter-of-fact, our feelings take on more subtle shadings and our thinking and acting are more precise, effective, and enjoyable. We can designate this as the level of "zest," where, as Dumas points out, even feelings that at more severe intensities would be unpleasant are felt as agreeable; we enjoy the tonic of mild fear, mild tension, mild anger, as when we ride on a roller coaster, read a ghost story, or engage in a lively debate. At a still higher level of intensity, our feelings become less precise and variegated but are more distinctly pleasant or unpleasant. We become more egocentric and are oriented more to action than to interaction—we become more an assailant and less an adversary, more a rapist and less a lover. It is at this level that the physiological changes associated with emotionality become clearly visible. Finally, arousal can be so intense that our ability to function breaks down in paralysis or incoherence or explodes in random violence. Young children, of course, can shuttle rapidly back and forth between minimal and ultimate arousal, as seen in the massive distress reactions of the infant and his miraculously rapid recovery when the cause of his distress is removed. The temper tantrums of the toddler are less easily neutralized, but once recovery sets in it is very rapid. Developmentally, there is an increasing tendency to function at the intermediate levels of emotionality, and, at the same time, for emotional states to persist well beyond the situations that caused them. Adults generally protect themselves against the autonomic riot of the final stage of emotionality by conscious efforts at self-control, by such devices as substitution or displacement activities, or by leaving the field. Even the lower species may escape from an intolerable situation via displacement, as when the bird about to be worsted in a fight suddenly shifts to grooming or feeding movements. As Lorenz[4] and others have pointed out, this can work the other way, too: mating rituals among birds, for instance, have many of the same features as threat rituals, and a wrong move may change a courtship display into mortal combat.

We must recall that our mobilizations to particular situations take place in the context of a more general mobilization toward reality at large, and so it is with our feelings, which are layered and interwoven and fused in countless complex ways.

It should be apparent that the development of consciousness and of ideation amounts to an elaboration of feeling states into a body of knowledge. Feelings are the substrate and the raw material of cognition as opposed to reflexive action, and our human capacities for thought are no greater than our human capacities for feeling. It may well be that capacity for feeling, whether innate or generated out of early parent-child relations, is the essential variable in intellectual differences. It is only those with strong feelings who can resist the secondhand formulations of experience handed down from their progenitors and can work to thematize reality afresh for themselves. Certainly it is possible to be retentive without great feeling, but learning without the understanding that emotion gives is barren and perhaps even dangerous.

Motivation

It is not easy to draw a sharp line between emotion and motivation. It is said that we are drawn to those objects and activities that promise us pleasure and shun those that threaten pain, which would make emotion motivating and motivational states a matter of feeling states. But this simple hedonistic doctrine is complicated in several ways. Developmentally, for one thing, we come to distinguish between trivial pleasures and solid satisfactions and to prefer the latter. Hand in hand with this change comes a tendency to operate increasingly in terms of long-range goals and less for immediate gratifications. This is not to say that all our motivations are of this lofty sort. We are possessed by lusts and goaded by jealousies and racked by anxieties; we do have to eat and eliminate and take measures to keep ourselves from freezing or broiling. But there are several points to notice. First, our needs and drives are not autonomous entities propelling us from without like an outboard motor. They are movements toward particular ways of being mobilized toward reality. True, in pathological development motives may take on the character of external agencies, and at crucial points in ego-differentiation, as during the seeming war that goes on between flesh and psyche in adolescence, one's motives may feel very alien indeed; but ordinarily motivations are experienced as states of oneself. Second, drives are not to be thought of as constant factors in behavior, like the Freudian Eros surging relentlessly toward expression. Even the male adolescent, who may be beset by spontaneous and untimely lusts and who may find sexual significance in the most innocent of situations, still engages in activities and thinks thoughts in which sexuality plays no role. Third, under favorable conditions even the most exigent fleshly motivations may be suppressed in favor of cognitively-directed pursuits. We have only to think of the artist starving for his art, the monk doing penance in his cell, the hero immolating himself on the battlefield. Needless to say, some of man's higher vocations may be rooted in urges of a baser sort: fear, greed, a desire for dominance, a search for a status that will win esteem, sadism, voyeurism, organ inferiority. But even when this is the case, we must recognize that the extrinsically motivated pursuit may become intrinsically satisfying and self-motivating—in Allport's term, functionally autonomous; in Freud's term, the original drives are sublimated. Fourth, the organism does not act only for the sake of returning to inactivity, to the Nirvana of perfect equilibrium. A number of writers have lately been challenging the homeostatic view of motivation; this challenge has been summarized most cogently by White:

> It seems to me that these contributions, though differing as to details, speak with unanimity on their central theme and would force us, if nothing else did, to reconsider seriously the whole problem of motivation. Boredom, the unpleasantness of monotony, the attraction of novelty, the tendency to vary behavior rather than repeating it rigidly, and the seeking of stimulation and mild excitement stand as inescapable facts of human experience and clearly have their parallels in animal behavior. . . . Even when its primary needs are satified and its homeostatic chores are done, an organism is alive, active, and up to something.[5]

Behavior addressed to homeostasis does sometimes take the foreground, just as does cognition-seeking behavior. But in the two cases we can regard such activity as the necessary prelude to activity of a quite different kind, as a putting of one's house in order so that one can go about one's business undisturbed. Finally, we must observe that we cannot even count on a survival instinct, since some people choose not to survive, as in suicide and also as in just giving up.

However, in connection with the concept of "growth motivation," which writers such as White have added to the conative spectrum, we must note that it is not as pure as we might wish. On the one hand, when the child becomes capable of some new learning or activity, he works hard at developing and perfecting it. He tries to understand his experience, he is curious about new things and new facts, he is eager for new adventures. On the other hand, the child's progressive, expansive tendencies are counterbalanced by the inertia of conservatism, by resistance to new learning and to changing old ways. He loses interest, he shrinks before new experiences and the menace of the unknown, he shirks decisions and responsibilities, he plays it safe. Here we have the principle of growth ambivalence, a lifelong phenomenon that can be modified in the direction of growth motivation only by appropriate learning early in life: the learning that gives us the environment as a stable, coherent, reliable theater of operations and that gives us a sense of ourselves as competent to master reality actually and symbolically.

The Motivating Environment

Henle [6] has pointed out that many writers on motivation seem to take it for granted that motives well up from inside the organism, and that such writers fail to take account of the motivational environment. The environment plays three major roles in motivation: in the genesis of motivational patterns, in the maintenance of drive level, and in the elicitation of transitory motivational states.

We can distinguish at least four ways in which conative development depends on environmental support, without mentioning the nutritional conditions for normal physical development. First, severe emotional and cognitive deprivation leads to both physical and conative debility. Less severe deprivation is likely to produce disturbed patterns of motivation, such as those of psychopathy. Second, the environment directly and indirectly fosters the development of particular motives. Here we must note that phylogenetically primitive species come equipped with "instinctual" forms of behavior that appear independently of particular environmental conditions—the weaver-bird, for instance, when it is biologically ready to build a nest, will, in the absence of nest-building materials, weave a nest out of thin air. At a more advanced level, instinctual patterns seem to require an environmental trigger, as in the case of imprinting objects.

However, we cannot be certain about the conditions for imprinting, since laboratory studies have concentrated so hard on the following response as an index of imprinting that they may have overlooked evidence of other identifications or attachments, as to peers or to home cages. At the human level, drives are mediated not only through objects but also through symbols. Let us look, for example, at some phenomena of human sexuality. The one-year-old boy is quite capable of genital arousal and pleasure. Such arousal first happens as a by-product of bladder tension or accidental self-stimulation, but may be followed by deliberate masturbation. There is absolutely no evidence, however, that the one-year-old has any notion of object-directed sexuality. Boys and girls of preschool age examine and play with each other's genitalia, but they do not spontaneously attempt intercourse.

Although it is obvious that a craving for a certain kind of experience can develop without particular environmental conditions, such cravings do not contain any innately given representation of complex behavior such as the sex act. Harlow points out that male monkeys raised under deprived conditions do attempt intercourse when given an opportunity, but have no idea how to go about it, attacking the female's body virtually at random.[7] According to Kinsey's findings,[8] female sexuality, with due allowance for individual differences, becomes an autonomous drive almost entirely as a product of specific learning. What these observations suggest is that human motivational states, even when they exist independent of learning, have a low degree of specificity and do not point to courses of behavior until their objects have been defined cognitively. That is, the mere presence of a structure does not predict a function. This lack of specificity, even at the level of physiological tension states, helps us to understand why substitute gratifications are possible. Pacifiers, food, alcohol, drugs, sex, aggression, myths, delusions, rituals, all may come to act as irrelevant but nonetheless effective satisfiers for a broad variety of needs. The schematization of motives and their objects, like all other schematizations, can take place as a by-product of a broader cultural identification—thus the appetitive specializations that Murphy [9] calls canalization, from food preferences to standards of sex appeal. Some motives may arise as a reaction against cultural precepts. It may be that the harder parents work to protect their children from sexuality, the more they contribute to the growth of libido; it may also be that today's more relaxed, permissive, enlightened attitudes toward infantile sexuality serve to lower sexual drive and perhaps even to devalue sexuality.

The third way in which the environment—increasingly, the social environment—contributes to motivational development is an extension of the second. Not only is the child taught to want certain things but his wants are placed on scales of good and bad and of pleasant and unpleasant: sex, an older generation learned, is naughty but nice. Fourth, the child learns about the expression and control of his motives, the conditions—if any—under which gratification is permissible and ways of managing motives that threaten to get out of control. Young men, for example, are taught that oppressive sexuality can be dissipated in athletics or damped down with a cold shower.

Thinking about conative development has been obscured by a dualistic use of the term *needs*. On the one hand, a need is a state of deficiency which may be subjectively represented either as a specific drive or as a diffuse discomfort. On the other hand, a need can be a requirement for sound development which is merely an objective fact and in no sense motivating. Children need the stabilizing effect of discipline, but it would be a tenuous assertion indeed to say that the child is motivated to seek it. He may, on the other hand, be made anxious or irritable by its lack.

The environment is important to adult motivation in that stimulation, at both sensory and social levels, is necessary to the maintenance of motivation.[10] The subject in a sensory-deprivation experiment, the patient hospitalized for a long period, the castaway, the prisoner in prolonged solitary confinement, suffer a loss of drive. The individual operating in terms of long-range ambitions must find an environment that reinforces his orientation or he may lose interest or forget what he started out to do. This, of course, is simply a different version of what we said earlier (p. 106) about the preservation of the self-image.

Finally, the environment is important in the provocation of immediate motivational states. One does not have to be in a state of sexual arousal to respond to erotic stimulation—this apart from the fact that when sexual desire is lacking, we may deliberately set about stirring it up. One does not have to be in need of nutrition to be made hungry by delicious foodstuffs or even by a description of a succulent meal. Nor must we postulate any antecedent need to account for someone's stroking a kitten, pinching a baby's cheek, testing fresh paint, watching an excavation crew at work, flipping through the latest issue of a magazine, and so on ad infinitum. We may, of course, have to postulate a stage of cognitive organization which enables us to be stimulated by such stimuli. We must also postulate a lack of competing motivation. If one is hurrying to catch a train, one does not linger to watch a fire or a wedding party. But it is evident that the environment solicits our attention and our participation with little regard to specific motivations.

Orientation to the Future

It is now time to take up the problem of future-oriented motivation. Let us make clear that we are not embracing a transcendental teleology. Yet it is perfectly obvious, as we have said, that people do define goals and work to achieve them. Indeed, an individual may locate the true meaning of life in the afterlife, so that material existence is largely devoted to the duties and observances that will qualify him for salvation. A number of people, it is true, live lives of stimulus-bondage, prisoners of their routines and of the rhythms of their surroundings. It must also be noted that changing interests and the impact of hard reality may cause an individual to revise the script for his projected autobiography, perhaps beyond all recognition. But these reservations do not alter the basic datum that some people regulate their current activities in accordance with anticipated future events.

The problem here is that of determinism. As long as we say that human beings behave in keeping with their biological makeup as it evolves in a social context, we are saying that behavior is in some sense determined. It is important for both theoretical and practical reasons to decide what this sense is. We behave in accordance with the demands of situations, including our own motivational states. What experience teaches us is ways of evaluating the demands of situations so that various possibilities become evident. It gives us a temporal and moral perspective on situations. It teaches us a logic of action, and it is this logic which is determining. Thus, past experience determines present behavior indirectly, by having made us the kinds of people we are, with the kinds of outlooks and understandings that we have. From one point of view we can say that our way of comprehending a situation forces us to follow a given course of action; from another point of view we can say that it enables us to act in certain ways. It is clear that self-control and self-direction vary directly with cognitive maturity, and especially with the ability to manipulate situations symbolically, to anticipate consequences, to weigh, to judge, and to decide between alternatives. It is equally clear that there are material and psychological barriers to anything approaching free will.[11]

One's concept of determinism has practical consequences for how one rears and educates children. If, like Skinner,[12] one believes that will is an illusion, that the individual is a helpless witness to his own externally determined history, then there is little point to the cultivation of will. Rather, one aims at the production of happy, industrious, cooperative robots, not too unlike the "organization men" described by present-day sociologists. For example, Skinner's program of education carefully eschews punishment, since punishment blocks overt expression of a response but perpetuates an impulse to respond and so may cause evil or antisocial motives to persist in the form of response tendencies. Without punishment, the individual grows up without strain or conflict and, presumably, has no need of a conscience. A contrary view would be that the capacity for an interior life is found most fully developed in the individual who is prey to and who recognizes in himself impulses of all kinds, and who controls them. One cannot say much for the sanctity of a saint who is never tempted. The person who knows himself and is confident of his self-control can exercise his more primitive tendencies freely in fantasy, in humor, and in creative thought. Self-knowledge and self-control arise when impulses are thwarted, first by parental authority and later by conscience—which is just another way of saying mediated, conscious, forward-looking behavior. Whichever style of education one chooses, the prophecy tends to fulfill itself and the point of view is vindicated.

It must be added that the psychic and historical determinisms of psychoanalysis and behaviorism are to be found in real life. But when they are found in anything like pure form, they are pathognomic. The normal individual past early childhood lives with an integral schema of self within which his motives can be his own and in terms of which he can regulate his own behavior. We must recognize four levels of psychological causation. Behavior can be set off by spontaneous physiological conditions within the body, by changes in the metabolic environment, by meaningful stimuli, and, finally, by the conscious, sentient, verbal organism itself.

Our concern has been with the individualization of the individual. It must not be forgotten, however, that he can become an individual and function as one only by virtue of his close attachments, primarily to people but also to animals, playthings, places, and—eventually—keepsakes, works of art, traditions, institutions, and ideas. It is the feelings he has about the things that surround him that form the stuff and substance of his consciousness and keep him oriented to reality. The individual outgrows old attachments—sometimes without noticing, sometimes regretfully, and sometimes brutally—but normally in favor of new ones. It is true that certain people grow out of attachments and into isolation—here we have the makings of suicide, of involutional melancholia, of senile psychosis—but sound cognitive development occurs in a context of communication, communication not merely of factual information but of the feeling states that are characteristically human.

Thematization and Theory: Some Theoretical Contrasts

We have said that each individual, on the basis of firsthand experience and of original and secondhand thematizations, builds up schematic principles according to which reality is organized and defined. The individual's total schematic orientation to reality is, in effect, a concrete theory from which he draws inferences and makes predictions, and in terms of which he values or disvalues, believes or disbelieves, attends or ignores, is amused or irritated or untouched by the things he encounters or hears about. Now we can try stating the converse proposition, that what we think of as theories are in fact personal orientations to all or part of reality. No matter how impersonally phrased, a theory has its origins in an individual faced with an array of phenomena. It is only this that permits a difference of opinion about theories along with full accord on the facts. In this view, logical implication is not a property of propositions but of a relationship between proposition and person. A theory is always an ordering of facts into figure and ground, important and unimportant, and such an ordering may follow from personal predilections and emotional investments as well as from the dictates of reality. Thus, it is probably inaccurate to say that a scientist derives logical hypotheses from his theory; rather, he has intuitions which can then be phrased as hypotheses—complete, if need be, with ex post facto justifications.[13] It seems likely, too, that adherence to and defense of theories long since and repeatedly shown to be inadequate can best be explained by the personal nature of theories. For to question a theory is to question the theorist's grip on reality—as we have said, in the final analysis all our arguments are *ad hominem*.

If we accept the personal nature of theories, we are confronted with an irreducible circularity. As Merleau-Ponty has said, psychological theories can account for everything except the psychology of their creators. Psychological theorists have been inclined to play God, to see things *sub specie aeternitatis*, egocentrically forgetting that as human beings they can have only a partial and fragmentary and situation-bound command of all the essential phenomena, but also forgetting how their own behavior transcends their own theoretical formulations.

Perhaps it is because of a new humility, a new relativism, that psychological theory-making in the grand manner has all but disappeared. The psychological landscape is dotted with the ruins of once-splendid theoretical edifices, among which are sprinkled the more modest, functional dwellings of modern microtheorists: theorists of perception, of personality, of information, of thinking, of small group processes, of development. One finds, too, occasional more ambitious structures pieced together with fragments plundered from the ruins, with the delicate geometric traceries of Hull nestled against heavy Freudian baroque. And, of course, there are the workshops in which psychologists turned mathematician or computer engineer tinker busily with their models.

To abandon our metaphor, it is nowadays difficult to define a theoretical position by contrast with others. First, eclecticism is the order of the day. A second problem is to find theories of language, and especially theories that treat language as central to human functioning. For instance, in spite of Freud's intriguing observations on paraphasias and unconscious symbolism, his essential biologism, his Lamarckism, and his etymological-symbolic notions [14] stood in the way of any real attack on the problems of language. The Gestalt psychologists, like the Freudians, seem never to have produced a theory of language development, apart from what Koffka [15] took over more or less wholesale from Bühler, Stern, and other early writers. Osgood is concerned with verbal mediating processes, but in his system language seems to be simply the outward manifestation of the neural mechanisms which are his real concern. The Pavlovian theory of conditioning provides a neat, if not necessarily correct, account of passive language learning. However, it deals with active language only by means of the "second signal system," an unidentified region or attribute of the human nervous system which makes symbolic behavior possible. The very vagueness of the concept of the second signal system is, in the present view, a positive virtue since it makes everything possible, and the notions put forth by present-day Pavlovian theorists correspond very closely to those contained in this book. In other words, the Pavlovian theorists operate dualistically, speaking now the language of Pavlovian neurology and now that of empirical phenomenology. It would appear that the second signal system is a verbal-magical device for unifying doctrinal materialism and optimistic humanism. It is interesting to read O. K. Tikhomirov's review of Skinner's *Verbal Behavior* [16] for the contrast it gives between a humanistic materialism and a reductionistic one.

O. H. Mowrer [17] has proposed a view of language which combines learning theory, phonetics, Freudian theory, and some essentially phenomenological strands. However, Mowrer's comprehensive account of language (*Learning Theory and the Symbolic Processes*, New York: Wylie, 1960) appeared after the present work had gone to press, and we cannot judge how successfully he has unified the several diverse traditions on which he draws.

Thus, it seems that our contrasts have to be drawn mainly with the work of B. F. Skinner. We have spoken unkindly of Skinner's formulations in these pages, as have the critics of his *Verbal Behavior*.[18] We must therefore indicate some approximate correspondences between his views and the present one. We agree with Skinner that the notion of "a language," such as English, French, Bantu, or whatever, can be misleading. The psychologist must be concerned with the ways the individual learns and uses the symbolic conventions of a "speech community." We believe that Skinner has advanced the cause of behaviorism greatly by substituting the notion of general "operant" for that of specific "response," even if he does not always carry through all the implications of his substitution. It is worth noting that while Pavlovian behaviorism lacks a genuine theory of active language, Skinnerian behaviorism lacks a theory of passive language except for the echoic reproduction of behavior to which the organism has been exposed. While we feel that Skinner, perhaps for polemical purposes, has overdone his doctrine of the empty organism, we agree with him that psychology has thought too much in terms of fixed physiological and mental structures and has given

too little attention to the role of the environment in shaping behavior—or, to talk our own language, in evoking and maintaining
the schematic mobilizations from which action emerges. Although
we hold that, in the course of development, one forms stable
schemata of self and world, they are only semipermanent, their
stability being contingent on appropriate environmental support.
We further agree with Skinner that psychology need not wait
upon physiological explanations of behavior, even though they
may in principle be possible and the search for them a fascinat-
ing endeavor. Carried further, this means that psychology can be
a descriptive science and need not at every point justify its organizing principles by reference to those of physiology or physics.
Unlike Skinner, however, we believe that the facts of human
behavior call for descriptive principles that include subjective
states as well as overt behavior. In fact, Skinner has implicitly
conceded as much by introducing various hypothetical mediational constructs into his account of verbal behavior.

Having granted existence to subjective states, Skinner is at a
loss what to do with them, so that the conscious person is left
hovering helplessly like an ectoplasmic cloud over his own material body. Here we must propose a principle: Reductionism
begets spiritualism. And, more generally, every metaphysical
axiom relentlessly generates its antithesis: nativism-environment-
alism, determinism-voluntarism, and all the rest. It is our thesis,
first, that one can accept the fact that living organisms have
properties distinguishing them from inanimate matter without
thereby becoming a vitalist, and that one can accept the fact
that human beings have properties setting them apart from the
lower species without subscribing to spiritualism. The problem is
one both of method and of conceptualization. As countless critics
have pointed out, psychologists should not tailor their subject
matter to fit a preconceived set of methods, but should devise
methods by which to study their subject matter. Similarly, when
their descriptive categories fail to match the phenomena, it is
time to scrap them in favor of new modes of conceptualization.
It is not enough that psychology take an option on the distinc-
tively human areas of functioning, meanwhile devoting itself to
the study of "basic" processes. If psychology does not soon exer-

cise its option, it will find the field usurped by philosophy, psychiatry, theology, and parapsychology. Unless we can reunite the ectoplasm of the person with his biological body, with his social history, with his cultural situation, and with his animal ancestry, he will remain fair game for mystics, and we shall have bought our scientific purity only at the cost of ignorance and superstition.

NOTES

(1) Otto Klineberg, *Social Psychology* (New York: Holt, 1954), pp. 187-188. See also: *Race Differences* (New York: Harper, 1935), ch. 15.

(2) Mark Zborowski, Cultural components in responses to pain, *Journal of Social Issues*, 1952, 8: 16–30.

(3) G. Dumas, *Traité de Psychologie* (Paris: Alcan, 1923), vol. I.

(4) K. Z. Lorenz, The role of aggression in group formation, in Bertram Schaffner, ed., *Group Processes* (New York: Josiah Macy, Jr., Foundation, 1959), pp. 181–252.

(5) R. W. White, Motivation reconsidered: The concept of competence, *Psychological Review*, 1959, 66: 297–333. See also: J. McV. Hunt, Experience and the development of motivation: Some reinterpretations, *Child Development*, 1960, 31: 489–504.

(6) Mary Henle, On activity in the goal region, *Psychological Review*, 1956, 63: 299–302.

(7) Personal communication. F. A. Beach reports (Normal sexual behavior in male rats isolated at fourteen days of age, *Journal of Comparative and Physiological Psychology*, 1958, 51: 37–38) that early isolation does not affect the later sexual behavior of white rats. This finding has been challenged by P. G. Zimbardo, who reports (The effects of early avoidance training and rearing conditions upon the sexual behavior of the male rat, *Journal of Comparative and Physiological Psychology*, 1958, 51: 764–769) that "males reared in isolation were significantly less active sexually than males reared in cohabitation." We must note that all subjects had normal rearing for at least the first two weeks of life, and we cannot safely ignore the developmental influences of such early contacts.

(8) A. C. Kinsey & associates, *Sexual Behavior in the Human Female* (Philadelphia: Saunders, 1953).

(9) Gardner Murphy, *Personality* (New York: Harper, 1947), pp. 161 ff.

(10) D. O. Hebb, The motivating effects of exteroceptive stimulation, *American Psychologist*, 1958, 13: 109–113.

(11) See the statement by Paul Fraisse (*Psychologie du Temps*, Paris: Presses Universitaires de France, 1957, pp. 172–173) on the psychological conditions of future perspectives.

(12) *Walden Two* (New York: Macmillan, 1948).

(13) American Psychological Association, Scientific Development Board, Education for research in psychology, *American Psychologist*, 1959, 14: 167–179; D. O. Hebb, The Estes Park report and Cervin's comments, *American Psychologist*, 1960, 15: 623.

(14) See, for example: Sigmund Freud, *A General Introduction to Psychoanalysis* (New York: Liveright. 1935), pp. 142–143.

(15) Kurt Koffka, *The Growth of the Mind* (New York: Harcourt, Brace, 1928) pp. 339–365.

(16) O. K. Tikhomirov, Review of *Verbal Behavior*, by B. F. Skinner, *Word*, 1959, 15: 362–367.

(17) O. H. Mowrer, The psychologist looks at language, *American Psychologist*, 1954, 9: 660–694.

(18) See, in addition to the review by Tikhomirov, *supra*, those by: Noam Chomsky (*Language*, 1959, 35: 26–58), D. E. Dulany (*Science*, 1959, 129: 143–144), Charles Morris (*Contemporary Psychology*, 1958, 3: 212–214), and C. E. Osgood (*ibid.*, 209–212).

BIBLIOGRAPHY

This bibliography includes, in addition to titles specifically referred to in the text a number of works which have influenced the author's thinking or are of some historical interest. It does not seek to be complete. For more nearly exhaustive listings, the reader is referred to the valuable compilations by Leopold and by McCarthy.

Adams, J. K. Laboratory studies of behavior without awareness. *Psychological Bulletin*, 1957, 54: 383-405.

Ajuriaguerra, J. de. Intégration de la motilité. *Enfance*, 1956, 2: 15-18.

Allport, G. W., & P. E. Vernon. *Studies in Expressive Movement*. New York: Macmillan, 1933.

American Psychological Association, Scientific Development Board. Education for research in psychology. *American Psychologist*, 1959, 14: 167-179.

Ames, L. B. The development of the sense of time in the young child. *Journal of Genetic Psychology*, 1946, 68: 97-125.

Ames, L. B. The sense of self of nursery school children as manifested by their verbal behavior. *Journal of Genetic Psychology*, 1952, 81: 193-232.

Angelino, Henry, & C. L. Shedd. An initial report of a validation study of the Davis-Eells tests of general intelligence or problem-solving ability. *Journal of Psychology*, 1955, 40: 35-38.

Arnheim, Rudolf. Experimentell-psychologische Untersuchungen zum Ausdrucksproblem. *Psychologische Forschung*, 1928, 11: 1-132.

Asch, S. E. On the use of metaphor in the description of persons. In Werner, H., ed. *On Expressive Language*. Worcester: Clark University, 1955, Pp. 29-38.

Asch, S. E., & Harriet Nerlove. The development of double function terms in children. In Kaplan, B., & S. Wapner, eds. *Perspectives in Psychological Theory*. New York: International Universities Press, 1960. Pp. 47-60.

Barber, T. X. Toward a theory of pain: Relief of chronic pain by prefrontal leucotomy, opiates, placebos, and hypnosis. *Psychological Bulletin*, 1959, 56: 430-460.

Barnes, Nellie. American Indian verse. *Bulletin of the University of Kansas*, 1921, 22, no. 18.

Barnett, H. G. *Innovation*. New York: McGraw-Hill, 1953.

Bartlett, F. C. Social factors in recall. In Newcomb, T. M., & E. L. Hartley, eds. *Readings in Social Psychology*. New York: Holt, 1947. Pp. 69-76.

Bayley, Nancy. Consistency and variability in the growth of intelligence from birth to eighteen years. *Journal of Genetic Psychology*, 1949, 75: 165-196.

Bayley, Nancy. On the growth of intelligence. *American Psychologist*, 1955, 10: 805-818.

Beach, F. A. Experimental investigations of species-specific behavior. *American Psychologist*, 1960, 15: 1-18.

Beach, F. A. Normal sexual behavior in male rats isolated at fourteen days of age. *Journal of Comparative and Physiological Psychology*, 1958, 51: 37-38.

Beach, F. A. "Psychosomatic" phenomena in animals. *Psychosomatic Medicine*, 1952, 14: 261-276.

Beach, F. A., & Julian Jaynes. Effects of early experience upon the behavior of animals. *Psychological Bulletin*, 1954, 51: 239-263.

Beauvoir, Simone de. *Mémoires d'une Jeune Fille Rangée.* Paris: Gallimard, 1958.

Beecher, H. K. Increased stress and effectiveness of placebos and "active" drugs. *Science*, 1960, 132: 91-92.

Benveniste, Emile. Animal communication and human language. *Diogenes*, n.d., 1: 1-17.

Berko, Jean. The child's learning of English morphology. *Word*, 1958, 14: 150-177.

Berkowitz, Leonard. Leveling tendencies and the complexity-simplicity dimension. *Journal of Personality*, 1957, 25: 743-751.

Birdwhistell, R. L. Kinesic analysis of filmed behavior of children. In Schaffner, B., ed. *Group Processes*. New York: Josiah Macy, Jr., Foundation, 1956. Pp. 141-144.

Boder, D. P. The adjective-verb quotient: A contribution to the psychology of language. *Psychological Record*, 1940, 22: 310-343.

Bolles, R. C. Group and individual performance as a function of intensity and kind of deprivation. *Journal of Comparative and Physiological Psychology*, 1959, 52: 579-585.

Boring, E. G., Karl M. Dallenbach. *American Journal of Psychology*, 1958, 71: 1-40.

Bradley, N. C. The growth of the knowledge of time in children of school age. *British Journal of Psychology*, 1947, 38: 67-78.

Brain, Sir Russell. *The Nature of Experience*. London: Oxford University, 1959.

Brian, C. R., & F. L. Goodenough. The relative potency of color and form perception at various ages. *Journal of Experimental Psychology*, 1929, 12: 197-213.

Brown, Carlton. *Brainstorm.* New York: Farrar & Rinehart, 1944.

Brown, F. A., Jr. Living clocks. *Science*, 1959, 130: 1535-1544.

Brown, Roger. Is a boulder sweet or sour? *Contemporary Psychology*, 1958, 3: 113-115.

Brown, Roger. Linguistic determinism and the part of speech. *Journal of Abnormal and Social Psychology*, 1957, 55: 1-5.

Brown, Roger. *Words and Things*. Glencoe: The Free Press, 1958.

Brown, Roger, & Jean Berko. Word association and the acquisition of grammar. *Child Development*, 1960, 31: 1-14.

Brown, Roger, R. A. Leiter, & D. C. Hildum. Metaphors from music criticism. *Journal of Abnormal and Social Psychology*, 1957, 54: 347-352.

Brownlee, Aleta. The American Indian child. *Children*, 1958, 5: 55-60.

Bruce, H. M. & D. M. V. Parrott. Role of olfactory sense in pregnancy block by strange males. *Science*, 1960, 131: 1526.

Bruell, Jan, & G. W. Albee. Higher intellectual functions in a patient with hemispherectomy. Paper given before the American Psychological Association, 1957.

Bruner, J. S. Going beyond the information given. In *Contemporary Approaches to Cognition*. Cambridge: Harvard, 1957. Pp. 41-69.

Bruner, J. S., J. J. Goodnow, & G. A. Austin. *A Study of Thinking*. New York: Wiley, 1956.

Brunet, Odette. Genèse de l'intelligence chez des enfants de trois milieux très différents. *Enfance*, 1956, 1: 85-94.

Bühler, Karl. Les lois générales d'évolution dans le langage de l'enfant. *Journal de Psychologie Normale et Pathologique*, 1926, 23: 597-607.

Bühler, Karl. On thought connections. In Rapaport, David. *Organization and Pathology of Thought*. New York: Columbia, 1951.

Buyssens, E. La conception fonctionelle des faits linguistiques. *Journal de Psychologie Normale et Pathologique*, 1950, 43: 37-53.

Cameron, Norman. Experimental analysis of schizophrenic thinking. In Kasanin, J. S., ed. *Language and Thought in Schizophrenia*. Berkeley: University of California, 1944. Pp. 50-64.

Carlson, V. R. Overestimation in size-constancy judgments. *American Journal of Psychology*, 1960, 73: 199-213.

Carr, H. A., & J. B. Watson. Orientation in the white rat. *Journal of Comparative Neurology*, 1908, 18: 27-44.

Carroll, H. A. *Genius in the Making*. New York: McGraw-Hill, 1940.

Cary, Joyce. *Art and Reality*. New York: Harper, 1958.

Cassirer, Ernst. *An Essay on Man*. New York: Anchor, 1954.

Cassirer, Ernst. Le langage et la construction du monde des objets. *Journal de Psychologie Normale et Pathologique*, 1933, 30: 18-44.

Chapman, D. W. Relative effects of determinate and indeterminate *Aufgaben*. *American Journal of Psychology*, 1932, 44: 163-174.

Chauchard, Paul. *Le Langage et la Pensée*. Paris: Presses Universitaires de France, 1956.

Chomsky, Noam. Review of *Verbal Behavior*, by B. F. Skinner. *Language*, 1959, 35: 26-58.

Cohen, Marcel. Observations sur les dernières persistances du langage enfantin. *Journal de Psychologie Normale et Pathologique*, 1933, 30: 390-399.

Cohen, Walter. Spatial and textural characteristics of the *Ganzfeld*. *American Journal of Psychology*, 1957, 70: 403-410.

Comalli, P. E., S. Wapner, & H. Werner. Interference effects of Stroop color-word test in children, adults, and aged. Paper given before the Eastern Psychological Association, 1960.

Conn, J. H., & Leo Kanner. Children's awareness of sex differences. *Journal of Child Psychiatry*, 1947, 1: 3-57.

Daniels, M. E. The effect of value and situational context on word definitions. Unpublished manuscript.

Darby, C. L., & A. J. Riopelle. Observational learning in the rhesus monkey. *Journal of Comparative and Physiological Psychology*, 1959, 52: 94-98.

Dashiell, J. F. The role of vision in spatial orientation by the white rat. *Journal of Comparative and Physiological Psychology*, 1959, 52: 522-526.

Davis, R. C., A. M. Buchwald, & R. W. Frankman. Autonomic and muscular responses, and their relation to simple stimuli. *Psychological Monographs*, 1955, 69, no. 405.

Davis, R. C., L. Garafolo, & Kolbjørn Kveim. Conditions associated with gastrointestinal activity. *Journal of Comparative and Physiological Psychology*, 1959, 52: 466-475.

Denenberg, V. H., & R. W. Bell. Critical periods for the effects of infantile experience on adult learning. *Science*, 1960, 131: 227-228.

Dennis, Wayne. Piaget's questions applied to a child of known environment. *Journal of Genetic Psychology*, 1942, 60: 307-320.

Dixon, J. C. Development of self recognition. *Journal of Genetic Psychology*, 1957, 91: 251-256.

Dukes, W. F. Psychological studies of values. *Psychological Bulletin*, 1955, 52: 24-50.

Dulany, D. E. Review of *Verbal Behavior*, by B. F. Skinner. *Science*, 1959, 129: 143-144.

Dumas, G. *Traité de Psychologie*. Paris: Alcan, 1923. Vol. 1.

Duncan, C. P. Recent research on human problem solving. *Psychological Bulletin*, 1959, 56: 397-429.

Duncker, Karl. On problem-solving. *Psychological Monographs*, 1945, 58, no. 5.

Elting, E. F. An experimental study of color and form perception at various ages. *Vassar Undergraduate Studies in the Behavioral Sciences*, 1958, 1: 33-39.

Empson, William. *The Structure of Complex Words*. Norfolk, Conn.: New Directions, 1951.

English, H. B., & A. C. English. *A Comprehensive Dictionary of Psychological and Psychoanalytical Terms*. New York: Longmans, Green, 1958.

Ervin, S. M. Grammar and classification. Paper given before the American Psychological Association, 1957.

Festinger, Leon. *A Theory of Cognitive Dissonance*. Evanston: Row, Peterson, 1957.

Flavell, J. H., & Juris Draguns. A microgenetic approach to perception and thought. *Psychological Bulletin,* 1957, 54: 197-217.

Flesch, R. A new readability yardstick. *Journal of Applied Psychology,* 1948, 32: 221-233.

Fraisse, Paul. *Psychologie du Temps.* Paris: Presses Universitaires de France, 1957.

Freud, Sigmund. *A General Introduction to Psychoanalysis.* New York: Liveright, 1935.

Gardner, Riley, P. S. Holzman, G. S. Klein, Harriet Linton, & D. P. Spence. Cognitive control. *Psychological Issues,* 1959, 1, no. 4.

Gardner, W. J., C. R. Licklider, & A. Z. Weisz. Suppression of pain by sound. *Science,* 1960, 132: 32-33.

Ghent, Lila, & Lilly Bernstein. The influence of orientation of geometric forms on recognition in children. Paper given before the Eastern Psychological Association, 1960.

Gibson, E. J. A re-examination of generalization. *Psychological Review,* 1959, 66: 340-342.

Gibson, E. J., & R. D. Walk, The "visual cliff." *Scientific American,* 1960, 202: 64-71.

Gibson, J. J. Pictures, perspective, and perception. *Daedalus,* Winter, 1960: 216-227.

Gibson, J. J. What is a form? *Psychological Review,* 1951, 58: 403-412.

Gibson, J. J., & E. J. Gibson. Continuous perspective transformations and the perception of rigid motion. *Journal of Experimental Psychology,* 1957, 54: 129-138.

Ginsburg, Norman. Conditioned vocalization in the budgerigar. *Journal of Comparative and Physiological Psychology,* 1960, 53: 183-186.

Goldstein, Kurt. Methodological approach to the study of schizophrenic thought disorder. In Kasanin, J. S., ed. *Language and Thought in Schizophrenia.* Berkeley: University of California, 1944. Pp. 17-39.

Goldstein, Kurt, & Martin Scheerer. Abstract and concrete behavior. *Psychological Monographs,* 1941, 53, no. 2.

Gorham, D. R. Verbal abstraction in psychiatric illness. Paper given before the 16th International Congress of Psychology, 1960.

Grégoire, Antoine. *L'apprentissage du Langage: Les Deux Premières Années.* Paris: Droz, 1937.

Griffin, D. R. *Listening in the Dark: The Acoustic Orientation of Bats and Men.* New Haven: Yale University, 1958.

Griffiths, Ruth. *The Abilities of Babies.* New York: McGraw-Hill, 1954.

Guilford, J. P. Morphological model for human intelligence. *Science,* 1960, 131: 1318.

Guillaume, Paul. Les débuts de la phrase dans le langage de l'enfant. *Journal de Psychologie Normale et Pathologique,* 1927, 24: 203-229.

Gulliksen, Harold. How to make meaning more meaningful. *Contemporary Psychology,* 1958, 3: 115-119.

Haber, W. B. Reactions to loss of limb: Physiological and psychological aspects. *Annals of the New York Academy of Sciences,* 1958, 74: 14-24.

Hadamard, J. *Psychology of Invention in the Mathematical Field.* Princeton: Princeton University, 1949.

Haldane, J. B. S. Animal ritual and human language. *Diogenes,* Autumn, 1953, 61-73.

Hall, G. S. The contents of children's minds on entering school. *Pedagogical Seminary,* 1891, 1: 139-173.

Haner, C. F., & E. R. Whitney. Empathic conditioning and its relation to anxiety levels. Paper given before the American Psychological Association, 1960.

Hanfmann, Eugenia. Analysis of the thinking disorder in a case of schizophrenia. *Archives of Neurology and Psychiatry,* 1939, 41: 568-579.

Hanfmann, Eugenia, & J. S. Kasanin, *Conceptual Thinking in Schizophrenia.* New York: Nervous and Mental Disease Publishing Co., 1942.

Hayek, F. A. *The Sensory Order.* Chicago: The University of Chicago Press, 1952.

Hebb, D. O. The Estes Park report and Cervin's comments. *American Psychologist*, 1960, 15: 623.

Hebb, D. O. Heredity and environment in mammalian behaviour. *British Journal of Animal Behaviour*, 1953, 1: 43-47.

Hebb, D. O. The motivating effects of exteroceptive stimulation. *American Psychologist*, 1958, 13: 109-113.

Hebb, D. O., & A. H. Riesen. The genesis of irrational fears. *Bulletin of the Canadian Psychological Association*, 1943, 3: 49-50.

Heidbreder, Edna. Problem solving in children and adults. *Journal of Genetic Psychology*, 1928, 35: 522-545.

Heider, Fritz, & Marianne Simmel. An experimental study of apparent behavior. *American Journal of Psychology*, 1944, 57: 243-259.

Heinemann, E. G. Review of *Über Aufbau und Wandlungen der Wahrnehmungswelt*, by Ivo Kohler. *American Journal of Psychology*, 1953, 66: 503-505.

Henle, Mary. On activity in the goal region. *Psychological Review*, 1956, 63: 299-302.

Henri, P. Cécité et verbalisme. *Journal de Psychologie Normale et Pathologique*, 1948, 41: 216-240.

Hernández-Péon, Raúl, Harald Scherrer, & Michel Jouvet. Modification of electric activity in cochlear nucleus during "attention" in unanesthetized cats. *Science*, 1956, 123: 331-332.

Herscher, Leonard, A. U. Moore, & J. B. Richmond. Effect of postpartum separation of mother and kid on maternal care in the domestic goat. *Science*, 1958, 128: 1342-1343.

Hovland, C. I., I. L. Janis, & H. H. Kelley. *Communication and Persuasion*. New Haven: Yale, 1953.

Hughes, Richard. *The Innocent Voyage*. New York: Harper, 1929.

Humphrey, George. *Thinking*. London: Methuen, 1951.

Hunt, J. McV. Experience and the development of motivation. *Child Development*, 1960, 31: 489-504.

Huntley, C. W. Judgments of self based upon records of expressive behavior. *Journal of Abnormal and Social Psychology*, 1940, 35: 398-427.

Hunton, V. D. The recognition of inverted pictures by children. *Journal of Genetic Psychology*, 1955, 86: 281-288.

Inhelder, Bärbel, & Jean Piaget. *The Growth of Logical Thinking*. New York: Basic Books, 1958.

Jenkin, Noël, & S. M. Feallock. Developmental and intellectual processes in size-distance judgment. *American Journal of Psychology*, 1960, 73: 268-273.

Jenkins, J. J., & Marjorie Schaefer. Word association phenomena at the individual level: A pair of case studies. In Jenkins, J. J., ed. *Associative Processes in Verbal Behavior: A Report of the Minnesota Conference*. University of Minnesota, Department of Psychology, 1959. Pp. 26-43.

Johansson, Gunnar. *Configurations in Event Perception*. Uppsala: Almqvist & Wiksells Boktryckeri AB, 1950.

Johnson, Wendell. Studies in language behavior: I. A program of research. *Psychological Monographs*, 1944, 56, no. 1.

Kagan, Jerome. Styles of conceptualization: Their significance for intellective and personality variables. Paper given before the American Psychological Association, 1960.

Kasanin, J. S., ed. *Language and Thought in Schizophrenia*. Berkeley: University of California, 1944.

Katcher, Allan. The discrimination of sex differences by young children. *Journal of Genetic Psychology*, 1955, 87: 131-143.

Katona, George. *Organizing and Memorizing*. New York: Columbia, 1940.

Kellogg, W. N. Echo ranging in the porpoise. *Science*, 1958, 128: 982-988.

Kinsey, A. C., & associates. *Sexual Behavior in the Human Female*. Philadelphia: Saunders, 1953.

Klebanoff, S. G., J. L. Singer, & Harold Wilensky. Psychological consequences of brain lesions and ablations. *Psychological Bulletin*, 1954, 51: 1-41.

Klineberg, Otto. *Race Differences*. New York: Harper, 1935.

Klineberg, Otto. *Social Psychology*, 2d ed. New York: Holt, 1954.

Klopfer, P. H. Influence of social interaction on learning rates in birds. *Science*, 1958, 128: 903.

Kluckhohn, Clyde. *Mirror for Man*. New York: Whittlesey House, 1949.

Koffka, Kurt. *The Growth of the Mind*. New York: Harcourt, Brace, 1928.

Koffka, Kurt. Problems in the psychology of art. *Art: A Bryn Mawr Symposium*. Bryn Mawr: Bryn Mawr College, 1940. Pp. 180-273.

Kohler, Ivo. On the development and transformations of the perceptual world. *Psychological Issues*, 1961, 2, no. 4.

Koupernick, C. Motricité et développement psychologique. *Enfance*, 1956, 2: 19-22.

Krasner, Leonard. Studies of the conditioning of verbal behavior. *Psychological Bulletin*, 1958, 55: 148-170.

Kreezer, George, & K. M. Dallenbach. Learning the relation of opposition. *American Journal of Psychology*, 1929, 41: 432-441.

Lacey, J. I. The evaluation of autonomic responses: Toward a general solution. *Annals of the New York Academy of Sciences*, 1956, 67: 123-164.

Lacey, J. I., & K. M. Dallenbach. Acquisition by children of the cause-effect relationship. *American Journal of Psychology*, 1939, 52: 103-110.

Lawrence, D. H. & G. R. Coles. Accuracy of recognition with alternatives before and after the stimulus. *Journal of Experimental Psychology*, 1954, 47: 208-214.

Lee, D. D. Being and value in a primitive culture. *Journal of Philosophy*, 1949, 46: 401-415.

Lee, D. D. Linguistic reflection of Wintu.' Thought. *International Journal of American Linguistics*, 1944, 10: 181-187.

Lenneberg, E. H. Review of *Speech and Brain Mechanisms*, by Penfield & Roberts. *Language*, 1960, 36: 97-112.

Leopold, W. F. *Bibliography of Child Language*. Evanston: Northwestern University, 1952.

Leopold, W. F. *Speech Development of a Bilingual Child.* Evanston: Northwestern University, 1939-1949. 4 vols.

Levine, Seymour, & G. W. Lewis, Critical period for effects of infantile experience on maturation of stress response. *Science,* 1959, 129: 42-43.

Lewis, M. M. *How Children Learn to Speak.* New York: Basic Books, 1959.

Lipps, Theodor. *Ästhetik. Psychologie des Schönen und der Kunst.* Hamburg: Leopold Voss, 1903, 1908. 2 vols.

London, I. D. Research on sensory interaction in the Soviet Union. *Psychological Bulletin,* 1954, 51: 531-568.

Lord, Edith. The impact of education on non-scientific beliefs in Ethiopia. *Journal of Scoial Psychology,* 1958, 47: 339-354.

Lord, Walter. Review of *Collision Course,* by Alvin Moscow. *New York Times Book Review,* March 15, 1959, 1 & 30.

Lorenz, K. Z. Morphology and behavior patterns in closely allied species. In Schaffner, B., ed. *Group Processes.* New York: Josiah Macy, Jr., Foundation, 1955. Pp. 168-220.

Lorenz, K. Z. The role of aggression in group formation. In Schaffner, B., ed. *Group Processes.* New York: Josiah Macy, Jr., Foundation, 1959. Pp. 181-252.

Luria, A. R. The directive function of speech: I. Its development in early childhood. *Word,* 1959, 15: 341-352.

Lynip, A. W. The use of magnetic devices in the collection and analysis of the preverbal utterances of an infant. *Genetic Psychology Monographs,* 1951, 44: 221-262.

Maier, N. R. F. Reasoning in children. *Journal of Comparative Psychology,* 1936, 21: 357-366.

Maier, N. R. F. Reasoning in humans: I. On direction. *Journal of Comparative Psychology,* 1930, 10: 115-143.

Markey, J. F. *The Symbolic Process and Its Integration in Children.* New York: Harcourt, Brace, 1928.

Marouzeau, J. Analyse syntaxique et analyse psychologique. *Journal de Psychologie Normale et Pathologique,* 1950, 43: 34-36.

Marquand, J. P. *The Late George Apley*. Boston: Little, Brown, 1937.

Marquart, D. I., & L. L. Bailey. An evaluation of *The Culture-Free Test* of intelligence. *Journal of Genetic Psychology*, 1955, 86: 353-358.

Mason, W. A. Development of communication between young rhesus monkeys. *Science*, 1959, 130: 712-713.

Matthews, L. H. Visual stimulation and ovulation in pigeons. *Proceedings of the Royal Society of London*, 1939, 126 (B): 557-560.

McCarthy, Dorothea. Language development in children. In Carmichael, Leonard, ed. *Manual of Child Psychology*. New York: Wylie, 1954. Pp. 492-630.

McFarland, J. H. The effect of body tilt on tactual sensitivity. Paper given before the Eastern Psychological Association, 1959.

McGranahan, D. V. The psychology of language. *Psychological Bulletin*, 1936, 33: 178-216.

Melzack, Ronald. The genesis of emotional behavior: An experimental study of the dog. *Journal of Comparative and Physiological Psychology*, 1954, 47: 166-168.

Merleau-Ponty, Maurice. Phénoménologie de la Perception. Paris: Gallimard, 1945.

Meyer, Edith. Comprehension of spatial relations in preschool children. *Journal of Genetic Psychology*, 1940, 57: 119-151.

Michotte, Albert. *La Perception de la Causalité*. Louvain: Institut Supérieur de Philosophie, 1946.

Michotte, Albert. Réflexions sur le rôle du langage dans l'analyse des organizations perceptives. *Actes du Quinzième Congrès International de Psychologie*, 1957. Pp. 17-34.

Moore, A. U. Studies on the formation of the mother-neonate bond in sheep and goat. Paper given before the American Psychological Association, 1960.

Morris, Charles. Words without meanings; Review of *Verbal Behavior*, by B. F. Skinner. *Contemporary Psychology*, 1958, 3: 212-214.

Morse, W. H., & B. F. Skinner. A second type of "superstition" in the pigeon. *American Journal of Psychology,* 1957, 70: 308-311.

Moscow, Alvin. *Collision Course.* New York: Putnam's, 1959.

Mowrer, O. H. The psychologist looks at language. *American Psychologist,* 1954, 9: 660-694.

Munn, N. L. *The Evolution and Growth of Human Behavior.* Boston: Houghton Mifflin, 1955.

Murphy, Gardner. *Personality.* New York: Harper, 1947.

Murphy, J. V., R. E. Miller, & I. A. Mirsky, Interanimal conditioning in the monkey. *Journal of Comparative and Physiological Psychology,* 1955, 48: 211-214.

Olum, Vivian. Developmental differences in the perception of causality. *American Journal of Psychology,* 1956, 69: 417-423.

Osgood, C. E. The cross-cultural generality of visual-verbal synesthetic tendencies. *Behavioral Science,* 1960, 5: 146-149.

Osgood, C. E. A question of sufficiency; Review of *Verbal Behavior,* by B. F. Skinner. *Contemporary Psychology,* 1958, 3: 209-212.

Osgood, C. E., G. J. Suci, & P. H. Tannenbaum. *The Measurement of Meaning.* Urbana: University of Illinois, 1957.

Oswald, Ian. Number-forms and kindred visual images. *Journal of General Psychology,* 1960, 63: 81-88.

Pangborn, R. M. Influence of color on the discrimination of sweetness. *American Journal of Psychology,* 1960, 73: 229-238.

Pap, Arthur. On the empirical interpretation of psychoanalytic concepts. In Hook, Sidney, ed. *Psychoanalysis, Scientific Method, and Philosophy.* New York: New York University, 1959. Pp. 283-297.

Parkinson, C. N. His law transforms Parkinson. *New York Times Magazine,* July 10, 1960, p. 58.

Penfield, Wilder, & Lamar Roberts. *Speech and Brain Mechanisms.* Princeton: Princeton University, 1959.

Piaget, Jean. *Language and Thought of the Child.* New York: Meridian, 1955.

Piaget, Jean. Motricité, perception, et intelligence. *Enfance,* 1956, 2: 9-14.

Poincaré, H. *Science et Méthode.* Paris: Flammarion, 1908.

Preyer, Wilhelm. *The Mind of the Child.* Part II: *The Development of the Intellect.* New York: Appleton, 1914.

Psychological Bulletin, 1929, 26: 241-338. (Special language number.)

Quine, W. V. O. *Word and Object.* New York: Wylie, 1960.

Rashkis, H. A. Cognitive restructuring: Why research is therapy. *A.M.A. Archives of General Psychiatry,* 1960, 2: 616-621.

Rechtschaffen, Allan, & S. A. Mednick. The autokinetic word technique. *Journal of Abnormal and Social Psychology,* 1955, 51: 346.

Révész, Géza, ed. *Thinking and Speaking.* Amsterdam: North-Holland Publishing Co., 1954.

Rheingold, Harriet, J. L. Gewirtz, & H. W. Ross. Social conditioning of vocalizations in the infant. *Journal of Comparative and Physiological Psychology,* 1959, 52: 68-73.

Richardson, Claudia, & Joseph Church. A developmental analysis of proverb interpretations. *Journal of Genetic Psychology,* 1959, 94: 169-179.

Riess, B. F. Genetic changes in semantic conditioning. *Journal of Experimental Psychology,* 1946, 36: 143-152.

Riggs, L. A., Floyd Ratliff, J. C. Cornsweet, & T. N. Cornsweet, The disappearance of steadily fixated visual test objects. *Journal of the Optical Society of America,* 1953, 43: 495-501.

Robinowitz, Ralph. Learning the relation of opposition as related to scores on the Wechsler Intelligence Scale for Children. *Journal of Genetic Psychology,* 1956, 88: 25-30.

Rock, Irvin, & Walter Heimer. The effect of retinal and phenomenal orientation on the perception of form. *American Journal of Psychology,* 1957, 70: 493-511.

Ronjat, Jules. *Le Développement du Langage Observé chez un Enfant Bilingue.* Paris: H. Champion, 1913.

Rosenthal, David, & J. D. Frank. Psychotherapy and the placebo effect. *Psychological Bulletin*, 1956, 53: 294-301.

Ruesch, Jurgen, & Weldon Kees. *Non-Verbal Communication*. Berkeley: University of California, 1956.

Russell, D. H. *Children's Thinking*. Boston: Ginn, 1956.

Sanford, F. H. Speech and personality: A comparative case study. *Character and Personality*, 1942, 10: 169-198.

Sanford, R. N. Age as a factor in the recall of interrupted tasks. *Psychological Review*, 1946, 53: 234-240.

Schaffner, B., ed. *Group Processes*. New York: Josiah Macy, Jr., Foundation, 1955, 1956, 1957, 1959. 4 vols.

Scheerer, Martin, & M. D. Huling, Cognitive embeddedness in problem-solving: A theoretical and experimental analysis. In Kaplan, B., & S. Wapner, eds. *Perspectives in Psychological Theory*. New York: International Universities Press, 1960. Pp. 256-302.

Scheerer, Martin, Eva Rothman, & Kurt Goldstein. A case of "idiot savant": An experimental study of personality organization. *Psychological Monographs*, 1945, 58, no. 4.

Schilder, Paul. *The Image and Appearance of the Human Body*. London: Kegan Paul, 1935.

Schneirla, T. C. The concept of development in comparative psychology. In Harris, D. B., ed. *The Concept of Development*. Minneapolis: University of Minnesota, 1957. Pp. 78-108.

Schneirla, T. C. Instinctive behavior, maturation—Experience and development. In Kaplan, B., & S. Wapner, eds. *Perspectives in Psychological Theory*. New York: International Universities Press, 1960. Pp. 303-334.

Scott, J. P. *Animal Behavior*. Chicago: The University of Chicago Press, 1958.

Shapiro, A. K. A contribution to a history of the placebo effect. *Behavioral Science*, 1960, 5: 109-135.

Sheldon, W. H., with the collaboration of S. S. Stevens. *The Varieties of Temperament*. New York: Harper, 1942.

Sheldon, W. H., with the collaboration of S. S. Stevens & W. B. Tucker. *The Varieties of Human Physique*. New York: Harper, 1940.

Sherif, Muzafer. A study of some social factors in perception. *Archives of Psychology*, 1935, no. 187.

Sigel, I. E. The dominance of meaning. *Journal of Genetic Psychology*, 1954, 85: 201-207.

Skinner, B. F. "Superstition" in the pigeon. *Journal of Experimental Psychology*, 1948, 38: 168-172.

Skinner, B. F. *Verbal Behavior*. New York: Appleton-Century-Crofts, 1957.

Skinner, B. F. *Walden Two*. New York: Macmillan, 1948.

Smith, C. J. Mass action and early environment in the rat. *Journal of Comparative and Physiological Psychology*, 1959, 52: 154-156.

Spearman, C. E. *Creative Mind*. New York: Appleton, 1931.

Staples, Ruth. The responses of infants to color. *Journal of Experimental Psychology*, 1932, 15: 119-141.

Stern, William. *Psychology of Early Childhood*, 2d ed. New York: Holt, 1930.

Stewart, G. R. *Names on the Land*. New York: Random House, 1945.

Stoddard, G. D. *The Meaning of Intelligence*. New York: Macmillan, 1943.

Stone, L. J. An experimental study of form perception in the thermal senses. *Psychological Record*, 1937, 6: 235-337.

Strauss, A. A. *Mirrors and Masks*. Glencoe: The Free Press, 1959.

Strauss, A. L. The development of conceptions of rules in children. *Child Development*, 1954, 25: 193-208.

Supa, M., M. Cotzin, & K. M. Dallenbach. "Facial vision": The perception of obstacles by the blind. *American Journal of Psychology*, 1944, 57: 133-183.

Taine, M. The acquisition of language by children. *Mind*, 1877, 2: 252-259.

Tatz, S. J. Symbolic activity in "learning without awareness" *American Journal of Psychology*, 1960, 73: 239-247.

Tikhomirov, O. K. Review of *Verbal Behavior*, by B. F. Skinner. *Word*, 1959, 15: 362-367.

Valentine, C. W. The colour perception and colour preferences of an infant during its fourth and eighth months. *British Journal of Psychology*, 1913-14, 6: 363-386.

Van Breda, H. L., ed. *Problèmes Actuels de la Phénoménologie*. Brussels: Desclée de Brouwer, 1952.

Vendryes, J. *Language*. New York: Knopf, 1925.

Vincent, M. Sur le rôle du langage à un niveau élémentaire de pensée abstraite. *Enfance*, 1957, 4: 443-464.

Von Frisch, Karl. *Bees, Their Vision, Chemical Senses, and Language*. Ithaca: Cornell, 1950.

Wallon, Henri. Importance du mouvement dans le développement psychologique de l'enfant. *Enfance*, 1956, 2: 1-4.

Wapner, S. The differential effects of cortical injury and retesting on equivalence reactions in the rat. *Psychological Monographs*, 1944, 57, no. 2.

Wapner, S., & H. Werner. *Perceptual Development*. Worcester: Clark University, 1957.

Wapner, S., H. Werner, & D. M. Krus. The effect of success and failure on space localization. *Journal of Personality*, 1957, 25: 752-756.

Wapner, S., & H. A. Witkin. The role of visual factors in the maintenance of body-balance. *American Journal of Psychology*, 1950, 63: 385-408.

Weinstein, S., & H. L. Teuber. Effects of penetrating brain injury on intelligence test scores. *Science*, 1957, 125: 1036.

Weizsäcker, V. von. *Der Gestaltkreis. Theorie der Einheit von Wahrnehmen und Bewegen*. Stuttgart: Georg Thieme, 1940.

Wenger, M. A. The measurement of individual differences in autonomic balance. *Psychosomatic Medicine*, 1941, 3: 427-434.

Werner, H. *Comparative Psychology of Mental Development*. Chicago: Follett, 1948.

Werner, H., ed. *On Expressive Language*. Worcester: Clark University, 1955.

Werner, H., & Edith Kaplan. The acquisition of word meanings. *Monographs of the Society for Research in Child Development*, 1950, 15, no. 1.

Werner, H., & S. Wapner. The Innsbruck studies on distorted visual fields in relation to an organismic theory of perception. *Psychological Review*, 1955, 62: 130-138.

West, Anthony. Our far-flung correspondents: The stranger. *New Yorker*, May 16, 1959, 109-129.

West, Michael. *Bilingualism*. Calcutta: Government of India, Central Publication Branch, 1926.

White, R. W. Motivation reconsidered: The concept of competence. *Psychological Review*, 1959, 66: 297-333.

Whorf, B. L. *Language, Thought, and Reality*. New York: Wiley, 1956.

Wohlwill, J. F. Developmental studies of perception. *Psychological Bulletin*, 1960, 57: 249-288.

Wolff, P. H. Observations on newborn infants. *Psychosomatic Medicine*, 1959, 21: 110-111.

Wolff, Werner. *The Expression of Personality*. New York: Harper, 1943.

Worchel, P., & K. M. Dallenbach. "Facial vision": Perception of obstacles by the deaf-blind. *American Journal of Psychology*, 1947, 60: 502-553.

Yacorzynski, G. K., & B. E. Tucker. What price intelligence? *American Psychologist*, 1960, 15: 201-203.

Zazzo, René. Le probleme de l'imitation chez le nouveau-né. *Enfance*, 1957, 2: 135-142.

Zborowski, Mark. Cultural components in responses to pain. *Journal of Social Issues*, 1952, 8: 16-30.

Zimbardo, P. G. The effects of early avoidance training and rearing conditions upon the sexual behavior of the male rat. *Journal of Comparative and Physiological Psychology,* 1958, 51: 764-769.

Zuckerman, C. B., & Irvin Rock. A reappraisal of the roles of past experience and innate organizing processes in visual perception. *Psychological Bulletin,* 1957, 54: 269-296.

INDEX

JOSEPH CHURCH is Professor of Psychology at Brooklyn College of the City University of New York. Before joining the Brooklyn College faculty, he taught at Vassar College in the Department of Child Study, at the New School for Social Research, and, most recently, at the University of Hawaii as a visiting professor. He is the editor of *Three Babies: Biographies of Cognitive Development*, a newly published Random House book, and co-author, with L. Joseph Stone, of the widely known *Childhood and Adolescence*, published by Random House in 1957 and regarded as a leader in its field. Professor Church is a graduate of the New School for Social Research and was awarded his master's degree by Cornell University and his doctorate by Clark University. During his undergraduate years in New York City he was a professional free lance writer, and while working for his Ph.D. received clinical training under the U.S. Veterans' Administration Clinical Psychology program. He is currently doing research on early cognitive development and on group differences in value systems.

VINTAGE WORKS OF SCIENCE
AND PSYCHOLOGY

VINTAGE FICTION, POETRY, AND PLAYS